MAP OF THE USSR c.1930

PRAISE FOR JOHN URE'S PREVIOUS BOOKS

'Ure's beautifully understated account of his adventures is in the best tradition of the travel book'
Daily Telegraph on *The Trail of Tamerlane*

'Anyone with red blood in his or her veins will be stirred by these stories' *Country Life* on *Shooting Leave*

'This is the stuff that travellers' tales are made of . . . makes one want to go straight back there oneself' Fitzroy Maclean

'Cheerful and elegantly written . . . and never boring'
Daily Mail on *The Cossacks*

'Ure's adventurous spirit sweeps across continents and through history' *The Sunday Times*

BEWARE THE RUGGED RUSSIAN BEAR

BY THE SAME AUTHOR

Cucumber Sandwiches in the Andes

Prince Henry the Navigator

The Trail of Tamerlane

The Quest for Captain Morgan

Trespassers on the Amazon

The Royal Geographical Society's History of World Exploration (contributor)

A Bird on the Wing: Bonnie Prince Charlie's Flight from Culloden Retraced

Diplomatic Bag (editor)

The Cossacks

In Search of Nomads

The Seventy Great Journeys in History (contributor)

Pilgrimage: The Great Adventure of the Middle Ages

The Great Explorers (contributor)

Shooting Leave: Spying Out Central Asia in the Great Game

Sabres on the Steppes: Danger, Diplomacy and Adventure in the Great Game

BEWARE THE RUGGED RUSSIAN BEAR

British Adventurers Exposing the Bolsheviks

JOHN URE

Illustrations by Toby Ward

First published in hardback in Great Britain in 2015 by Old Street Publishing
8 Hurlingham Business Park, Sulivan Road
London SW6 3DU

www.oldstreetpublishing.co.uk

ISBN 978-1-908699-58-9

10 9 8 7 6 5 4 3 2 1

A CIP catalogue record for this title is available from the British Library.

Printed and bound by CPI Group (UK) Ltd, Croydon, CR0 4YY

Typeset by JaM

For my grandson

RORY RAMSAY

Who at nine months old already shows signs of being an adventurer

CONTENTS

“Seek not by reason to discern the soul of Russia,
or to learn her thoughts by measurements designed for other lands.”
– lines by the Russian “people’s poet” Tiutchev, translated by Paul Dukes

“If you must live among wolves, then howl, too, as the wolves do!”
– Old Russian saying

CHRONOLOGY

	Events in Russia	*Characters' Lives*
1904	The Russo-Japanese war reveals the weakness of the Russian armed forces.	Maurice Baring visits Russia for the first time to report on the Russo–Japanese war. He becomes an ongoing commentator on the subsequent revolutions.
1905	The January march on the Winter Palace in St Petersburg leads to a period of protracted violence by Tsar Nicholas II's Cossacks against peaceful protesters. In October, the Tsar feels obliged to call an elected *Duma* (or parliament).	
1910		Stephen Graham sets off on a series of 'tramps' through Central Asia, the Caucasus and northern Russia, and establishes himself as the leading expert on Russia. Ranald MacDonell takes up his appointment as a British vice-consul in Baku on the Caspian Sea and is in situ to run a ring of secret agents when Turkey threatens to take over the Caucasus.
1912		Robert Bruce Lockhart is appointed vice-consul in Moscow, and stays on to become the British prime minister's personal representative to the revolutionary leaders.
1914	Russia declares war on Germany and Austria, and is joined by France and Britain.	

1915 The Tsar takes personal command of the Russian army at the Front, but proves ineffectual.

1916 Rasputin, the self-proclaimed 'Holy Man' who exercises unacceptable influence over the Tsar and Tsarina, is murdered by Prince Youssoupoff.

1917 In March, Tsar Nicholas II abdicates.

In October, Kerensky's ministers are arrested, and power passes from the Provisional Government into the hands of the Bolsheviks.

In December, Lenin sets up the Cheka – a secret police force charged with eliminating counter-revolutionary activity.

Somerset Maugham is sent by the British secret service to Petrograd, to try to shore up the Provisional Government there, and to prevent the Russians making a separate peace with Germany.

Sidney Reilly is transferred from Germany to Russia to work for the British secret service against the Bolsheviks.

Paul Dukes is sent to Russia, under cover of the Boy Scout movement, to assess the strength of the Bolshevik regime.

George Hill arrives in Petrograd, rescues Romanian gold from the Kremlin, and goes on to run a network of secret agents in Moscow.

1918 In March the Bolshevik government signs a peace treaty with Germany at Brest Litovsk.

In July the Tsar and his family are murdered by the Bolsheviks at Ekaterinburg.

In August, Dora Kaplan, a young Jewish woman belonging to the Social Revolutionary party, shoots

Edward Noel is kidnapped by Jungalis while trying to contact anti-communist intervention forces.

Reginald Teague-Jones is accused of ordering the murder of 26 Soviet Commissars from Baku.

Bruce Lockhart is arrested on suspicion of involvement in a plot to assassinate Lenin.

	at Lenin and seriously wounds him. Throughout the year, Western intervention forces, including British troops, land in the Archangel region, in the Caucasus and in Siberia in an effort to overthrow the Bolshevik regime.	Frederick Bailey is sent to Tashkent in Central Asia to monitor and try to undermine the Bolshevik takeover there, and escapes the following year. 1918–22 Percy Etherton, as British consul in the western Chinese province of Sinkiang, persuades the Chinese to resist Soviet incursions from neighbouring Russia.
1919		Hugh Walpole publishes his novel, *The Secret City*, about life in revolutionary Russia.
1920	The remaining Western intervention forces evacuate from the Crimea, leaving Bolsheviks in overall command of Russia.	
1924	Formation of the USSR, incorporating those regions of Central Asia, the Caucasus and the Ukraine which had remained independent. Britain formally recognises the new Soviet State. Lenin dies.	John Buchan publishes his anti-Bolshevik novel *Huntingtower*.
1925	Stalin takes over and develops doctrine of 'socialism in one country', abandoning expectation of early revolutions throughout Europe.	
1929		Alfred Gough, vicar of Holy Trinity Brompton church in London, exposes the forced labour camps in northern Russia which are supplying timber to the British market.

1930	1930–39 Stalin's reign of terror purges the ranks of the old Bolsheviks, the armed forces and the civil service.	
1934		Peter Fleming travels overland from China to India and subsequently publishes his *News from Tartary*, revealing the extent of Bolshevik intervention in the western Chinese province of Sinkiang since Etherton's time there.
1938		Fitroy Maclean reports from Moscow on the purges and show-trials of Stalin's rivals, and goes on to explore Soviet Central Asia.
1939	The Nazi–Soviet (Ribbentrop–Molotov) Pact is signed in August, helping to precipitate the Second World War.	

A CAST OF ADVENTURERS REVEAL A SECRET LAND

Introduction

All friendly nations are friendly in more or less the same way; every unfriendly nation is unfriendly in its own particular way. So it has been with Britain and Russia. From early in the 19th century until early in the 20th, Britain and Russia were almost continually in confrontation with each other. Only once – during the Crimean War of 1854 to 1856 – did this confrontation break into open hostilities. For the rest of the time, it was mainly confined to the activities of adventurers from both sides in the region of Central Asia, where imperial Russia was forever encroaching on the territories of Bokhara, Samarkand, Khiva, Tashkent and other independent khanates and emirates, while at the same time drawing ever nearer to the frontiers of British India – on which she was assumed to have predatory designs. The Great Game – as this shadow conflict was called – lasted from the beginning of the reign of Tsar Nicholas I in 1825 till the murder of the last Tsar, Nicholas II, in 1918. When it was over, many in Britain were disposed to welcome the new regime; change must – they felt – be for the better. There was a natural reluctance to embark on a fresh quarrel with Russia. Could not the revolution be seen as evidence of progress, rather than as a cause for further confrontation?

The only people who gave a clear and alarming answer to this question were a group of British adventurers who were infiltrated, or found their own way, into the embryonic Soviet Union and who reported back – to their government, to the intelligence services and in some cases directly to the public – about what was really happening. Such adventurers, who are the subject of the chapters that follow, often had to begin their exploits by overcoming the challenge of entering Russia in the first place. Apart from a few – like Robert Bruce Lockhart – who were sent under diplomatic or consular protection, they had to smuggle themselves or be smuggled by others across closed and often frozen frontiers. But infiltrate or be infiltrated they must, because having one's own man (it was rarely a woman) on the ground was essential in an environment where there were no foreign newspaper correspondents or radio commentators. Having arrived in this forbidden land, they faced the further challenges of securing accurate information and then getting their reports and impressions home: they were entering a country which had always been an enigma and which – with the revolution – had become more opaque than ever; and this was a era – a hundred years ago – when carrier pigeons and semaphore, messages in cleft sticks and dispatches sewn into the hems of greatcoats, were more familiar techniques to undercover agents than were photographs, photocopies and telephone calls, and when emails, faxes and iPads had yet to be invented.

The complacency in Britain about the effects of the upheaval in Russia was of course tempered from the start. Even in its pre-Lenin stage, the revolution had raised some grave anxieties. Would the new regime rush to make peace with Germany in the middle of the First World War, in which Britain and Russia had so far been allies? If so, would not the whole might of the Kaiser's army be shifted to the western front to overwhelm the French and British armies? And was not a dangerous streak of anarchism likely to replace the ordered – if autocratic – regime of the Tsar? After all, the First World War had been triggered by the assassination of a member of a European royal house by a dissident Slav in Sarajevo, and some of the Provisional Government ministers in Russia – notably Boris Savinkov – were self-confessed assassins. It was this fear of the infection of anarchy, and of social and economic upheaval, that led King George V to decline to give his cousin the Tsar and his family refuge in Britain, fearing that their presence might trigger unrest or even revolution in England's green and pleasant land.

The Bolsheviks did their reputation abroad much harm by the brutal murder of Tsar Nicholas II and his wife and children, but until that tragic event in July 1918 there were many in Britain and the West who were inclined to give Kerensky's Provisional Government, and then the Bolsheviks, the benefit of the doubt. Many in England had seen the Tsar as 'a tyrant wielding a knout'. On hearing the news of the Tsar's abdication, Arthur Bonar Law (then leader of the House of Commons) quoted Wordsworth's well-known lines on the French Revolution: 'Bliss was it in that dawn to be alive, but to be young was very heaven'; Lloyd George (as Prime Minister) telegraphed to the Provisional Government with his 'sentiments of profoundest satisfaction…the Russian Revolution had revealed that the war was at bottom a struggle for popular government'. A French socialist minister telegraphed 'fraternal greetings' to Kerensky. The United States government promptly afforded official recognition to Kerensky's Provisional Government, and was encouraged to join the Allies' cause in the First World War by the fact they would no longer be fighting alongside an autocratic monarchy: the President referred to the 'wonderful and heartening' things that had been happening in Russia. And even after the Bolsheviks had taken over from Kerensky, with Lenin's arrival and the storming of the Winter Palace, the revolution still had its apologists outside Russia – in England and elsewhere.

So while there was a fear in many quarters of the consequences for Britain and for the western world of the Russian Revolution, there was also a naive reluctance to condemn – let alone confront – a social change in Russia which appeared to many to be overdue, and to some to have resulted in a more egalitarian form of government. This reluctance was most evident among left-wing intellectuals and working-class activists, as well as in artistic circles. When Maxim Gorky was incarcerated in the Peter and Paul Fortress in St Petersburg, among those who had canvassed for his release were the sculptor Auguste Rodin, the writer Anatole France and the medical genius Marie Curie: creativity was seen to be on the side of the forces of change. Socially progressive and militant writers such as George Bernard Shaw and H.G. Wells (both of whom visited the embryonic Soviet Union) and John Galsworthy found that their works were promptly translated into Russian after the revolution. These works – together with the novels of Charles Dickens – served to encourage those who were intent on toppling the old order and replacing it with a 'dictatorship of the proletariat'. Such writings – be they *David Copperfield*, *Mrs Warren's Profession* or *The Silver Box* – were represented as reflecting a contemporary, repressive and decadent Britain, despite the fact that Dickensian London had long since ceased to exist. Trade union leaders (the General Strike of 1926 was only a few years ahead) and left-wing politicians (Mr Ramsay MacDonald's first Labour government was elected in 1924) were actively flirting with the concept of communism, even if many – like MacDonald himself – were later to reject it.

While the writings of authors such as H.G. Wells were treated inside Russia as evidence that England – and indeed the whole western world – was living in an outdated and unjust society, in England the views of such authors – especially when they had visited Russia – were widely read and accepted as evidence that conditions inside Russia had been vastly improved by the Bolshevik revolution. In his book *Russia in the Shadows* (1920), Wells does two things: first, he paints a gloomy and highly critical picture of the imperial Russia that preceded the revolution and, second, he is laudatory and uncritical about Lenin and most aspects of the new Bolshevik regime. He writes of pre-revolutionary Russia: 'by its own inherent rottenness and by the thrusts and strains of aggressive imperialism, the Russian part of the old civilized world…is now gone'. Wells goes on to argue that it was not the Bolsheviks who destroyed the civilized elements of pre-revolutionary Russia, but the 'unsound system' that had collapsed of its own volition; and he claims that Russia fell into its miserable state through 'the moral and intellectual insufficiency' of its ruling class. About the Bolsheviks, on the other hand, he finds much good to say: while the rest of Russia was apathetic, only the communists were prepared to act; the communists embodied an idea that could be relied upon; the Bolshevik government was 'as securely established as any government in Europe'; Marxists had 'his very warmest sympathy'; with communist activists he found he had 'the freemasonry of common indignation'; he believed that anyone who attempted to destroy the Bolshevik regime 'would destroy what was left of law and order in Russia'; of the worst atrocities of the revolution, he found 'the Bolsheviks...about as responsible as the government of Australia'; Vladimir Lenin alone had the 'vision of a world changed over and...built afresh'; he concluded that 'the only possible government that can stave off a final collapse of Russia now is the present Bolshevik government'; it followed from this that 'there is only one being in Russia with whom the western world can deal, and that is the Bolshevik government itself'. These were the widely disseminated views of a popular and much respected author, who had visited Bolshevik Russia and had long, meaningful conversations with Lenin, and whose ties with that country were to be consolidated by his long-standing and intimate relationship with Moura Budberg (the sometime mistress of both Bruce Lockhart and Gorky). It was going to take a lot of evidence – daringly and dangerously accumulated – to countersay such considered and apparently informed views coming from an intellectually and socially revered writer such as H.G. Wells.

Among westerners familiar with Russian literature, there was an awareness that Russian aristocracy had already been trying to grapple with the long-standing inequalities of social life before the revolution: Tolstoy's sympathetic figure of Leo Levin (in *Anna Karenina*) was not alone in working alongside his peasants and trying to understand their way of life – indeed, Tolstoy had been practising this himself. Novelists such as Fyodor Dostoevsky and Nikolai Gogol had dramatised the need for radical reform and the abandonment of the old system with all its rigid hierarchies. In England and elsewhere there was a sympathy for radical change that – to judge from such Russian literature – seemed to be a force for good. When Kerensky and the Provisional Government took over from the Tsar in March 1917, there was therefore a general tendency to welcome this as a progressive move – particularly since Kerensky seemed inclined to keep Russia fighting against the Germans on the eastern front.

Against this background, it was not only the intellectuals and the left-wingers who were seduced by the reports of life in Bolshevik Russia. According to the chief of the imperial general staff in London, General Sir Henry Wilson, Prime Minister Lloyd George had 'pronouncedly Bolshevist' sympathies. The *Daily Mail* also accused Lloyd George of falling victim to the influence of the 'international Jewish financiers' who were thought to be behind the Russian Revolution; the American President's advisers at the Paris Peace Conference in 1919 were anxious to settle 'the Russian question' on terms acceptable to Lenin; President Georges Clemenceau of France was reluctant to engage French troops in support of the White Russian cause, not only because his men were war-weary, but also because they sympathized with the Bolsheviks and might mutiny in consequence; events in Bavaria suggested that many of the prisoners of war, captured by the Russians and subsequently allowed to return home, had become brainwashed with the idea of a communist utopia; in Hungary there was a movement to declare a 'People's Republic' in 1918. Everywhere it seemed that the Bolsheviks were making progress, and Lenin's vision of western Europe following the revolutionary example of Russia could not be discounted.

One element that might have been expected to rally to the support of the Tsar and the old regime was military opinion. But by 1917 the reputation of the Tsar's military and naval forces was so low that it commanded little respect abroad. Between January and October 1905 the Tsar had deployed his army (generally the Cossacks) 2,700 times 'in support of civil power' – that is, to put down insurrections and disturbances; this was not a use of the military which garnered respect at home or abroad. Even more unhelpful to the military reputation was an event in Petrograd in October 1916, when two infantry regiments were called out to disperse an unruly crowd of striking workers and, instead of doing so, turned their rifles on the police. Four regiments of Cossacks were required to repel the infantry, more than a hundred of whom were executed by firing squad for their mutinous behaviour. Such chaotic and brutal incidents did nothing to rally foreign opinion behind the Tsar's army as a moderating force.

The Russo-Japanese war of 1904–05 had been a humiliating disaster for the Tsar, largely owing to poor leadership and planning. One affair in particular which had turned British military opinion against the Tsar's armed forces was an encounter in the North Sea: Russian admirals were so nervous after the destruction by the Japanese of a large part of their fleet in the Pacific that even in European waters they feared an attack by Japanese warships – possibly sailing under false colours. When in 1905 one such nervous admiral was cruising off the Dogger Bank, he found himself surrounded by small vessels and – imagining they might be Japanese gunships – he opened fire on them. After sinking one, he steamed off, leaving the scuppered sailors to drown. When it transpired that the small ships had been innocent British fishing vessels, the Tsar reluctantly paid damages and sent a telegram to his Uncle Bertie (King Edward VII) expressing – quite inadequate – regrets. It had not been an endearing incident as far as British opinion was concerned. In fact, the Russian navy was becoming an embarrassment: the mutiny on the battleship *Potemkin* in June 1905 had raised fears of a general mutiny in the Black Sea fleet.

Equally, the Tsar's inability and reluctance to give a lead to his army at the outbreak of the First World War, and the poor quality of the leadership in general – which appeared to have learnt nothing from the Japanese war – did little to inspire a feeling of solidarity and comradeship with the Russian regime in military circles in Britain.

Another reason the West, and the British in particular, was slow to condemn or confront the Bolsheviks was that people had been shocked by what they heard of the conspicuous consumption and extravagance of the Russian aristocracy. The Sheremetev family was known to employ 340 domestic servants at their palace in St Petersburg (a footman or chamberlain at every door), while the Duke of Devonshire managed to get by with a mere 18 at Chatsworth. It was felt that the Russian aristocracy, in its feverish efforts to become 'European', had ended (as Orlando Figes has pointed out) by becoming foreigners in their own land.

Nor had those in exile in Paris or London done much to alert their host countries to the deplorable state of affairs in the Russia they had left behind. Although some three million Russians – mostly from the aristocratic or professional classes – had left or fled the country between 1917 and 1929, they tended to confirm western opinion that they were an over-privileged and outdated ruling class. Many lived – at least to start with – off the proceeds of the treasures they had managed to smuggle out of the country: jewellery, Fabergé eggs and boxes, ancient icons and other objects of *vertu*; one Grand Duke financed himself by the sale of old Tsarist coins which he had secreted in his clothing. They lived in largely closed communities centred around Orthodox churches, Russian schools, Russian publishing houses, Russian cafés, and clubs dedicated to celebrating the works of Alexander Pushkin (himself compulsorily exiled from St Petersburg for much of his life, but always an ardent patriot). They inter-married and consolidated their own communities rather than reaching out to the leaders and thinkers of their host countries, and did little to enlighten English or western opinion about the horrors that were occurring in the land they had abandoned.

In part, this was because they mostly considered their exile as a temporary condition. They could not believe that Bolshevism would last long, and looked forward to an early return to their estates and property. Writers such as the Nobel-Prize-winner Ivan Bunin (whose short stories were published by Stephen Graham alongside those of Anton Chekhov, Gogol and Dostoevsky) evoked nostalgically the relaxed and leisured life of the Russian countryside, as if this had been suspended but not permanently destroyed. Bunin recreated such a world in house parties with Sergei Rachmaninov, Vladimir Nabokov and other creative exiles, where they surrounded themselves with Russian servants, Russian food and drink, and Russian memories of their motherland. They relished recollections of a former and apparently enduring lifestyle, rather than sounding the alarm about the current state of affairs in their beleaguered home land. Blinded by their own wishful thinking, these émigrés were ill-equipped to expose to their hosts the sinister and irreversible nature of the change in their homeland. As the Ballets Russes danced its way into the hearts and imaginations of an enchanted Europe in the 1920s, few people – at least until Sergei Diaghilev's death in 1929 – were inclined to dwell on the darker side of the Bolshevik state; the world of *Swan Lake* left little room for contemplation of the world of the gulag. Perhaps an even more significant indicator that nothing was too badly wrong in Soviet Russia was the fact that so many prominent and creative exiles chose to return. Even Gorky, who had at various times fallen out dramatically with both Lenin and Stalin, chose to revisit Russia in 1928 and permanently to resettle there in 1931; and the composer Sergei Prokofiev returned there from Paris in 1936. Surely – it must have seemed to many – not much could be wrong with a country to which its own most celebrated exiles chose voluntarily to return. Few – and certainly not Prokofiev himself – realized that they were returning at the very height of Stalin's horrendous purges.

And all the time, while there was ignorance about the current state of affairs, there were reminders of how dire the lives of the workers had been in pre-revolutionary Tsarist Russia – and how antiquated and stultifying life had been even in more elevated social circles. Although serfdom was formally abolished in the mid-19th century, the poverty and exploitation of the peasantry was still an all too visible part of Russian country life well into the following century. Paintings such as Ilya Repin's 'Barge Haulers on the Volga' (1870–73), with its vivid portrayal of suffering and dignity, made a deep impression outside as well as inside Russia. The hostile attitude of the Tsarist police to artists like Repin, as well as to many writers, seemed evidence of their fear of any exposure of the grim realities of rural life; the plays of Chekhov (notably *The Cherry Orchard*, which was to become the most frequently performed play of the whole 20th century) were not wistful exercises in nostalgia, but sharp comedies deriding the old-fashioned attitudes of a fading and irrelevant gentry. The Orthodox Church, with its role in forcibly arranging peasant marriages, was also considered overdue for reform.

Indeed, given that the Orthodox Church was almost as much a target for the Russian revolutionaries as the Tsar and the aristocracy, it might at first have seemed strange that Christian communities across Europe did not react more promptly and strongly in support of the Russian clergy and in condemning the revolutionaries. But the Church in Russia was seen by both Russians and outsiders as an instrument of the autocratic regime. Tsar Nicholas II saw himself as the embodiment of 'Holy Rus', in the way that most Tsars before Peter the Great but few since had done; he claimed a divine as well as a temporal authority. (In this as in other ways, he was more like Charles I of England than his contemporary and cousin George V.) Church sermons were expected to endorse and defend the role and status of the Tsar and his court, and to denounce any subversive loose talk. In a country where the peasantry was still largely illiterate, the influence of the pulpit was greater than it had been in western Europe since the 17th century. It was rumoured that the clergy reported evidence of any subversive behaviour to the police – even if the evidence was based on the confessional. The Church also played a role in the aggressive Russification of the outlying provinces of the Tsar's empire, subjecting Catholic, Protestant and Muslim communities to heavy-handed missionary work. Meanwhile, it failed to reach out to the new industrialized cities, its strength remaining in backward rural communities, where icons found a place in even the simplest dwellings. Here too, though, abuses were known to be widespread: for instance, priests often made excessive demands for payment in return for even the most basic services, such as marriages and funerals.

Yet regardless of the specific failings of the Orthodox Church, the fact was that western Christendom was generally out of sympathy with a doctrine that seemed to them lost in the Middle Ages. The icons and cupolas, the shovel-hatted monks and the subservience to the monarch all seemed as ripe for change and modernization as the civil state had been. One English clergyman, Canon John Douglas – who had devoted much of his life to trying to reconcile the Anglican and Orthodox Christian Churches and had seen for himself something of the workings of the newly emerged Bolsheviks – was stirred to write a number of pamphlets exposing the persecution to which Christians were being subjected in communist Russia. But 'the world did little heed nor long remember' his warnings. It was left to the few more adventurous British observers to reveal to the world that the Russian Church, like the bourgeois classes, the civil service and an ordered society, had become the casualty of a ruthless and destructive Bolshevik movement.

Opinion outside Russia was, therefore, aware of the failings of the Tsar's regime, in Church as well as in state, but it was also under the impression that wholesome reforms had already been under way well before the 1917 revolution. Following the emancipation of the serfs, there had been a 'populist' movement among the intelligentsia, whose aim was to forge closer contact with peasant communities. Tolstoy was not alone in his social experiments at Yasnaya Polyana: as early as 1874, a group of aristocratic Russians had attempted to live among the peasants in order to gain a better understanding of a class which they saw as constituting 'the soul of Russia', and in 1862 Nikolai Chernyshevsky had written a novel entitled *What Is to Be Done?*, which outlined a new society and was said to have inspired Lenin. Ivan Turgenev and Fyodor Dostoevsky were also deeply aware of the injustices of Russian society and struggled to bring these to wider attention and to find remedies. Many artists and intellectuals had suffered under the Tsar for their forward-looking 'revolutionary' ideas. Dostoevsky had spent four years of forced labour in a Siberian salt mine on account of his association with a supposedly seditious political group.

The events of 1905, insofar as they were known to the outside world, tended to confirm the view that revolution in Russia was not to be feared as a world-shattering event, but rather to be welcomed as an overdue correction of the Tsar's autocratic form of government. The march on the Winter Palace at St Petersburg, led by Father Gapon on 9 January 1905 – or 'Bloody Sunday', as it was ever afterwards to be known – was not intended as a violent affair, or even as a protest against the Tsar, but rather as a means of conveying a petition to him.

Gapon was an Orthodox priest who had been a prison chaplain. His gathering of factory workers, mill workers and peasants was inspired not by revolutionary motives but by a desire to protest at the harsh and unfair treatment meted out to them by corrupt and greedy managers and officials. They felt that their 'Little Father' – the Tsar – would be on their side once he knew the facts. What consolidated public opinion – both within Russia and abroad – in favour of the hymn-singing protesters was the brutal manner in which their peaceful march was put down and dispersed. As they converged on the Winter Palace (where, incidentally, the Tsar was not in residence, having gone to his more rural home on the outskirts of the city), the police and then the Cossack cavalry first charged the crowd and then fired, not over their heads but deliberately into them. Many were killed or injured, and more fled – but when those who had fled quietly reassembled, the troops again fired on them and the killing continued. In one sense, the Tsar had an alibi: he was not even at the Palace when the shooting occurred. On the other hand, as the father of his people, he could hardly distance himself from any massacre, particularly one inflicted in part by his own elite corps of guards and outside his own palace. There was widespread understanding of the decision of the merchant clubs in the capital to close their doors to guards officers as a protest. Both at home and abroad the Tsar began to be viewed less as the protector of the common people and more as their autocratic oppressor. The need for change was recognized by all observers of the scene. So when that change came – at first in the form of the Tsar's abdication and the installation of a Provisional Government bent on constitutional reform – it seemed natural to welcome it. It took time – and the intervention of the adventurers who are the subject of this book – to recognize that the original revolution had, with the arrival of Lenin and the Bolsheviks, transformed itself from an overdue liberal experiment into something altogether more menacing.

Outcry against the treatment of the marchers in St Petersburg prompted some salutary reforms. After 'Bloody Sunday' public meetings were no longer prohibited, and even an occasional soap-box speaker was to be heard at street corners. For the first time the press was publishing not only comment on government policies, but actual criticisms of them. There were even occasional cartoons depicting the Tsar and his court. In the outlying regions of the empire – in the Caucasus, the Ukraine and the Baltic States – local languages began to be taught in the schools, and Russian was no longer imposed as the sole *lingua franca*. Could the Bolsheviks not be merely a continuation of this wholesome process? Many liberal observers were inclined to regard the events of October 1917 as no more than a further step along the desirable road which had been opening up through the later half of the 19th century, which had received a boost from the disturbances of 1905, and which had come to fruition in the abdication of Nicholas II earlier in 1917. The brutal nature of the October Revolution was easily overlooked by those who had no love for the Tsarist regime and no inside knowledge of the country.

Those who favoured active military intervention in Russia to topple the Bolsheviks, as did Winston Churchill, were in a minority and viewed by many as wild warmongers. The jury of public opinion was still out on the question of whether the Bolshevik experiment was a bogey or a beacon, a grim warning or an enticing will-o'-the-wisp. As the revolution unrolled, Britain awaited those with the courage to explore the facts, and the skill to communicate their findings.

The history of the White Russian forces, backed by 'bourgeois' western governments, who attempted unsuccessfully to overthrow the communist regime is well remembered and still resented in Russia, and is well documented in the West. What is less well known is the part played by individual Britons – most of them Scotsmen – who penetrated the embryonic Soviet Union to discover what life under communism was really like, and who exposed in their writings the deadly flaws of a regime which was very different from the utopia that left-wing intellectuals and others imagined it to be.

The adventures of these buccaneers were every bit as dangerous as the exploits of their predecessors – the explorers, young officers and secret agents who had played the leading roles in the Great Game in the previous century. Some, like Robert Bruce Lockhart, found themselves – despite diplomatic or consular cover – imprisoned in the Kremlin and condemned to death. Others, like the Highland chieftain Ranald MacDonell, found themselves running spy rings in Soviet Black Sea ports, taking part in roof-top chases and escaping from Russia as stowaways.

Some, like Sidney Reilly and Frederick Bailey, actively plotted and intrigued against the Bolsheviks. Another intrepid traveller, Stephen Graham, who had explored the remoter corners of Russia before the revolution, eventually managed to convince London society and the world at large that all was not as it seemed – Lenin and Stalin were not, as had been suggested, the spiritual descendants of Tolstoy and Dostoevsky. A few, like Peter Fleming (the elder brother of the creator of James Bond), travelled around Tartary and the fringes of the Soviet Union, collecting material which was a revelation to western readers. One young diplomat, Fitzroy Maclean, managed to escape from the hothouse of embassy life in Moscow to travel – dogged and harassed all the while by the secret police – to parts of Soviet Central Asia which had been unseen by any westerners since the revolution. Meanwhile, at home, John Buchan (who published *Huntingtower* in 1922) was penning novels about anarchistic Bolshevik villains who kidnapped young maidens and terrorized people far beyond the frontiers of Russia: readers of *The Thirty-Nine Steps* thrilled at a new set of national enemies – not Germans but Bolsheviks. So it came about that these Scotsmen and others were at the forefront of those revealing to the world that communist Russia posed a more alarming and far-reaching threat than that which had for so long been perceived as emanating from Tsarist Russia.

Nor did it fall only to male adventurers to expose the true nature of Bolshevism. From well before the first stirrings of trouble in Tsarist Russia, there had been a steady trickle of British residents there who were uniquely well qualified to observe and report. These were the English, Scottish and Irish governesses who were employed by aristocratic Russian families to teach and look after their children. Although French was still the preferred language of the upper classes, and German had enjoyed some additional currency from the fact that the last empress was German, English was recognized as an increasingly useful international language. British girls were also considered less flirtatious than French governesses and more 'wholesome' than German ones. They often became respected and trusted members of the families for whom they worked, and many stayed on after the revolution broke out to look after their young charges, rather than rushing home to safety. Their employers, under pressure of every sort, often turned to the English governess to perform such risky and responsible tasks as hiding the countess's jewels, burying the family silver and even throwing the odd incriminating revolver into the lake. When they did come back to Britain – some of them having had remarkable escapes by sleigh through wolf-infested forests – they had quite a tale to tell, and it was a tale which did as much as the more formal reports of diplomats, secret agents and trans-continental travellers to expose the rigours and horrors of the new Bolshevik set-up.

It is the story of these adventurers that will be told in the following chapters. Their tales may have been individually known at the time – in the 1920s and 1930s – but have been overtaken in most memories by a Second World War and a protracted Cold War. Many of them were more likely to have packed a revolver than a dagger in their luggage, along with their cloaks; all of them packed a fountain pen and a notebook; and all of them shared their discoveries with a wide and influential circle of readers. They were whistle-blowers on a revolution which had turned cruel and brutal. To speak and write as they did was a valuable contribution to exposing Bolshevism for what it was, and to gather the raw material necessary for such whistle-blowing was a dangerous, lonely and secretive occupation. This is why their exploits were often so dramatic.

My own interest in the exploits and achievements of these compatriots stems in part from my friendship with some of the protagonists in this book: I travelled in Russia with Fitzroy Maclean some twenty years after the exploits he described in *Eastern Approaches*, and he told me many details of his adventures which had never appeared in print. I also knew Stephen Graham at the end of his life, and he too told me something of the rigours and risks of travelling in Russia. Robert Bruce Lockhart's nephew and confidant

– who followed the same diplomatic career as Bruce Lockhart and myself – passed on to me some of his uncle's unrecorded experiences. Peter and Ian Fleming were also acquaintances who discussed their experiences with me. One of the Scottish governesses, who had been charged with the upbringing of an upper-class Russian family's children, was still anxious to pass on her reminiscences when I was serving at the British embassy in Moscow forty years later. As I explain in more detail in the personal epilogue to this book, this untapped material has tempted me to resuscitate, expand and interpret stories most of which last saw the light of day some decades ago.

Another motivation for telling these tales was that I had myself followed in the footsteps of many of the subjects I was writing about – not only in Moscow and St Petersburg but also in Central Asia, the Caucasus and other more remote parts of Russia. I did this at a time – in the 1950s while Ian Fleming was writing *From Russia with Love* and his other early James Bond stories – when, though many of the essential features of the Soviet regime were known in the West, the feelings of the indigenous population of such parts of the Soviet Union as Armenia, Chechnya, Georgia, Kazakhstan and all the other '-stans' were still a mystery. Did they want to be independent or were they happy to be a part of a communist superpower? My own adventures, though less considerable than those of some of the protagonists whom I have mentioned above, were nonetheless stimulating and revealing. There were moments when I was tempted to ask for a dirk or a dagger to be sent out in the diplomatic bag, and when I felt that disappearing without trace was a fate that was not impossible. After all, this was a period when even major air accidents or national disasters were not reported in the Soviet press. The disappearance of a solitary wayward westerner – even one who could claim 'diplomatic immunity' – would not have been even the smallest news item in the columns of *Pravda*.

When I first started to gather material, I was very struck – having Scottish ancestry myself – at how many of the adventurers who confronted and exposed the early Bolsheviks were Scotsmen: Robert Bruce Lockhart, Ranald MacDonell, Stephen

Graham, Peter Fleming, Fitzroy Maclean and so on. I even contemplated calling the book *Dirk & Pen against Hammer & Sickle* before I realised that to limit the cast of characters exclusively to Scotsmen would distort the overall picture. Nevertheless, it remains the case that the Scottish spirit of adventure and inquiry was a major factor in lifting the curtain on the nefarious activities that were taking place, not only behind the lofty walls of the Kremlin, but also across the smoky urban cities and the misty steppes and forests of Russia. Sir Walter Scott in his Waverley novels made all Scotsmen aware of the tradition of adventure that had always lurked in their veins, and he would not have been surprised that, almost exactly a hundred years later, a generation of his compatriots were to show just how alive that tradition was. They played a major part – *the* major part – in revealing the true nature of what was happening in the largest and most obscure country on earth, in a way which the present age (almost exactly another hundred years on), with its love of transparency, must surely admire. I hope that the following chapters will help readers to recall how this was done, and to re-live and admire those old adventures in a new context.

Robert Bruce Lockhart

POLITICAL AGENT & SUSPECTED ASSASSIN

Robert Bruce Lockhart

As Acting British Consul-General in Moscow, the 29-year-old Robert Bruce Lockhart had a ringside seat as the dramatic succession of events that led to the Russian Revolution began with the abdication of Tsar Nicholas II in March 1917. After the Bolshevik seizure of power in October of that year, he was thrust even closer to the centre of the action, appointed by Prime Minister Lloyd George as his personal – if unofficial – representative to the new leadership. Menaced by the Russians among whom he was living, and harassed by his political masters in London, Lockhart trod a delicate path with courage and skill. He survived, and made his reputation as an adventurer, emerging from a death-row cell in the Kremlin to inspire generations of later Scottish adventurers.

It was hardly surprising that twenty years later, he was still in the thick of the action.

In the bleak mid-war summer of 1941, Sir Robert Bruce Lockhart, now director of the political warfare executive in the Foreign Office, called a meeting with Fitzroy Maclean, a young diplomat recently returned from Moscow, and with Ian Fleming, then a young officer in naval intelligence. Seldom can three musketeers with such a sense of adventure have been gathered together at such a critical time. Lockhart had already done much to expose and confront the Bolshevik regime in Russia in the years during and immediately following the Russian Revolution. Maclean had already witnessed and reported on the horrors of the Stalinist terror in the 1930s and was later to share his impressions with the millions of readers of his Eastern Approaches. Fleming was to enlist an even wider readership to relish James Bond's exploits in confronting the machinations of the Soviet Union during the Cold War. Lockhart was the pioneer, and his track record by the time of this meeting was a remarkable and unexpected one.

No one could have been more intensely and passionately a Scotsman than the young Robert Bruce Lockhart. For the first seventeen years of his life he never left his native shore, and when eventually he went to continental Europe it was before he had ever seen London, or even set foot across the border with England. Much later, after publishing his bestselling book *Memoirs of a British Agent* in 1932, he found that his "misfortune lies in the fact that I have the label of adventure attached to me...my readers expect from me stories of international intrigue with great figures strutting across the stage and the adventurer himself pulling the strings in the background".

His readers had every reason to expect this. After leaving Fettes school and his native Scotland, he had completed his education in Berlin and Paris. He had then set off to be a rubber planter in Malaya, where he had a series of escapades which he was later to record. One such begins by describing how, having "oiled his revolver" and slipped a torch into his pocket, he walked by night through narrow jungle paths and over rickety bamboo bridges to a private rendezvous; it was not, he declared, a journey he would have made for money. This episode turned out to be the prelude to an unsuitable love affair with a Malay girl of royal blood and led to threats against his life. Lockhart was clearly already a young man not to be deterred by danger from achieving his objectives. The incident was a curtain-raiser to more dramatic events that were to follow in Russia a year or two later.

Lockhart had to leave Malaya and his prospects of making a fortune out of the rubber boom because of a bad bout of malaria. After returning to Scotland, where his ill health and rumours of his romantic royal affair pursued him, his father decided that his new career should be in the British consular service. To everyone's surprise

– including his own – he passed the highly competitive entrance exam and was in due course appointed as vice-consul in Moscow in 1912. The glamour of Russian high society and artistic life, as well as the drama of the political scene, were concentrated around the Tsar's court in the capital – St Petersburg – and life in Moscow for a junior official was distinctly drab. Despite this, Lockhart managed to persuade an Australian girl he had met in Scotland to marry him, and she joined him in Moscow. But with the outbreak of the First World War in 1914, everything was to change.

Moscow suddenly became the centre of Russian discontent, of grumbling about the Tsar and his German wife, of exposure to the huge numbers of wounded and disgruntled soldiers returning from the war front, of riots in the streets and of pessimism about the chances of winning a war in which the Tsar had now – at least nominally – taken direct control of the army. There was much to report and much to do in order to influence Russian opinion. Lockhart, from being a junior vice-consul with largely clerical duties, suddenly – while still in his twenties – became an acting Consul-General with a huge burden of political duties, among them advising the ambassador in St Petersburg. He shone in his new role, making friends with rising men such as Maxim Gorky (who was already a popular author and who had been imprisoned for his activities during the abortive 1905 uprisings) and reaching out to subversive layers of Russian society which were beyond the reach of the embassy in the capital.

When in March 1917 the first stage of the revolution erupted on the streets of Moscow, Lockhart reckoned that the Russian people's patience had simply broken down – that the widespread inefficiency and corruption had become too much for them. He considered that no other nation would have put up with these conditions for so long. He was not out of sympathy with the revolutionaries, or with Kerensky – their new and temporary leader – whom he saw as the victim of the bourgeois hopes which his initial success had aroused. In his view Kerensky was a necessary interlude between the Tsarists and the Bolsheviks.

Every effort was made during this interregnum to keep Russia in the war against Germany. Lockhart himself made a stirring public speech to the Soldiers' Soviet in a packed Moscow theatre. Shortly after this, in the autumn of 1917, he was recalled to London, ostensibly because he was showing signs of exhaustion after all his labours in Moscow, but in reality because the ambassador in St Petersburg had learnt that Lockhart was having a romantic affair outside his marriage: he had formed an attachment to a Russian Jewish woman whom he had met casually at the theatre, and in consequence had made himself talked about.

Back in London, where his hard work in Moscow had been much appreciated and where the scandals of his private life were unknown, Lockhart found himself fêted and consulted by the great and good. He had meetings with Mr Lloyd George at 10 Downing Street, and with such luminaries as Lord Milner, Lord Curzon, General Smuts and John Buchan. He was questioned about the likely durability of Lenin and Trotsky, and argued that – however short their probable time in power – it would be foolish not to make contact with the men who were now running Russia. Finally, the Prime Minister, impressed with his knowledge of the emerging figures of the revolution, declared that "Mr Lockhart [is] obviously a man whose right place [is] in Russia and not in London."

By early 1918 Lockhart was indeed on his way back to Moscow. Although he was in effect the personal representative of the Prime Minister, he had been given only the vaguest of instructions about how he might establish relations with the Bolshevik leaders. He carried a letter from Litvinoff (the Bolsheviks' man in London) to Trotsky recommending him as "a thoroughly honest man who understands our position". Despite this, his standing was – at best – equivocal, since Britain had not officially recognized the revolutionary government and so he had no formal diplomatic status. None of this deterred Lockhart: as far as he was concerned, he had been given the opportunity for a great adventure, a mission as difficult as it was exciting. Those difficulties and excitements began in Finland before he even reached Russia: a blown-up bridge across the frontier had to be negotiated at midnight by lantern-light. Creeping across the bridge with an armed escort had been an eerie performance. Far more hair-raising experiences were to follow.

The first weeks after his return to Russia offered depressing evidence of the way in which both St Petersburg and Moscow had become run down and disorganized under the new regime. The streets were full of rubbish; many of the mansions of the aristocracy had become the squatting pads for anarchist groups. When Lockhart called on Trotsky at the Smolny Institute in Petrograd – which before the revolution had been a seminary for young girls of good breeding and had "resounded to the gentle tramp of girls' slippers", but which had become the Bolshevik headquarters – he found that "now all was dirt and confusion…sailors, red guards and working men lounging against the walls…none of them looked as if they had washed for a fortnight".

The few remaining western diplomats were busily trying to get out of the country. At one point Lockhart managed to shuffle the passport of a colonel in British intelligence – who had been working assiduously against the communists and so was on the list of those not allowed to leave – into a pile of passports that were being stamped with exit visas. He achieved this by chatting up and distracting the pretty girl presiding over the passports; he was never one to play too closely by the rules.

One encouraging aspect of his first few weeks back was that the new Soviet leaders – including Lenin and particularly Trotsky – were readily accessible to him. He had numerous significant conversations with them, which he duly reported back to London. Trotsky, who was well aware that Britain was keeping in touch with all elements in the Russian scene, commented to Lockhart that Lloyd George was like a man playing roulette who scattered chips on every number on the board. Lockhart, for his part, developed a certain respect for Trotsky; although he did not share the view of Raymond Robins (head of the American Red Cross mission) that Trotsky was "the greatest Jew since Christ", he recorded in his diary on 15 February 1918 that Trotsky struck him "as a man who would willingly die fighting for Russia providing there was a big enough audience to see him do it." When it came to assessing the relative power of Lenin and Trotsky, though,

Lockhart had no doubts: Trotsky was as incapable of standing against Lenin "as a flea would be against an elephant".

The Bolsheviks were negotiating in a muddled and divided way with the German government about a separate peace settlement. On the one hand they feared that the German army would reinstate the bourgeois classes in Russia and that they would cooperate with the Japanese or other interventionists. On the other, they were desperate to stop the war – one of the main planks of their original programme. There was nothing Lockhart – or probably anyone else – could have done to keep Russia as an effective ally for Britain and France. At times he felt he was a shuttlecock between the Bolshevik leadership and his own government in London.

For all the upheavals, disorder and squalor in the streets, not to mention the champagne-drinking and nightclub carousing of the Russian bourgeoisie who still hoped a German army was coming to reinstate them, the terror of later months and years had not yet begun. The main danger to life during those early days of the revolution was not from the Bolsheviks but from the anarchist bandits who roamed the streets. Lockhart recorded that, when he went out at night, he never went out alone and he kept his finger tight on the gun in his overcoat pocket.

Despite his official preoccupations, it was during this period that Lockhart – whose wife had not accompanied him back to Russia – first met and fell under the spell of Moura von Benckendorff. She was to be a much larger factor in his life than the Jewish woman whose relationship with him had been the cause of his earlier recall. He described Moura as "then twenty-six...a Russian of the Russians with a lofty disregard for all the pettiness of life and a courage that was proof against all cowardice...where she loved, there was her world". Moura had already been romantically involved with Gorky and was to go on to have affairs with H.G. Wells, among others. But her relationship with Lockhart, although it did not develop immediately, was to be deeply significant when it did. It was at this time too that Lockhart first encountered a strongly built man with a sallow face, a black moustache and heavy eyebrows, who did not seem of sufficient importance to deserve his attention: this turned out to be Stalin.

The mixture of normality and violence continued throughout the year, as it does so often in a revolutionary situation. Lockhart attended the ballet, where the same dancers were performing as before, as well as the cabarets which the bourgeoisie continued to frequent. On one occasion, twenty masked men rushed in and relieved the audience of their jewellery and cash. On discovering that Lockhart was British, they returned his money and his watch, explaining that they did not rob Englishmen, and apologizing for being reduced to earning a living by robbery.

One of Lockhart's few soul-mates during these difficult early days of the revolution was the resident Russian-speaking correspondent first of the *Daily News* and later of the *Manchester Guardian* – Arthur Ransome. Lockhart describes him as a "Don Quixote with a walrus moustache", a sentimentalist, a champion of the underdog and – more dangerously – one whose imagination had been fired by the Russian Revolution. Lockhart recounts how Ransome would spin a fairy tale out of anything, how he was an ardent fisherman – and how he was certainly not guilty of the charges of being a Bolshevik agent which were later to be levied against him. Like Lockhart, Ransome was not impervious to the charms of Russian ladies. He courted and eventually married Evgenia Petrovna Shelepina, an attractive girl who was secretary to Trotsky and who helped Lockhart on various occasions – not least in ensuring that the newly arrived German diplomatic mission were refused accommodation at the hotel where Lockhart was living. The future creator of the Swallows and Amazons stories was a civilized and welcome companion, and Lockhart saw him almost daily during a period when good company was difficult to come by.

In fact, Arthur Ransome was a more complex and troubled character than Lockhart acknowledged. He had been quick to recognize – as Lockhart had been – that only Lenin and the Bolsheviks were in a position to exercise any real degree of control over revolutionary Russia. He came under the spell of Lenin, whom he likened to Oliver Cromwell, and in whom he could see little fault. His journalistic contributions were alarmingly uncritical of Bolshevism: so much so that the Bolsheviks took to circulating his articles in translation, not only within Russia but outside too, as evidence of how ill-judged foreign intervention would be. Ransome felt that – as a writer with no political background – he was able to take a more objective view than other commentators. Like Lockhart, he saw himself as an invaluable interlocutor between the British government and the Soviet hierarchy. But unlike Lockhart, he had no official role. Also unlike Lockhart, when the British government finally became involved in intervention against the Bolsheviks, Ransome continued to oppose this vocally and provocatively.

By 1918, Arthur Ransome was being viewed very differently from different quarters. On the one hand, the British intelligence agencies were using him to keep them informed about events and opinions within the Soviet machine, and he was in regular social and working contact with the few remaining British embassy personnel. On the other hand, his by-now-notorious involvement with Trotsky's secretary – Evgenia – was causing scandal and suspicion. He was, after all, already married to an English wife from whom he had not sought a divorce, while Evgenia was still deeply involved with Bolshevik personalities and policies. When Ransome travelled to Sweden and was later joined by Evgenia there, he carried not only a British passport but also Soviet documentation – as well as a large supply of roubles to finance Bolshevik activities and propaganda abroad. Nobody was sure he could be trusted and, when he returned to England in the spring of 1919, he was promptly arrested and taken for interrogation by the head of Special Branch at Scotland Yard. In the event, he was quickly released. But the former Rugby schoolboy, the dedicated fisherman, the teller of children's tales and the tweedy English gentleman was clearly never quite the innocent figure that he liked to represent himself as being. Lockhart might have done well to have kept him at slightly greater arm's length: he was struggling to keep up his own credibility with HMG, and his association with Ransome, however agreeable socially, did not help his reputation in London.

As the Bolsheviks became ever more firmly established, Lockhart did not forget or neglect those earlier and more moderate figures of the revolution who had been his friends. Chief among these was Kerensky, the interim revolutionary leader and president of the Provisional Government. Following the Bolshevik coup in November 1917, Kerensky had not so much been marginalized as declared an "enemy of the revolution". He decided he had to flee the country for his own safety, disguising himself as part of a platoon of Serbian soldiers who were returning home via Murmansk. For this plan to have a chance of success, he needed a visa to enter Britain to show to the British representative in Murmansk. The British consulate (now an ineffective body no longer under Lockhart's control) had declined to issue such a visa. Lockhart had no authority to issue a visa himself without referring the matter to higher authority, and he knew that any attempt to do so would not only hold things up, but be liable to interception by the Soviets. Meanwhile, Kerensky's life was in imminent danger. At any moment he might be betrayed, arrested and shot. Lockhart – not for the first or last time – decided to disregard the rules and do what he thought was right. He therefore took the Serbian passport which Kerensky had procured and wrote out an improvised visa, sealing it with a rubber stamp which he hoped would prove convincing. Kerensky set off immediately for Murmansk, from where he managed to reach England and safety. He remained deeply grateful to Lockhart, with whom he kept in touch for the rest of his life.

Lockhart's period of being in relative favour with the Bolshevik leadership was coming to an end. Until June 1918 he had enjoyed easy access to Trotsky and had regular meetings with most of the other Soviet leaders. But now the British government was starting to despair that Russia would provide any real help in drawing German military resources away from the western front. It was all too clear that Lenin was far more interested in fermenting a communist revolution in Germany (and elsewhere in Europe) than he was in confronting the Kaiser's armies. London was also becoming impatient with Lockhart's arguments for retaining a dialogue with Lenin and Trotsky, and his continued objections to any Allied intervention in support of the bourgeois opposition to the Bolsheviks. His long-suffering wife warned him – in letters and telegrams from London – that he was losing credibility in Westminster and Whitehall. He was being viewed in London as soft on communism, and in Moscow as being soft in his resistance to intervention. It was with reluctance that he accepted that his masters in London were intent on military intervention against the Bolsheviks despite all his arguments. In spite of the war-weariness of the British nation, and in spite of the reluctance of Lloyd George to embark on another perilous foreign venture, Winston Churchill successfully led a popular movement for armed intervention against the Bolsheviks. It was a crusade after his own heart, which (like the Gallipoli campaign) was to end in disaster and a set-back for Churchill's reputation.

Lockhart himself wondered whether he should resign and return home, but concluded that this would have felt rather like deserting his post in the face of the enemy. Where he differed from the view in London was that, while he had no great sympathy for the Bolsheviks, he nonetheless felt there was an idealistic background to Bolshevism which lifted it above the level of a mob movement. He also discounted the idea that it was led by German agents. Despite these reservations, however, the stark realities of Bolshevism were beginning to dawn on Lockhart. He was becoming ever more aware of the brutality of a system which attached no value to the individual but all value to the party or the state. His change of position – from opposing intervention to supporting it – was not (as Arthur Ransome and others suggested) dictated by considerations of his own career prospects and self-interest, but by a more fundamental change of view.

Despite the clear dangers of his new position – he now represented a government openly hostile to the Bolsheviks – Lockhart felt duty-bound to stay in Russia. Another factor in this decision was undoubtedly his growing affection for Moura. As things went from bad to worse, she would offer him a lifeline just when he most needed it.

Between June and August 1918, while Britain – with Lockhart's help – planned an armed intervention in Russian affairs, life in Moscow became more and more disturbing. Lockhart lost access to Trotsky; the Soviets began to cut off food supplies to western representatives in

Moscow; an attempt by the moderate left to overthrow the Bolsheviks was put down; the Tsar and his family were murdered at Ekaterinburg; the Allied embassies – or what remained of them – fled to Archangel from where they could escape the country for good. Although a few consular officials remained behind in Moscow, Lockhart himself – a "British agent" yet no longer part of either the diplomatic or consular staff – became more isolated than ever.

On 4 August news reached Moscow that the Allies had landed a strong military force at Archangel, and were advancing on Moscow. The bourgeois elements who still resisted the Bolsheviks went wild with excitement: their reinstatement on their lands and property seemed imminent. But the rumours were inaccurate: although the Allies had indeed landed, their force was ridiculously small (some 1,200 men in all). The intervention was the worst of both worlds – enough to infuriate the Bolsheviks, but not to have any chance of overthrowing them. The British consulate building was raided by the Cheka (the Bolshevik secret police); while consular officials were being cross-questioned on one floor, the intelligence officers busily burned their cypher books and compromising documents on another.

At this point the Bolsheviks would have liked to arrest all western diplomatic representatives, but they did not want to violate the immunity of diplomatic premises more than was necessary, particularly after most of the remaining westerners had congregated in the Norwegian embassy. They decided it would be easier to starve them out. They surrounded the embassy with troops, and cut off not only food supplies but also water and electricity.[1] But what the Bolsheviks did not know was that the embassy cellars held substantial supplies of food, candles and even tobacco. Moreover, they had overlooked one of the water taps, which was still functioning. The trapped diplomats acted the part of being desperately thirsty.

---

1 The author had similar experiences as British ambassador in Cuba. Whenever Mrs Thatcher (then Prime Minister) made a speech criticizing Cuban involvement in Africa or Central America, the utilities would regularly be cut off from the ambassador's residence, which was particularly disturbing when – with the food shops empty in Havana – the capacity to carry out any diplomatic entertaining depended entirely on the functioning of the deep freezer.

When it rained, they made sure to put out buckets to collect every last drop of water – although in fact they had no need of this. They spent the evenings playing poker and smoking and drinking behind closed curtains. In this way they survived until the time came for a safe departure.

Reluctantly – because he did not believe it could ever succeed – Lockhart did all he could to help the anti-Bolshevik resistance movements. His help was mostly financial. This was not easy because the banks were all closed, and dealing in foreign currency was illegal. However, many disaffected Russians were only too willing to hand over their roubles to Lockhart in exchange for promissory notes on London; they liked the idea of building up some capital abroad for the time when they might have to flee their own country. Meanwhile, Lockhart established contact with a dubious character called Captain Sidney Reilly (the subject of a later chapter) who was busily plotting against the Bolsheviks, and who was later to become a source of embarrassment.

On 31 August 1918 an event occurred which was to put Lockhart in serious and immediate danger. A young Jewish girl called Dora Kaplan, a Socialist Revolutionary, fired twice at Lenin with a pistol as he was leaving a workers' meeting at a Moscow factory. One bullet penetrated his lung, close to his heart, and the other his neck. He appeared to be mortally wounded. Lockhart heard the news within half an hour and quickly surmised that it could have sinister implications for him. He was right. At half past three the next morning, he was awakened by a man pointing a revolver at him. He was ordered to get up and get dressed. There were some ten other armed men in his bedroom. He was informed he was being taken to the Lubyanka – the Cheka headquarters and prison. When he arrived there, he was interrogated by a Bolshevik official called Peters, whom he had met before. As he had foreseen, he was immediately asked whether he knew "that Kaplan woman"? And did he know Reilly, and where he could be found? Lockhart held to the line that he was a diplomatic representative of his government (which strictly he was not) and that as such he would answer no questions. He was told it would be better for him if he spoke up and spoke the truth.

During this interrogation, Lockhart suddenly felt in his breast pocket the notebook in which he had recorded the money he had paid to the opponents of the regime to encourage their resistance. It was a potentially fatal piece of evidence. In the circumstances, flushing it down the loo seemed the only possible way to get rid of it. He asked to go to the lavatory, but was disconcerted when his two armed guards would not allow him to close the door, and instead continued to stand over him menacingly. But he was saved by the insanitary character of the place: "There was no paper. The walls were smeared with stains of human excrement. As calmly as I could, I took out my notebook, tore out the offending pages and used them in the manner in which the circumstances dictated. I pulled the plug. It worked, and I was saved."

He had not long to wait in his cell at the Lubyanka before another prisoner was sent in to join him. She was a dark-haired girl who looked as if she were in her twenties and who had Jewish features. It was Dora Kaplan. He was relieved when she gave no sign of recognizing him. She did not stay with him long. The sentries soon took her out again – this time to be shot.

Lockhart always maintained – even to his own family – that he had played no part in the plot to shoot Lenin, but it seems likely that he had at least met Dora Kaplan, hence his alarm at the prospect of her recognizing him in prison. By the summer of 1918, he was – as the *Oxford Dictionary of National Biography* confirms – "closely involved in negotiations with various groups hostile to Bolshevik rule". His book, *Memoirs of a British Agent,* almost certainly understates his involvement in the various conspiracies that were being hatched against Lenin and his circle during the summer and autumn of that year.

The day after his encounter with Dora Kaplan, somewhat to his surprise, Lockhart was released and allowed to go home. Lenin was still in a critical state, and the city was largely deserted apart from the posses of soldiers at street corners. There was an unaccustomed atmosphere of terror. Newspapers were full of reports of the "Lockhart plot" against Lenin's life. Anxious about the fate of Moura, who had been arrested separately, Lockhart, with his accustomed boldness, walked back to the Lubyanka to inquire after her whereabouts. He was received by his former jailor – Peters – who declared that Lockhart had saved a lot of time and trouble: there was a fresh warrant out for his arrest. He was detained again, and this time he was to be a prisoner for much longer.

Although he was not ill-treated, Lockhart's second detention was much more alarming than the first. He was allowed to read the local newspapers, which carried reports of workers' meetings demanding his trial and execution. He found sleep difficult, as his prison room was continually occupied not only by his jailors but also by other prisoners coming and going. Lockhart pinned his hopes for survival on two factors: the recovery of Lenin and the recovery of the Allies' fortunes on the western front. He watched as other prisoners were sent off to their executions, and was informed that he was to be transferred to quarters in the Kremlin that had just become vacant following the execution of their previous occupant. Lockhart was well aware that the Kremlin was reserved for only the most unfortunate political prisoners, and that hitherto not one had left alive. The betting among his guards was two to one that he would be shot. A single ray of hope was that he heard that Litvinoff – the Bolsheviks' man in London – had been arrested, and was being held against his own release.

Despite his own fears and discomforts, Lockhart was still deeply concerned on behalf of Moura. He appealed to Peters, who seemed still to be in charge of political prisoners, to release her – an innocent woman. Lenin was now well on the way to recovery and, in this somewhat more encouraging atmosphere, Peters not only agreed to release her, but he also allowed her to visit Lockhart in the Kremlin jail. She brought with her clothes, books, tobacco and various other luxuries. For all his adventurous and even reckless ways, Lockhart was still a serious scholar: his prison reading included Thucydides and Macaulay, and – appropriately – Carlyle's history of the French Revolution. During one visit, Moura signalled to him (when no one was looking) that she was placing a note for him inside one of his books. As soon as she had left, he fetched the hidden note. It read simply: "Say nothing – all will be well." This filled his heart with hope.

Shortly after this visit, Peters informed Lockhart that he was to be released and allowed to leave Russia. He also tried to persuade his former captive not to leave the country, but to make a new life in revolutionary Russia, where he would be able to stay with Moura. Peters argued that Lockhart had no future in England: he would never be forgiven for his earlier opposition to intervention – and in any case capitalism was doomed and the future lay with the new world of communism. Lockhart, with his earlier reservations about the Allies' policy of intervention, and with his deep affection for the brave woman who had stood by him in his adversity, was tempted by the offer. Several French diplomats had decided to stay on in Russia. But the pulls towards home proved stronger than any of these considerations. He had begun to see the inherent flaws in the communist ideal, and the huge efforts made on his behalf by his own and other governments could hardly be rejected. He also hoped he would somehow and somewhere meet up again with Moura.

Once he had resolved to go, he wanted to return home as soon as possible. Yet this was no easy matter. The British government did not trust the Bolsheviks, and were reluctant to let Litvinoff out of England until Lockhart was safely back. The Russians, for their part, resented being treated as kidnappers rather than as a responsible government. In the end, a compromise was reached: once Litvinoff reached Norway on his return journey to Russia, Lockhart would be allowed to leave Russia on his return journey to England. He and his companions spent four hours sitting in a motionless train waiting with mounting apprehension for it to begin its journey from Moscow to the frontier. After innumerable snorts and false starts, it set off at two in the morning. When they finally reached the Russian–Finnish frontier, they found that there was no Finnish train to which they could be transferred, and – worse – that there was no news that Litvinoff had reached Norway. Once again, everything was on hold. Some of Lockhart's companions suggested making a dash for it across the frontier before the Soviets changed their minds and they were taken

Moura von Benckendorff

back to Moscow. Lockhart's morale was very low: not only did he feel that he had deserted Moura, he also feared that his professional career might be over. His wavering on intervention – at first hotly opposing it before offering lukewarm support – had, it seemed, left him with no friends and few admirers. He saw his expertise as being discredited. His years of hardship and danger appeared to have been endured to no end.

Lockhart need not have worried too much about Moura's fate after he left Russia. She quickly went to work as an assistant, secretary and translator for Maxim Gorky, living in his house and – it is generally assumed – becoming his mistress. Eventually she managed to leave Russia for her native Estonia, and then moved on to London. Here she became the long-term mistress and companion of H.G. Wells, who was already well established as a bestselling author, and who was among those who – even after prolonged visits to Russia – could see little wrong with the Bolshevik regime there. But she did not lose touch with Bruce Lockhart. When he was en poste as a diplomat in Prague – some six years after they had parted – he visited her and they reminisced affectionately about old times in Moscow. Moura – who by this time had remarried and become Baroness Budberg – made her life in Britain, working during the Second World War on the Free French service of the BBC, where Harold Nicolson found her (according to his diaries) "one of the most delightful people I have ever known". She went on to be for many years an advisor – primarily on all things Russian – to the film director Alexander Korda. (It was in this capacity, towards the end of her life, that I met her, and found her to be one of those older women who – having had notable success in earlier life with a succession of prominent men – still assumed that all men would pay admiring attention to her every whim and tantrum: we did.) Even after her death in 1974, she remained a controversial figure: many people thought she was passing information to the People's Commissariat for Internal Affairs (NKVD, the successor of the Cheka), while others thought she was acting as a British agent. However, it seems likely that her main motivation in life was not political intrigue but a wholehearted commitment to whoever happened to be her current lover.

Lockhart may have been depressed on leaving Moscow, but it was not the case that his mission had been a failure or that it had ruined his reputation. Like others, he had shifted his position, but Lockhart's contribution to the British – and indeed the western – understanding of the Bolshevik revolution was substantial. His charm, youth and enthusiasm had enabled him to establish closer relationships with the Bolshevik leaders than any other official representative. This, coupled with his open-mindedness towards the motivation of the revolutionary leaders – whom he refused to classify as stooges or agents of the Germans or of the Jews – meant that his eventual disillusionment about the Soviet regime, and his support for military intervention against it, had carried all the more weight. While Arthur Ransome had compromised himself through his too-close affiliation with the Bolshevik leaders, Lockhart – despite his doubts and fears on this score – had not. He returned, not to arrest like Ransome, but to a hero's welcome, and was offered a further appointment as a British diplomat abroad. His eventual conclusion that the Bolsheviks could neither be reliable allies nor political friends of England proved to be the case. And this message – from so brave and enterprising a young official – went straight to the heart of government.

Ranald Macdonell

A TEAM OF AGENTS IN THE CAUCASUS

Ranald MacDonell

The Caucasus, lying as it does between the Black Sea and the Caspian, is a region of spectacular mountains, deep ravines and rushing torrents. The only thing more romantic than the scenery is the population – a highland people of dashing warriors and beautiful maidens. Few people could have been better suited to engage with this dramatic region during the tumultuous years of the Russian Revolution than Ranald MacDonell, himself a Highland chieftain – in fact, the twenty-first chief of the Clan Glengarry.

After a brief spell working in Fleet Street, MacDonell's first adventures in life had been – like Bruce Lockhart's – in the East. He had gone to Ceylon as a tea planter and had stayed there for five years. When his father, brother and sister all died in Scotland rapidly one after another, he returned to his native land, promising his mother that in future he would remain somewhere "nearer home". Nearer home turned out to Moscow, where he had "been offered a post" about which he is rather vague in his memoirs. This post was to shape his future life. He learnt to speak and read Russian, and even more importantly became familiar both with the Russian temperament and the weaknesses of the country's administrative and social structure under the Tsarist regime. Outsiders often assumed that it was the conspicuous, wealth-flaunting aristocracy who ran this huge and complex land, with its sophisticated capital city of St Petersburg, its sleepy rural Chekhovian countryside and its vast snowbound steppes. MacDonell grasped that this was not the case: "It was a popular mistake to think that the aristocracy were the governing class… the governing class were the officials drawn from the people, and paid to govern the country so that the aristocracy might not be bothered. Hence all the bottling of the bother, and the final bursting of the bottle." He also learnt to enjoy traditional Russian sports, including wolf hunts, and in his memoirs describes vividly the difficulties and perils of trying to shoot wolves from a fast-moving troika – a three-horse sledge.[2] He was becoming absorbed in all things Russian.

After some months in Moscow, MacDonell moved in 1909 to a job in Baku, the oil-mining port on the west coast of the Caspian. This would later be the scene of many hair-raising adventures during the latter stages of the First World War, but meanwhile he was determined to see something more of the interior of Russia. He sailed to Astrakhan on the north coast of the Caspian, and from there set out up the Volga River. Having satisfied himself that he understood the role of that great river as a highway through Russia, he then – on his next excursion from Baku – turned southwards and explored the interior of Iran – or Persia, as it was still more generally called. He was a restless and inquisitive character. But he always returned to his pedestrian job on the oilfields at Baku and – long before the violence following the revolution broke out – had diagnosed this part of the Caucasus as a potential trouble spot.

With its eighteen distinct races and forty-eight different languages and dialects, MacDonell recorded that "from Biblical times the country has been swept by successive struggles for supremacy by these various races…what a cauldron of trouble!" Although the Tsars had over the previous century steadily incorporated the different elements of the Caucasus (Georgia, Armenia, Chechnya, Dagestan and so on) into their imperial domains, there remained many distinct

---

2 Wolf-hunting was still an active pursuit in the forests north of Moscow when the author was there in the late 1950s and, being just forty years after the revolution, most of the "ghillies" had been working there since Tsarist days. The Personal Epilogue to this book includes a description of such wolf hunts..

The Caucasus
RUSSIA
Volga
Sea of Azov
Astrakhan
River Kuban
CIRCASSIA
ABKHASIA
Kislovodsk
River Terek
Grozny
Black Sea
Caspian Sea
GEORGIA
Batumi
Tbilisi
Trabizond
ARMENIA
Yerevan
Baku
TURKEY:
OTTOMAN EMPIRE
River Aras
N
NE
E
SE
S
SW
W
NW
PERSIA
Enzeli
0
100
200 miles

ethnic elements. Chief among these were the Tartars, who were traditionally descended from Genghis Khan and his nomadic Mongol hordes, and who could still be identified by their Muslim faith and their Turkic language. At the time MacDonell was in the Caucasus, there were nearly a million and a half such Tartars there. Their religious and linguistic connections made the Tartars natural supporters of Turkey, and so a potential threat to the British in the First World War – Turkey being allied to Germany. The strategic importance of the region was increased by the presence of vast oil reserves, which were shipped from Baku, the main port of the Caucasus and the hub of the oil industry. The place was indeed "a cauldron of trouble" waiting to erupt – and erupt it did, in spectacular fashion.

In his memoirs MacDonell records the latent antagonism between the Christian Armenians and the Muslim Tartars in Baku. In 1910 the acting British vice-consul in the city was the target of an assassination attempt by Armenian dissidents. He survived, but he was badly shaken and it was deemed improper and too dangerous for him to stay on. He was recalled to Britain, and the vacancy was filled by MacDonell, the only British official on this turbulent scene. For the first time in his hitherto disoriented career, he was now serving his country rather than his own personal interests. It was a turning point in his life and, unconventional though his methods might have been, the service he delivered was to prove of the highest value.

MacDonell's early time as a vice-consul was taken up with the usual preoccupations of a consular office: assisting British businessmen and sorting out the problems of visitors. This continued for the first two years of the First World War, then everything changed dramatically. The region's internal conflicts and rivalries suddenly became significant on the world stage. Baku – poised on the edge of the Caucasus, with its rich oil reserves and its strategic position on the perceived route for any invading army heading towards India – became the centre of intrigue and infighting, not just between the traditional factions, but between the Muslims supporting Germany's ally Turkey, the Armenian and Georgian Christians, the Bolsheviks, the Mensheviks and the Socialist Revolutionaries (the former supporters of Kerensky), as well as all the other emerging and aggressive groupings that had been spawned by the Russian Revolution and the global conflict. In 1917 MacDonell was given a commission in the British army, promoted to the rank of major, and effectively recruited to run secret service operations. Where before he had spent his days giving commercial advice to itinerant businessmen and rolling out the red carpet for VIP visitors, he was now confronted by a completely new challenge – and he rose to the occasion.

The first of his many clandestine duties was surreptitiously to finance – with "mounds of paper roubles" – all those who could be persuaded or bribed to fight against the advancing Turks. These were not only Armenian and Georgian Christians but – at least to start with – Russians of both the old and the new communist order. However, it quickly became clear that the Russian enthusiasm for fighting Germany had evaporated. MacDonell records seeing a troop train leaving for the front: "their womenfolk lay on the line to prevent the train leaving; the soldiers refused to remove them, and they had to be removed forcibly by Cossacks". He comments that the Cossacks would undertake any task, however unpleasant.

Tbilisi was the focal point of attempts to rally resistance to the Turks, and MacDonell set about making regular trips from Baku to that city, concealing his stash of roubles not only in his clothes but also in the upholstery of the train compartments. These journeys could be eventful. The trains were often stopped and searched; sometimes they were derailed; frequently railway stations were set on fire; and on one occasion they were fired at by a Russian count who had joined the revolutionaries and was determined to thwart MacDonell's efforts to finance the "reactionary forces". Whatever the provocation, MacDonell strictly forbade his companions to shoot back at their opponents, convinced that this would precipitate a blood bath. Sometimes he travelled with an escort in luxury railway coaches hooked onto the back of refugee trains; at other times he travelled for days alone, sitting on his suitcase in an overcrowded goods wagon with no "facilities" except a shared bucket. There was no room for protocol in the dangerous game the vice-consul was now playing.

By 1918, in addition to running roubles into Tbilisi, MacDonell was engaged in Scarlet-Pimpernel-like exploits smuggling Tsarist Russians out of the country. Some were senior army officers with a price on their heads. One particularly vulnerable escapee was General Polovtsov, who had distinguished himself in an attempt to overthrow the Bolshevik coup in St Petersburg the previous year. He had a price of 50,000 roubles on his head – "dead or alive". Many of the Russian troops on the train between Tbilisi and Baku were deserters from the Tsar's army and active revolutionaries; more alarmingly, some had actually served in Polovtsov's own regiment and knew him well by sight. If they discovered him in their midst, they would shoot him and his wife without compunction and claim their reward.

It was decided to smuggled the General onto the train disguised as an American missionary. The missionary in question had died some time before, but MacDonell had managed to get hold of his and his wife's passports, and it was on these that the Polovtsovs travelled. Even so they dared not expose themselves to view, and spent five full days shut up in their compartment, letting it be known that the missionary was very ill and that his wife was nursing him.

This particular train journey was one of MacDonell's worst. At one point the engine driver ran out of water to generate steam, and it took hours to find a working water cock. The passengers were frequently on the point of mobbing the driver. At several stations they were forced to fight off Tartar tribesmen led by Turkish officers – one battle lasted four hours before they were able to get their train through the station, which was already in flames. MacDonell noted that it was "highly entertaining that these Bolshevik soldiers on the train should fight a path to freedom for the General [whom they would have shot if they had recognized him] and his wife". Somehow the Polovtsovs got through to Baku, where MacDonell installed them in his apartment until he could "by various subterfuges" get visas stamped on their American passports and smuggle them onto a tramp steamer sailing for Persia. One of the difficulties throughout their escape by train and ship had been that – although both spoke excellent English – they found it hard to conceal the fact that their first language was

Russian, and tended to respond visibly to anything said in their hearing in Russian. MacDonell was sad but also relieved to part company with such an enterprising and charming couple.

In parallel with these secret service activities, MacDonell still had some consular duties to perform. Most challenging of these was rescuing the small British community left behind in the Caucasian town of Grozny, some 300 miles north of Baku in Chechnya. The town had been taken over by the Bolsheviks, who were running it as a model communist community: "everybody who had never been anybody was now a member of some committee". The town had been surrounded by hostile Muslim Chechens, who shelled the place often enough to force the population to dig themselves protective trenches and shelters – a task that usually fell to the expatriate community because the Russians were too busy sitting on their committees. Food was short, money was even shorter, and the Bolsheviks found that the best way of raising cash was periodically to arrest some member of the British community and oblige him or her to pay a ransom for their release. The community clearly needed rescuing. MacDonell required three separate passes to get through the strife-torn territory between Baku and Grozny; one of his problems was knowing which pass was required at which checkpoint – to produce the wrong one would prompt indefinite delay or detention, despite his consular status. When he finally arrived – the last obstacle being an electrified barbed-wire fence that surrounded the town – he was met with a blank refusal to allow any of the British men to leave with him. Wives and children were permitted to depart, though some of the wives felt it their duty to remain with their husbands whatever the risks and hardships. MacDonell was later to feel that by bringing these refugees out of Grozny and back to Baku he had taken them out of the frying pan and into the fire. Be that as it may, he had seen for himself – at a time when much western opinion was still undecided on the merits or otherwise of communism – something of the reality of life in a model Bolshevik community. He had not been impressed.

***

On many of his train runs between Tbilisi and Baku – including the one on which the Polovtsovs had been ferried to safety – MacDonell had been accompanied by a remarkably fearless and enterprising intelligence officer who had first appeared in the Caucasus carrying a large quantity of smuggled roubles from Tehran, and with similar instructions to those which MacDonell had received. This was Captain Edward Noel, and he was soon to have a very dramatic adventure of his own.

Captain Noel was an officer from the Indian Political Service who in 1912 had – most unusually – spent a whole year in Russia learning the language. Although he had some Scottish blood, Noel was more an Englishman than a Scotsman, but he had in common with MacDonell an aristocratic background: his grandfather was the Earl of Gainsborough. He has sometimes been thought to be the role model for John Buchan's character Sandy Arbuthnot: like Arbuthnot, he was a fine linguist, a good shot, a splendid horseman and an intrepid adventurer in eastern parts. However, this seems unlikely. Buchan first introduced Arbuthnot to his readers in his novel *Greenmantle* which was published in 1916, and Noel's first publicized adventures began only in 1918, although he had achieved a certain notoriety among his contemporaries for having bicycled from England to India in 1909 and – as if once was not enough – again in 1910, camping en route with various tribes and nomads who were not renowned for their hospitality to foreign travellers. He had a gift for making himself acceptable in surroundings where his compatriots were seldom seen and even more seldom accepted.

This was the man who joined MacDonell in the perilous activity of running illicit funds into Tbilisi to finance resistance among the Georgians, Armenians and any others who might be bribed or cajoled into resisting the Turkish advance into the Caucasus. On one occasion when his rail compartment stuffed with roubles was about to be searched, Noel had the brilliant idea of suggesting that the Persian Consul-General (who happened to be present) should make an impartial supervision of the procedure, knowing perfectly well that this strictly correct consular official would be embarrassed by any involvement in searching an Englishman's – particularly a fellow consul's – compartment, and so would ensure that the process was as unintrusive as possible. Sure enough, the rail compartment was subjected to less-than-thorough scrutiny and the hidden roubles remained undetected. Noel was proving himself to have the skills of a secret agent as well as those of a soldier and a political officer.

By the end of February 1918 any hope of fostering real resistance to the Turks in Tbilisi had evaporated. The field of activity moved to Baku, though conditions there were scarcely more auspicious. Noel was later to write that "nobody knew who was really governing… there were Socialist Revolutionaries, the Bolsheviks, the Mensheviks, the Tartars, the White Russians, the Armenians…and a host of other potential aspirants to power". He would look back on his time in Baku as an unreal nightmare made up of midnight meetings, clandestine assignations, plots and desperate schemes. He busied himself handing out cheques to anyone prepared to resist the Turks until such time as the British General Lionel Dunsterville and his interventionist force – in which all hopes were now vested – arrived.

However, Dunsterville and his troops remained stuck at Kasvin in Persia, and eventually Noel decided to travel south in order to make direct contact with the army and try to find a way to speed its progress. The first stage was to take a ship down the Caspian coast to Enzeli; he would then ride overland from there. At Enzeli he was met by the director of customs, who turned out to be an old friend and invited him to stay. It turned out to be a disastrous invitation.

One of the reasons why Dunsterville had been making such slow progress through Persia was that the forested terrain between Kasvin and Enzeli was the haunt of a gang of Muslim extremists known as the Jungalis. This gang had been staunch enemies of Tsarist Russia – and so by extension of Russia's allies, including Britain. They had now thrown in their lot with the Bolsheviks, and were well aware of Noel's anti-Bolshevik activities in Baku. They had also learnt of his departure for Enzeli and his stay with the customs director there. On the first night, while he was dining upstairs, a party of Jungalis arrived at the front door of the house and announced they had come to kidnap him. Noel overheard what was going on, and with his customary quick-wittedness threw his diplomatic and cypher papers into the Russian stove in the dining room. He then went downstairs and allowed himself to be captured.

Initially he was guarded by just four men, and held in a ground-floor room from which he could see parties of Russian troops wandering up and down Enzeli's quayside in search of a ship that might take them home. Mindful of the accepted wisdom that the best moment for a prisoner of war to escape is immediately after his capture, and thinking that he would throw himself on the goodwill or mercy of the Russians, Noel decided to make a bid for freedom. He dashed past his guards, belted along the quayside and hurled himself into the arms of the startled and bemused Russian soldiery. A curious scene then developed: Noel tugged at the beard of a friendly-looking Russian and pleaded for protection; the Russian adopted a protective manner; the Jungalis arrived in hot pursuit; the local Persian dock workers crowded round to witness or join in the scrap. "A tug of war ensued, in which I was the rope," Noel recorded. Alas, the Jungalis won the day and, stowing their captive in a small boat, took him offshore to a safer prison – where, with surprising gallantry and no recriminations, they offered him tea and cigarettes.

Noel was not one to give up easily. His first escape attempt had failed; now he began thinking up another. While enjoying a quiet cigarette, he noticed that his captors were smoking more seriously – opium pipes, in fact. Noel knew that opium had a soporific effect: perhaps if he could keep them at it his guards might become too drowsy to bother preventing another escape attempt. He decided that the best way to achieve this would be to pay for his own pipe and, having joined them in their indulgence, to await developments. Unfortunately he set about his task with too much enthusiasm, and by the time his guards were showing signs of drowsiness, he himself was too far gone to try another escape: "I postponed from minute to minute the decision to act." He had been caught in his own trap.

Soon Noel was in the hands of less drowsy guards and, having been rowed through a series of lagoons, he was taken ashore by his captors and mounted on a pony for a long ride into the forests. Eventually, having lost all sense of direction, he arrived at a forest encampment where he was confined in a hut under the vigilant eye of an Islamic guardian. It was here that his serious troubles began.

A few days later he was brought before a self-appointed court and accused of the murder of Tartars and other Muslims in Baku. In fact this massacre had been perpetrated by Armenians – who were a Christian minority and themselves often the victim of persecution – and had taken place shortly after Noel had left the city. Noel pleaded that he knew nothing about the massacre, but his abrupt departure just before it happened suggested to his captors that he had set it up and then cleared off in time to avoid the consequences. More damning still was his chequebook, which had been discovered, and the stubs of which revealed that Noel had paid large sums of money to Armenians – perhaps even to the murderers themselves – before he left Baku. (The stubs of course related to the bribes he had dispensed in the hope of winning support against the invading Turks.) Noel cursed himself for not having burnt his chequebook along with his diplomatic cyphers at the moment of his arrest. His inability to explain the payments proved fatal, and the kangaroo court condemned him to death by firing squad the next day.

The following morning, after several unsuccessful attempts to make him "confess" by suggesting that this would cause his execution to be suspended, Noel was led out by a firing squad to a clearing in the forest. Then, at the last moment, he was told that his execution had been postponed – and shortly afterwards, that it had been permanently suspended.

He was not to be freed, however, and one of his guards tried to persuade him to part with his gold pocket watch to finance a further escape attempt. Noel was instinctively – and, it turned out, rightly – suspicious of the man, and declined the offer, although he did begin to hoard food secretly in readiness for another get-away. When his hidden supplies were discovered, he was moved again – blindfolded and at night – to a camp even deeper in the forest, and warned that any attempt to run away would end inevitably in his becoming "hopelessly entangled in the thorn brambles and bog".

Noel never accepted that this jungle clearing was escape-proof: he could see snowcapped and inviting mountains a mere ten miles away. If he could just survive those ten miles of dense undergrowth and swamp he would reach friendlier, nomad-populated country. Once again he began to secrete supplies for the journey, this time in a hollow wooden beam. He also prepared a cover story in case he ran into anyone in the forest. He had overheard conversations about an Armenian merchant who had bought timber rights in the locality; if challenged, he would try to pass himself off as a Russian agent of this merchant.

There remained one big problem: his guardians removed his shoes at night and kept them on the ground floor next to the family's dog, while Noel slept on the floor above. To make it through the dense forest would be hard enough if properly shod; to do so barefoot would be quite impossible. Noel began to tie his shoe laces together before surrendering his shoes at night. He then constructed a hook out of a piece of abandoned metal, and attached it to a string made out of cotton thread. With this device he planned to fish silently for his shoes through a hole in the floor, and retrieve them without waking the dog.

He decided that the only chance of success was to make his bid for freedom at full moon and under a clear sky that would allow him to navigate by the stars. After one abortive attempt, a spell of bad weather forced him to put his plans on hold for another month. At last the opportunity presented itself. He tiptoed past his sleeping guards, successfully fished for his shoes, slid down a pole, and made off into the jungle. His captors had not been exaggerating about the thorn brambles and the difficulty of the terrain: soon Noel's trousers were in tatters and his shoes encased in mud. He pressed on. After a time he reached a clearing in the forest given over to rice cultivation and manned by watchmen and guard dogs. All attempts to elude them were in vain, and Noel – looking very like the escaped convict he was – found himself trapped by men and dogs. It was here that his cover story proved its worth: he explained that he was the Russian agent of the Armenian timber merchant, and – to his relief and surprise – they accepted his tale without demur. He was on his way again. His legs were lacerated, and his feet were so swollen that he had to cut open his shoes with an old razor blade. As he staggered on, he became ever more careless of his safety. After a night spent in an empty woodcutter's cottage he had chanced upon, he found himself on a track which – since it appeared to be virtually untrodden – he failed to recognize as a caravan route. Eventually he arrived at a hostelry, where he slept on a shelf with other weary travellers.

In the morning Noel was rudely awakened. After a desperate hunt when they discovered his escape, his captors had lost his tracks in the jungle and all but given up hope of finding him. Then, by sheer chance, they had stumbled on the same caravan track as he had. His tiredness and swollen feet had delivered him into their hands. This time they had no intention of allowing him to try his tricks again. His feet were shackled together with heavy irons and he was taken still further into the jungle to yet more remote place of custody. His guards, who now believed him to have supernatural powers of escape, planned to take no further chances with their Houdini-like prisoner. It was a start of a long period of close confinement, of lonely self-recrimination, of trying to maintain sanity by reciting all the poetry he knew by heart, of losing weight, losing his health, and losing any hope of freedom. Although there was evidence that Dunsterville's force was nearing – in the form of bombing raids on Jungali camps in the forest – Noel was continually told about the heavy losses inflicted on British troops by the Jungalis. Rescue seemed ever more unlikely.

Just when he was on the point of despair, everything changed. Without warning, he was released from his shackles, taken to more civilized surroundings and invited to participate in a generous meal. It transpired that the Jungalis had made peace with General Dunsterville, and that one of the conditions of this had been the release "safe and sound" of Captain Noel.

The only problem was that he was not "sound". He was desperately thin, covered in sores from his shackles and looking altogether haggard. His captors decided they could not hand him back in this condition.

There followed a period of embarrassment and frustration while the Jungalis tried to fatten him up as if he were a duck for market, and he tried to "grow a paunch and a double chin as rapidly as possible". Eventually all concerned realized that they were never going to make a plump Persian out of a lean British officer, and he was handed over as he was to the nearest British military commander. Noel was allowed to join up with Dunsterville's force, by now in Baku, and he resumed his part in the struggle against the Bolsheviks. In his own words: "I was once again back in life."

One of the things that had most frustrated Noel during these adventures was that he felt himself to be missing out on the action. When he was captured, he wrote that he "was filled with wild regret at the prospect of no longer taking a hand in what seemed to me the making of history". And indeed history was being made. On Noel's first arrival in the Caucasus after the collapse of the Tsar's army, his prime duty had been to encourage resistance to Turkey's advance into the region. But with the growing international alarm at the way in which the Russian Revolution was developing, the emphasis had changed. Henceforth the main task was the containment of Bolshevism: a far more prolonged, difficult and far-reaching endeavour. In this wider task, Noel had even before his capture played a significant role, as evidenced by the high regard in which he was held by MacDonell, who was masterminding anti-Bolshevik activities.

Now he was to rejoin MacDonell who, during Noel's detention, had found himself virtually alone among the Bolsheviks in Baku, and badly in need of such support.

***

Ranald MacDonell may have been feeling lonely among the Bolsheviks in Baku while Noel had been undergoing his ordeal with the Jungalis, but he had not been idle. The Bolshevik commissars had grasped effective control of the port and town, and – although MacDonell had established good relations at a personal level with the chief commissar – he knew that he was being closely followed by the commissars' secret agents, who were interested in ascertaining all they could about his contacts. He used to delight in teasing his minders by taking long walks in the heat of the day which exhausted them more than him, and then asking them cheerfully how they were enjoying themselves.[3]

There were good reasons for the Bolsheviks to keep MacDonell under close observation. He was running a network of agents, many of them young girls from aristocratic families who were determined to help overthrow the revolutionaries in any way possible. One such girl approached MacDonell with what seemed the unlikely claim that she knew of anti-Bolshevik elements who could be mobilized in the aviation school and even in the oilfields. There were also, she said, "hundreds of Tsarist officers in hiding". Believing she was an *agent provocateur*, he politely rejected her offer of help, but then she burst into tears so convincingly that he changed his mind and recruited her on the spot. She and her friends passed subversive messages to other agents, including to an Orthodox priest who even communicated secrets at the communion rail. Others carried messages in the soles of their shoes or in the leather buttons of their coats. He thought of them as "little heroines" and later commented that the young lady who had first approached him "proved to be one of those wonderful Russian women who often make one feel ashamed of being a mere man".

It was true that there were lots of former Tsarist officers in hiding in Baku, but MacDonell was not always impressed with them. He wrote that "every Tsarist Captain had gazetted himself Colonel or General, and the whole thing was rather like a comic opera". Nor was the comic effect restricted to the Tsarist elements in society. MacDonell's domestic servants had decided that, under the new regime, he should no longer be addressed as "Master", which was "a sign of serfdom", but as "Comrade". They also wanted to eat in the dining room with their Comrade/Master and sit with him in the drawing room afterwards.

---

3 When the author was at the British embassy in Moscow in the late 1950s, he found that he was similarly followed by the KGB (successors of the NKVD). There were various well-tried methods of shedding one's followers, but it was generally found best to do this only when there was some special reason for needing to be untracked. Repeated teasing of the minders only resulted in ever closer and more intrusive surveillance.

MacDonell's response was to welcome the proposals and say that he looked forward to them joining him in listening to classical music, reading political economy and studying the arts. Predictably this was not the sort of evening entertainment his domestic staff had in mind, and he heard no more of their suggestions for sharing his dinner table and drawing room.

MacDonell had more serious things on his plate than the tiresome foibles of self-important Tsarist officers and stroppy Bolshevik servants. A plot was being devised to overthrow the regime of the commissars in Baku, and he had a central part to play in that plot. The plan was that the workmen on the oil fields (infiltrated with opponents of the new regime) would call a strike and stage a peaceful demonstration. The commissars would undoubtedly send the police to deal with the demonstration; with the police distracted from their normal protection duties, the Tsarist officers – hitherto in hiding – would emerge with their revolvers and arrest the commissars, thereby terminating the Bolshevik regime. The aviation school, with its old-fashioned seaplanes, and the offshore fleet would both support the coup. MacDonell's role was that of coordinator and paymaster. Everything depended on total secrecy – and the coded messages carried by MacDonell's *débutante* couriers to the priests and officers.

Like many another well-laid plan, it went awry. One of the key conspirators was arrested on the eve of the intended strike. MacDonell saw him being carried off by the Bolshevik police, and rushed into a shop to avoid the risk that the detained man would show any sign of recognizing him. He then called on the priest, who philosophically remarked that if the arrested plotter succumbed to "the persuasive atmosphere of a Bolshevik prison", then he, MacDonell and the others behind the plot would certainly be arrested. On the other hand, if he did not succumb, by the following night "there would be no Bolsheviks left to arrest us". They decided to go ahead as if nothing had happened, and not to alarm the other plotters by telling them of the arrest.

By the next morning it was clear that the coup had been aborted. MacDonell found no strikers on the sea front, the shops were open as usual, and the Russian to whom he had entrusted his clandestine funds had fled across the Caspian. At the cafés and bars where the conspirators had gathered were now only empty chairs at empty tables. MacDonell found himself under much more obvious and intense surveillance, and it seemed only a matter of time until he too would be arrested by the commissars.

As he pondered his next move, he received a secret message from the priest, giving details of a rendezvous for that night. On arriving at the specified time and place, MacDonell was asked to climb a ladder, then spirited away over vertiginous rooftops – "Don't go near the edge," he was warned – before passing "through another hole and down another ladder, at the foot of which was a young girl". He was back under the protection of the network of Tsarist *débutantes* which he had so hesitantly set up. This was just the first stage. He was now invited to don the boots and uniform of a Red Army soldier. He thought of protesting that it was neither "meet nor proper" for a representative of His Majesty's Government to masquerade as a Bolshevik soldier, but on reflection decided it was best to go along with what the young ladies proposed. So – now disguised in an ankle-length military greatcoat – he set off again, this time for a meeting with three unknown conspirators. They told him that he was shortly to be arrested; that he should accept the legal adviser his captors would assign to him; and that he should not worry – all would be well. MacDonell retraced his path over the rooftops and returned home.

As predicted, he was arrested the following evening and taken by the head of the secret police to the Bolshevik commissars' council chamber. Sure enough, a lawyer was produced to defend him, and MacDonell raised no objection. Next, the lawyer showed him some letters that were alleged to have come from a fellow conspirator. Having been briefed on what to look out for, MacDonell pointed out that the typewriter on which they were written had certain distinctive abnormalities. He then produced from his pocket a letter he had received from the senior commissar – this had identical abnormalities. Clearly both documents originated in the senior commissar's office. Did it not follow that the commissar had manufactured the evidence and fabricated the plot as an excuse to arrest his enemies and take power? This, MacDonell declared, would be his line of defence. After much worried consultation it became evident that the senior commissar had no wish for these accusations to be aired in public. The charges were withdrawn, and in the small hours of the morning MacDonell was escorted home. It had been a strangely devious way of undermining the charges against him, and it showed that his friends – be they Tsarist officers or aristocratic young ladies – had allies in unexpected places.

Though he was no longer under immediate threat of being convicted of the capital offence of plotting against the commissars, Baku was no place for MacDonell to linger. It would only be a matter of time before he was re-arrested if he stayed on. However, his good luck continued. He found a Bolshevik police officer who was worried about his gambling debts: if MacDonell would settle these, he could arrange for him to get away by ship to Enzeli, a port on the Caspian coast where he would be able to meet up with the representatives of General Dunsterville. MacDonell reckoned it was £200 of British taxpayers' money well spent. He was stowed away in the engine room of a steamer bound for Enzeli, hidden behind a red-hot boiler with only a small bucket of water to help him survive. But survive he did, and soon he was among other British officers on the Persian coast and no longer the lonely figure he had been in Bolshevik-dominated Baku.

During his final weeks in Baku, MacDonell had been joined by Captain Reginald Teague-Jones, also a British intelligence officer. Teague-Jones had brought the news that the British government had finally decided they could not work with the Bolsheviks, who had now made peace with Germany and were therefore no longer allies. From now on, undermining Bolshevism was to be a top priority both for MacDonell and his colleagues.

MacDonell had not been long at Enzeli before he heard disturbing news from Baku. In his absence his trial had been reopened – now that he was out of the country, there was no fear that he would discredit the commissars by revealing the typewriter abnormalities.

Unable to defend himself, he had been found guilty of plotting against the commissars' regime and condemned to be shot. It turned out that had escaped in the nick of time: several other plotters who had stayed behind had already been executed.

One of MacDonell's first objectives in Enzeli was to make contact with General Dunsterville in order apprise him of the situation in Baku. This he did at Kasvin in Persia, halfway between Enzeli and Tehran, where Dunsterville was still waiting with his small task-force of British troops for the right moment to intervene in Baku. Now, quite suddenly, encouraging news began to filter through from that city. The Turks had advanced so close to the port that gunfire could be heard in the centre of the town, and the frightened anti-Turk forces – comprising some elements in the Bolshevik regime, the Socialist Revolutionaries, the Armenians and the offshore fleet – had finally decided they had no choice but to invite Dunsterville and his British troops ("Dunsterforce") to intervene before the Turks captured and looted the town. Twenty-six of the hard-line Bolshevik commissars – including the senior commissar – had not been prepared to accept British military support and attempted to flee across the Caspian to a safe haven, but they had been intercepted and brought back to jail in Baku.

The way was clear for MacDonell to return to Baku and prepare the ground for Dunsterforce's arrival. But when this British force finally came, on a ship called the 'Kruger', it proved disappointingly small, consisting mostly of officers and advisers and with less than a thousand fighting troops. Dunsterville himself described the predicament: "A British General on the Caspian, the only sea unploughed before by British keels, on board a ship named after a South African President and whilom enemy, sailing from a Persian port, under a Serbian flag, to relieve from the Turks a body of Armenians in a revolutionary Russian town." The whole venture was too complex; the force too small; the timing too late; the support on the ground too confused and half-hearted. One local resident was later to speak scathingly to MacDonell of how the British had talked of sending an army and then arrived with two batmen, a Ford van and a general. Soon Dunsterville had to face the fact that either his force would be captured or annihilated, or he had to withdraw it by sea while he could. He chose the latter option, for which he was much criticized and relieved of his command. But MacDonell for one thought he had done the right and honourable thing.

Meanwhile the twenty-six imprisoned Bolshevik commissars had been shipped away by their influential friends – having been told they were bound for Astrakhan. This town on the northern shore of the Caspian was firmly in Bolshevik hands and they would have been safe there. Dunsterville had been delighted to see them go to a destination where they could cause no further trouble to him, and MacDonell actually went on board to see the senior commissar off, as he had good personal relations with him. But once at sea, for reasons that remain unclear (possibly a question of fuel, or else a political decision on the part of the captain), the ship changed course for Krasnovodsk, a port on the eastern coast of the Caspian which was under the control of the Socialist Revolutionaries. This group – Kerensky's former supporters – were no friends of the Bolsheviks. They promptly arrested the commissars, and some time later put them on a train, from which they were unloaded in the desert and peremptorily shot.

The British agent who was held responsible by the Communist Party for decades to come for this brutal and fatal sequence of events was not MacDonell, but the intelligence agent who had been sent to join him at Baku – Captain Teague-Jones. This officer had already had his share of dangerous exploits.

***

In some ways Captain Reginald Teague-Jones was not unlike Noel: both had a flair for languages; both had a background in the Indian Foreign and Political Service; both had experience of working in disguise in the tribal regions on the north-west frontier of India; and both had lived and studied at an impressionable age in Russia. As a young teenager Teague-Jones had witnessed the abortive Bloody Sunday demonstration against the Tsar in St Petersburg in 1905, and – as an innocent bystander – had almost been crushed to death as a result of the Cossacks' brutal treatment of the demonstrators. He learned at an early age that revolution was a rough business.

In July 1918, as a promising young intelligence officer, Teague-Jones was dispatched to the Caucasus, disguised as an Armenian trader. He was sent by General Wilfrid Malleson, the head of the British intelligence station in Persia, and his mission was two-fold: first, he was to try to find out what was happening at Baku (where so many disparate elements were struggling for power and control of the oilfields) and to report back; and second, he was to convey to MacDonell the decision of the war cabinet in London to end their confused and vacillating policies towards the Russian revolutionaries and to commit themselves firmly to opposing the Bolsheviks (this was the same decision that had been conveyed to Bruce Lockhart in Moscow). As we have seen, this new policy of outright hostility to the Bolsheviks placed MacDonell in a more difficult position than ever: he would now be operating inside what was effectively enemy territory, and against an ever more brutal opponent. Less than a week after Teague-Jones arrived in Baku, the Bolsheviks would murder Tsar Nicholas II and his family at Ekaterinburg.

Having completed his twin missions in Baku, Teague-Jones took ship for Krasnovodsk on the eastern coast of the Caspian Sea. Here a new challenge awaited him. Krasnovodsk was crowded with Russian cargo-boats loading up cotton and about to set sail for Bolshevik-occupied Astrakhan, an important port at the mouth of the Volga River on the northern shore of the Caspian. To many observers, this might not have seemed of great significance. However, Teague-Jones – with his intelligence training – knew that cotton was a vital ingredient in the manufacture of explosives. He also knew that the Bolsheviks in Astrakhan were desperately short of cash and were almost certain to sell the cotton on to the Germans, with whom Britain was still at war. The cotton cargo ships must at all costs be prevented from reaching Astrakhan. But how?

Having rejected on practical grounds the idea of burning down or blowing up the cotton warehouses or the ships, Teague-Jones made contact with a Russian acquaintance who was of the Tsarist old school and therefore fiercely – if secretly – opposed to the Bolshevik cause. The pair concocted a plan: first, they would draft a spurious message, purporting to come from the Bolshevik authorities in Astrakhan, that instructed the port authorities at Krasnovodsk to cease forthwith all loading of cotton, to unload any already aboard, and to send the cargo-boats away for other duties elsewhere; second, they would bribe an employee at the telegraph office to infiltrate this false message among genuine ones; third, as soon as the message had been received and accepted at face value, they would ensure that the transmitters broke down and were not repaired until all the spurious instructions had been carried out (so that no compromising messages could be received from the real Bolshevik authorities). On this last point, according to Teague-Jones's diaries, the telegraph repairer commented: "As a matter of fact, it is much easier to arrange for it to break down than it is to keep it going, the way things are being run at present."

Everything depended on the fellow conspirators' cooperation, and this needed lubrication by some extensive bribery. Teague-Jones was up to the challenge. He produced a penknife, split open the lining of his clothes and unloaded a very substantial amount of roubles. These were handed over to his Tsarist contact, who passed them on to the operatives inside the telegraph office. All went according to plan: the message was accepted as genuine and the cotton shipments ceased. Predictably, there was much speculation in Krasnovodsk as to the reasons for this reversal: some people thought it was to free up shipping for an evacuation of Baku; others that it was to enable the ships to bring in British interventionist troops from Persia to attack the Turks. But, as Teague-Jones commented, "all that mattered was that not a bale of cotton left Krasnovodsk".

The cotton bales had a further part to play in Teague-Jones's story. Hydraulically compressed cotton bales were so dense that they were bullet-proof, and it was suggested to him that they might be used as part of the defences of Krasnovodsk – and of the railway carriages which ran from there to Ashkabad, a line liable to come under unfriendly fire. A trial run was set up and Teague-Jones was invited to witness first-hand the effectiveness of the cotton bales by remaining inside a rail truck while shots were fired at it. Fortunately, he declined: it turned out that the bales had been compressed by hand, and the bullets went straight through them.

Teague-Jones was now anxious to return to Mashad in Persia to report on the position in Baku to General Malleson. He started the journey by rail, on a line that had been built by the Russians across the Karakum desert between Krasnovodsk and Ashkabad. It was a line that would have facilitated any Tsarist advance towards India, and it remained a strategically important route. One of Teague-Jones's self-imposed tasks was to calculate how easy or difficult it would be to sabotage it. This depended on the number and positioning of the culverts and bridges beneath which explosive charges could be laid. The Captain therefore sat in a window seat and quietly noted these features. As darkness fell, the only position from which he could continue his observations was the platform at the back of the train, but the guard on the train became suspicious and ordered him to go inside. Undaunted, Teague-Jones soon found an excuse to go out again: he chatted up a pretty girl and invited her to continue their flirtation in the privacy of the rear platform. This time no one disturbed them – and he managed to note down every culvert.

When he reached Ashkabad, he found that the Bolshevik regime there had been overthrown in a violent coup by reactionary Turkmen elements. He pressed on southward to Mashad, travelling by hired mule, in order to report as soon as possible this new and dramatic development to the British consulate and the intelligence officers there. After several days of struggling through the mountains, cajoling officials at checkpoints and frontiers to let him pass, persuading a doctor to let him through a quarantine zone, pushing and kicking his mule over passes in the middle of the night – "poor little brute, I am afraid I was very cruel to it" – and even "practically carrying the beast" at one point, Teague-Jones eventually reached Mashad. At the consulate, he was disconcerted to be informed that General Malleson "had gone to bed, not to be disturbed". All his battling against the elements, the terrain and the obstructions en route were as nothing next to the overriding priority of the general's good night's sleep!

Captain Teague-Jones

The general did eventually listen to Teague-Jones's report, and he was duly dispatched back to Ashkabad to try to consolidate resistance to the Bolsheviks there. From Ashkabad, however, he was advised to retrace his tracks to Krasnovodsk, and from there back to Baku. It seemed after all that the decisive action was likely to be there. For most of the remaining months of the First World War, Teague-Jones shuttled back and forth between Baku (on the west coast of the Caspian) and Russian Transcaspia (on the east coast). His constant task was to resist the steady Bolshevik advance into the Tsar's earlier territories. Usually he was plotting behind the scenes, but from time to time he was exposed at the point of confrontation. Once he was wounded in crossfire.

A more lasting wound was the fact that the Bolsheviks – and all subsequent communist governments – would hold Teague-Jones responsible for the murder of the twenty-six Soviet commissars from Baku who had tried to flee as Dunsterforce approached. In fact, these commissars had been arrested by their Socialist Revolutionary opponents, and Teague-Jones had been among those who tried unsuccessfully to have them transported as prisoners of war to India, in order to keep them away from any opportunity to make more trouble. But his efforts were in vain: the commissars were sent by sea to Krasnovodsk then put on a train to Ashkabad, before being unloaded at a barren spot in the desert, made to dig their own shallow graves, and shot in cold blood. Teague-Jones had left the meeting at which this murderous execution had been planned before any decision about the commissars' fate was taken. He was not to blame for their murder. Nevertheless, many continued to hold him responsible for the atrocity, and he was forced for his own safety to change his name and to assume a new and secret persona – under which he continued to work in British intelligence for the rest of his life.

***

Ranald MacDonell reckoned that, with the withdrawal of Dunsterforce from Baku, there was nothing more that he could do there. His days of plotting and scheming against the Bolsheviks were over.

Yet leaving Baku was neither an easy nor a happy decision. He had lived in the town a long time; his son had been born there; he had acquired an eight-roomed apartment and filled it with his collection of Persian and Caucasian rugs and other treasures. All his belongings and most of his cherished memories would be left behind him on the western shores of the Caspian. From Baku he made his way to the Persian port of Enzeli, where, to make matters worse, he fell seriously ill and spent a long period in hospital. It was four months after the end of the First World War – well into 1919 – before MacDonell was once again fit for action of any sort. And then he found himself without any possessions, with no money and with no job.

Eventually the British government, mindful of his clandestine activities on their behalf, came to his rescue. He was granted "the maximum compensation allowed for loss while on government service" and found a job in the Foreign Office in London, where he was given the Transcaspian Desk (this was a new post created specially for him) and where his duties were more similar to those he had exercised as a consular officer than those he had pursued as a secret agent. He continued to be deeply concerned about the Bolshevik regime, which by then was consolidating itself throughout the Caucasus, and wrote that "in the Foreign Office we still cling to our hope that the Republics [Georgia, Armenia and Azerbaijan] would be persuaded to make a united stand against Bolshevism". This hope, of course, would not be fulfilled. He also warned that indiscriminate support for former Tsarist elements in Russia might have the effect of unifying revolutionary elements behind Lenin and his Bolsheviks. By 1920, the last of the Georgian aristocracy were leaving, mostly for Paris, and abandoning all their lands, houses and possessions.[4] MacDonell was appalled at the savagery with which the Bolsheviks were establishing

4 One such Georgian aristocrat was Prince Amilakvari (on whose estates Stalin's father had worked as a shoemaker) whose family were later to teach the author Russian in Paris, before his posting to the British embassy in Moscow. The prince escaped with virtually nothing, and joined the Foreign Legion in the ranks, serving with them in North Africa. By the time of the Battle of Alamein, he was commanding his regiment and was killed leading an assault – becoming a legend for bravery in the Legion.

their totalitarian regime. He recalled the old saying that if you scratch a Russian, you find a Tartar, and recorded his own version of it: "If you scratch a Soviet, you find a Russian, and under that a Tartar with an inbred doctrine of – When in Doubt – Kill!" Occasionally his duties brought him into contact with Soviet officials, but – once they learnt who he was – they refused to have any dealings with him on the grounds that he was "a White spy" who had been found guilty of plotting against them and condemned to death – albeit in absentia.

MacDonell had not been among the very first to see the dangers of Bolshevism, and he had tried to work with the Bolsheviks as long as there seemed any prospect they would remain allies in the war against the Kaiser's Germany. But once he accepted that the Bolsheviks were themselves the enemy, he was courageous, imaginative and indefatigable in confronting and exposing them. He inspired both Edward Noel and Reginald Teague-Jones in their own exploits. While others believed that Lenin's regime would be a short-lived aberration, MacDonell was less optimistic. He was cynical about the motives of many of those whom he recruited and ran as secret agents. Most conspirators, he declared, had only two things in common: they hated the Bolsheviks and they wanted money – usually his money. His life before his appointment as vice-consul at Baku had been a series of unconnected chapters – in Ceylon, Fleet Street and St Petersburg; and his life after his flight from Baku was a gradual, anti-climactic decline from that period of daring exploits which he himself described as being like a story from the *Boy's Own Paper*. In the end he became something of a grumpy old man: his son, Air Commodore Donald MacDonell CB DFC (who served as air attaché at the embassy in Moscow with the author), described his father in print as being on occasion "arrogant and offensive".

When he came to record the highlights of his time as a British agent, he called his book *And Nothing Long*, a quote from Dryden's couplet:

"Stiff in opinions, always in the wrong,
Was everything by starts, and nothing long."

He might have applied the whole couplet to his life. It had indeed been erratic. Yet he had confronted the Bolsheviks with bravery and determination at a crucial moment in their schemes and, having identified their motives, informed others about what he had discovered. This had been his finest hour.

THE PROPHET OF DOOM

Maurice Baring

Maurice Baring is often described in books about the Russian Revolution as a journalist, which he was. But he was also many other things: a poet and a renowned man of letters; a sometime diplomat who had served in Paris; an aristocrat who was the son of a peer and the nephew of an earl; a scion of the famous banking family; a close friend of many of the most celebrated contemporary literary figures, including G.K. Chesterton; and a recognized authority on Russian life and literature.

Baring first visited Russia as the correspondent of the *Morning Post*, charged with covering the Russo-Japanese war of 1904–05 in Manchuria, and after the war ended he stayed on as the paper's resident correspondent in St Petersburg. He took the job seriously, learning Russian to a very high standard and travelling – usually in crowded third-class train carriages – not only to Moscow but all over the country. He also journeyed down the Volga River into Central Asia, and to the far north. What set him apart from other British or western travellers was his facility for engaging in meaningful conversations with people of all regions and of all classes – from members of the newly established (and soon to be dissolved) parliamentary Duma, to the peasants and soldiers in whose close company he so frequently found himself. Nor was it only standard conversational fare that Baring enjoyed with his fellow travellers. He was enthralled by the folk stories (of frogs and princes, of cobblers and courtiers) which chance acquaintances would tell him. And he was a good storyteller himself – a valuable asset on a long-distance train or a Volga River steamer. Baring's dealings with these informal and often intimate contacts helped him, both in his contemporary reporting and particularly in the books he wrote later, to reveal to his readers the fatal shortcomings of the old Tsarist regime and the appalling dangers of the new Bolshevik order.

One early impression he reported back was the low morale of the armed forces – not only during the Russo-Japanese war but after the concluding peace, which was widely viewed as a humiliating one. When war was originally declared, the crowds in the cities had been wildly enthusiastic, carrying officers on their shoulders through the streets. By the time Baring arrived, this had changed. The Japanese, with their tactic of mounting sudden, surprise attacks, had inflicted severe defeats on land and at sea, and these had been exacerbated by the inadequacy of the Russian response. The paucity of any hard news about what was happening did not help: soldiers were begging for the sight of a newspaper to find out what was going on at their own front line. Towards the end of the war, in 1905, as he travelled back west on the Trans-Siberian express, Baring learnt from officers and their wives about the recent mutinies in the Black Sea fleet. His interlocutors predicted "if not a revolution, at least a great change in Russia in the immediate future". Already there was a feeling of living on the edge of a volcano that might at any moment erupt.

On this journey, Baring also became aware of the internal tensions within the army: he saw how Cossacks refused to share accommodation with ordinary soldiers, regarding themselves as an elite military caste. He had the impression "that a revolution was [already] going on": there were strikes on the railways of unpredictable duration, which seemed more like mutinies than normal industrial action. Gangs of convicts were working at the stations, and Baring noted that there was a general sympathy for them as victims of the old regime. They were often referred to as "unfortunates" rather than as convicts and were given cigarettes by passing passengers.

In November 1905, now in Moscow, Baring witnessed violent clashes between "liberal" students on the one hand and extremist supporters of the Tsar – known either the "Black Gang" or the "Hooligans" – on the other. The occasion for the confrontations was the anniversary of Nicholas II's accession. The police did little to quell the violence, and forays by Cossack troops – usually in support of the Hooligans – only added to the atmosphere of resentment and confusion. The lawlessness went on for three days and convinced Baring that complete anarchy was very close. The students were demanding a total amnesty for all political prisoners, as well as expressing their acute frustration at the conservatism of the Tsar's ministers, whom they viewed as inherently allergic to all change. The police and Cossacks were brutal in their repressive measures. It was an explosive mix, but even so Baring felt that the deaths and destruction could have been avoided with more effective and responsible policing.

As so often in Russia, the theatres continued to put on performances throughout the disturbances, but in time the febrile atmosphere penetrated even within these hallowed walls. One audience was reduced to hysterics by violent scenes on stage: they had seen "enough…friends killed in the streets without going to the play for such a sight". By the following month, the theatres had closed and strike action had brought most of Moscow to a standstill.

Baring was disenchanted with the existing regime, but he was alarmed at the alternative. He reported that the man in the street in Moscow was hostile both towards the strikers and towards the government, while the wealthier and educated classes felt either "intense sympathy or violent indignation with the revolutionaries". The revolutionaries, for their part, were obsessed with trying to prevent western banks from continuing to finance with loans the excesses of the Tsarist government. One Socialist Revolutionary, having discovered that Baring stemmed from the family of the famous banking house, threatened personally to shoot him dead if he gave a penny to the government.

Yet even after the events of Bloody Sunday, Baring discerned a willingness on the part of Russians to make a distinction between the Tsar as "father of his people", and the government as instruments of repression. Many attributed the Tsar's trust in the loyalty of the army to the fact that he came into contact only with his own Guards regiments, whose special privileges made them unrepresentative in their affection for their monarch. If only the Tsar could be seen to reach out to his people over the heads of their government, it was felt, then all might still be well for him.

As early as 1904, when the Russo-Japanese war broke out, Baring viewed the army as being the likely trigger for future discontent. The regime, he wrote, could not survive a larger-scale or a more protracted war, in which the army would become both disillusioned and disaffected. (This was exactly what was to happen between 1914 and 1917.)

For the moment, though – even after the disturbing events of 1905 – Baring judged that the lack of leadership among the potential reformers and revolutionaries was holding the movement back. The so-called liberals tended to be lawyers, professors, journalists, doctors and intellectuals rather than men of action. However incompetent and corrupt the Tsarist government might be, as long as the opposition lacked a true leader it would remain too ineffectual to bring about any radical change. Not until the emergence of a charismatic figure would any real revolution occur. (This was exactly what would happen with the emergence of Lenin.) Baring also thought that the longer the forces of the old regime held back the tide of history, the more violent change would be when it did occur. In this again, he was to prove all too accurate.

There had been alarming signs of the coming cataclysm even at the time of his earlier visits to Russia. When an assassination attempt on the unpopular governor-general of Moscow failed, killing two of his aides instead, Baring heard people in the streets talking about the attempt "as if they had narrowly missed backing a winner". There was a general loss of moral compass, with even middle-class people considering that throwing bombs was justified according to a kind of – almost natural – lynch law.

Baring received some advance warning of the impending violence of the revolution through the conversations he continually had with people of all classes, ranging from peasants, soldiers and taxi drivers to members of the Duma. It was only a matter of time before St Petersburg would be looted, he forecast. As he strolled through the park at the Peterhof Palace on a Sunday afternoon in May 1906, the Empress Alexandra rode past in her open carriage: "I could not help thinking of Marie Antoinette and wondered whether ten thousand swords would leap from their scabbards on her behalf". It depressed him that no such reaction was likely, and he shared Burke's forlorn conclusion that "the age of chivalry is gone!".

It is a recurring theme of Baring's that the Tsar did little or nothing to help his own cause. He reports that when the president of the Duma requested an audience to present a formal address on behalf of the people, the Tsar refused to receive him. It seemed that Nicholas II had learnt nothing from the events of Bloody Sunday the previous year. By June 1906 the political atmosphere had become sultry, if not explosive. "We shall kill all the rich [if the Duma is dissolved]," Baring was told by one interlocutor. Every piece of new writing seemed to be revolutionary in tone. Indeed, everything in Russia was now "tinged with one colour, and that colour was red".

One peasant startled Baring by telling him that he knew that the English thought of all Russian peasants as being no more than "wolves and bears". The same peasant went on to express his anger with the Russian Orthodox priests, who habitually deceived and threatened the people. Scepticism and resentment at the Church, it seemed, were only just below the surface. At the same time, there was a disconcerting tendency to credit the miraculous healing powers of village sages, even in the surroundings of Moscow. It was "like finding witchcraft in Surbiton", commented Baring wryly.

With his contacts straddling the social classes, Baring became aware of how much resentment had built up between these classes. One cab driver pointed out to him a man who regularly used his cab and never paid for the fare. When Baring asked why he allowed him to get away with it, the driver answered, "There's nothing to be done – he is an officer." Just as the Tsar did little to help his own cause, so the privileged classes continued to abuse their position, regardless of the hostility that this provoked.

The traditional forces of law and order also seemed to be losing their enthusiasm for keeping the peace. The Cossacks – for so long the instrument of last resort – were beginning to resent being used as police reinforcements. Army cadets were reluctant to be commissioned as officers if this meant that they were to be used solely for policing duties. Fewer and fewer were willing to incur the disapprobation that followed firing into an unruly crowd or charging into a turbulent mob.

Meanwhile the priesthood, aware of its growing unpopularity, was becoming wary of being used as a political instrument, encouraging reactionary violence or anti-Semitism from the pulpit. "They stay at home and tell others to kill," was how one man described the clergy to Baring. Yet despite widespread mistrust of the Church, religious feelings continued to exert a powerful grip on the peasantry. Baring heard the story of one ardent socialist who, to prove the non-existence or ineffectualness of God, spat upon an icon and defied the Almighty to strike him down with fire from Heaven. When the icon was defiled and broken up, and no retribution followed from on high, he said to the peasants, "You see – God has not killed me." "No," replied the peasants, "God has not killed you, but we will" – and they did.

If condemning the Jews in their sermons did nothing to popularize the clergy, the anti-Semitism of the Tsarist regime was all too apparent. On one occasion a Russian aristocratic family with whom Baring was staying was approached by the local Jewish community with a request to be allowed to store their possessions in the stables of his host's country house. The community had heard that a party of thugs was on the way by train, with orders to carry out a one-day smash-and-grab raid on Jewish homes and shops. An appeal to the police was pointless: the authorities were behind the raid. Such pogroms were an inevitable fact of life. Baring was shocked, and was later not surprised that many blamed the revolution largely on Jewish influence – or that many of those who supported or led the revolution found it necessary, as Trotsky did, to conceal or deny their own Jewish origins.

It was clear that Russia needed to change, but the available instruments of change seemed to Baring unsuited to this unique land. European institutions such as parliaments were impractical and inappropriate in a country that was still more oriental than western. The intelligentsia had lost their native Tartar traditions, but not yet assimilated those of western Europe. Slavic hands were not capable of upholding the banner of western values, he was told. Baring also detected a lethargy and resignation among large sectors of the population. Some peasants would not vote even if given the chance, fearing that such action would sooner or later land them in prison. Others were prepared to accept bribes to stay loyal as the line of least resistance (sailors were said to have received 150 roubles each if they declined to join in one of the recurrent mutinies).

Yet whatever the failings and shortcomings of the old regime, and whatever the blindness of the Tsar and his supporters towards the real need for change, Baring could see no prospect of the opposing revolutionary elements being the answer to Russia's woes. He observed that the word "expropriation", which had come into vogue among the revolutionaries, meant that they thought they had only "to stretch out their hands to take by right anyone else's property". Autocracy and authority, it seemed, would all too likely be replaced by vandalism and the rule of the mob.

Baring was a scholarly figure who spoke seven languages and was dauntingly erudite about Russian literature and history; but one of the reasons why people – on trains and in cafés, on ships and in private houses – opened up to him in conversation, sharing their hopes and fears, was that he also had a humorous and even clownish side to his character. He recounts in his autobiography (*The Puppet Show of Memory*) a conversation on a steamer going down the Volga with a Cossack who remarked rather impertinently on his bald head. Baring – far from being offended – recounted his efforts to encourage hair growth by everything from rubbing his head with onions to painting it with tar. The Cossack told him he should not worry – his baldness was clearly the will of God. John Julius Norwich – who was Baring's godson – tells in his own autobiography (*Trying to Please*) of how when he was a child Baring used to amuse him by doing conjuring tricks and "balancing a full glass of port on top of his egg-bald head". This was a much more approachable man than might be imagined.

Baring's observations about the state of Russia were based on visits between the uprisings of 1905 and the revolutions of March and November 1917. Although he was at one point accused of being a spy, in reality he never had any clandestine brief. He managed to leave Russia – more by luck than good judgement – only a few days before the outbreak of the First World War. His articles in the press appeared at intervals throughout his time in Russia, but his books, which give a more thoughtful assessment, did not appear until the 1920s, when the full horrors of the Bolshevik reign of terror were just beginning to seep out from that troubled land.

He was therefore not so much a whistle-blower as some of the adventurers who had travelled in Russia during the earliest, most formative and most secretive years of the Soviet Union. Yet he was an adventurer by the standards of scholars, if not by those of spies, and he went on to be a pioneer member of the Royal Flying Corps in the First World War. Baring's revelations were published at that crucial moment in the early 1920s when the first Labour government and the first general strike were in the offing – a time when there was still an alarming degree of ignorance in London about the realities of life in Petrograd and Moscow. There was a vacuum in informed opinion until Baring – the supreme Russian pundit – weighed in. His pessimism regarding Russia's future was evident from his reports: at one point he recounts how he had attended, on the eve of the revolution, the ceremony of smelting a new church bell. He had thrown a silver rouble into the furnace in the hope that this "would sweeten its utterance, and that it might never have to sound the alarm which signifies battle, murder and sudden death." He concluded that this had been "A vain hope – an idle wish."

Baring contributed a sensitive and highly civilized mind, linked to an acutely sharp ear for conversations with all manner of men in the streets, in the Duma, in the marketplaces, and in that essentially Russian environment – the long-distance railway train. His writing was at once highly critical of the privileged world of the Tsar and his court, and starkly revealing of the crudity and violence of the Bolsheviks. Its impact was all the more powerful for the fact that his love of Russia – that land of snows and sins – and his sympathy for its citizens shone throughout. He has plenty of criticism of the Orthodox church and its clergy, yet he also writes movingly about the Russian Easter Day church service, when people of all ranks and classes embrace each other with cries of "Christ is risen!" His was not the voice of a cynical and detached commentator, but of a committed Russophile. As he explains in his autobiography, you do not have to be a Russian to fall under the spell of all things Russian; you only have to live in the country for a while to succumb to its charm and never be quite free from it again. Baring found the Russian soul to be filled with a simplicity and sincerity that could be discovered nowhere else. Here was a true disciple of Tolstoy.

Sidney Reilly

THE ARTFUL DODGER

Sidney Reilly

Sidney Reilly is the odd man out in this collection of adventurers. More has been written about him than any of the others, yet the accounts of his life contradict each other, and the mystery that hung over him during his life persisted after it – and indeed still persists. He himself wrote an autobiographical sketch, which was completed by his last wife after he died. Robin Bruce Lockhart (the son of Sir Robert, who worked with Reilly in Moscow between 1918 and 1920) wrote a lively and dramatic biography of him in 1967. There was a major ITV series about him in the early 1980s, and (possibly prompted by this) Michael Kettle wrote his "true story" at the same time. There have been numerous other accounts of his exploits, some more fanciful than others. As Robin Bruce Lockhart pointed out, even Reilly's employers in the British intelligence services were uncertain about his identity and his origins: this was a man who spoke seven languages, who was said to possess eleven different passports and as many wives, who veered constantly between extravagant expenditure and bankruptcy, and who was reviled and admired in equal measure by different people and different nations. But not to include him in my gallery of adventurers who confronted the early Bolsheviks would be to leave an inexcusable gap. All one can do is to piece together as accurate a picture as one can of a man who spent much of his life trying to confuse and bewilder all those who were trying to pin him down – and whose death is as mysterious as his origins.

Reilly, though he was regarded as British by both the British and

Russian governments, was of Polish-Jewish extraction. He was born Sigmund Georgievich Rosenblum in 1874, to parents who were landowners with an estate in the Russian-dominated part of Poland.

The young Sigmund came early in his life to London, where he joined a large community of Polish and Russian exiles living in the East End – at that time a hotbed of anarchist plots against the Tsarist and other established regimes. Having assumed a largely fictitious Indian-colonial background – and the name Sidney Reilly – he married a young English widow in 1898. Around this time the British secret service, who kept a close eye on the activities of anarchist groups, appears to have recruited him, or at least to have been in contact with him. He trained as a mining engineer and went on to study at Trinity College, Cambridge, where he did research in civil engineering.

Reilly then embarked on a career in the oil and armaments industries, first in Persia and then in Tsarist Russia. Only a year or two had elapsed since the war with Japan, in which the Russians had suffered severe naval disasters, and the country was anxious to rebuild its navy. Reilly found employment as the Russian agent of a German firm which was helping in this process. With a characteristic eye for a profit, he topped up the commission he earned from this work by secretly selling the German naval designs intended for the Russians to the British government. This gave him a further entrée to those intelligence circles in London which were soon to become the central part of his life.

Meanwhile he was enjoying the rarefied existence of pre-revolutionary St Petersburg, mixing with the socially elite and high-spending society around the Tsar's court that was so soon to collapse. He was a noted womanizer, and having sent his first wife home, he soon married (presumably bigamously) a glamorous Russian lady who had divorced her previous husband. His personal life was already becoming a labyrinth of deceits and fabrications; professionally, he continued to work in the field of naval procurement, spending time both in Japan and the United States in this connection.

After the outbreak of the First World War, Reilly moved from the United States to Canada – leaving his Russian wife behind in New

York – and enlisted in the Royal Flying Corps before returning to London. Here he reactivated his links with the Secret Intelligence Service, and was employed on several undercover missions into Germany in an effort to discover further naval secrets. However when the Russian Revolution broke out in 1917, it was felt that he would be of greater use to Britain as an agent inside revolutionary Russia than inside Germany. From then until the disastrously premature end of his life, his convoluted espionage activities would be concentrated on Anglo-Russian intrigues.

As the Russian Revolution progressed and the Bolsheviks began to reveal their true colours, the British government – particularly its Prime Minister, Lloyd George – became increasingly aware of its ignorance as to what was really happening inside Russia. Lloyd George had already sent Robert Bruce Lockhart to Moscow to be his official interlocutor with Lenin and Trotsky, but – as we have seen – Lockhart's reports and opinions were not always what his government might have wished. Lloyd George decided he needed another less official agent to report back on the fast-moving developments in Moscow – one whose reports would be complementary to those of Lockhart and based on information obtained by more clandestine means. The British Admiralty and the secret services drew Reilly to the attention of the Prime Minister. With his background in espionage, he seemed the obvious man to provide the new dimension.

Having received his marching orders, Reilly called on Maxim Litvinoff, the Bolsheviks' man in London, presenting himself as a fellow Bolshevik and Russian émigré. Litvinoff took the bait and promptly issued him with a visa or pass to return to Russia.

Once he had arrived, Reilly set about trying to contact Lenin in the Kremlin, but he got nowhere. The British government remained undecided on what action they should take vis-à-vis the new regime. Should they attempt to blow up Russian warships before the Germans captured them? Intergovernmental discussions with the French and the Americans only confused the issue further. For a while it seemed that Reilly, like Lockhart, would be left without clear directions. Meanwhile it was becoming more and more clear to Reilly himself, even before it was to the British government, that the Bolsheviks were a broken reed as an ally against Germany, and that they were becoming a serious enemy in their own right. He decided to turn all his energies to plotting against them.

In early 1918 Reilly travelled from Moscow to Petrograd (as St Petersburg had now become) and was horrified at the changes that had occurred in the three years since he had last been there. There seemed to be no trace of the lavish lifestyle Reilly remembered from pre-revolutionary days. The bread queues had grown even longer since 1915 – and now people were not only queuing but starving. The Bolshevik terror had begun: people avoided each other's gaze as they walked down the streets (where no public transport was available). Even a flicker of recognition could be dangerous in a city where no one trusted anyone.

He started to make contact with some of his former friends, but it was not easy: some had fled, some were dead and some were under official suspicion, making any contact risky. So widely had the Cheka agents penetrated the city that even children, parents, lovers or childhood friends might now be reporting on every indiscreet criticism let slip about the new communist regime. *Agents provocateurs* were everywhere, fomenting imagined plots to entrap would-be conspirators. Those arrested were tortured until they betrayed their friends to save themselves. The authorities seized private property, including furniture, and claimed it belonged to the state. The social scene had moved on too: the literate, civilized citizens who had supported Kerensky were now themselves viewed as bourgeois enemies of the revolution. The lack of education of the new proletarian masters could on occasion help their opponents: those who could not read could not check or detect false personal documents. One British agent had travelled across communist Russia with his sole documentation consisting of a receipted bill on impressively headed writing paper, with a flamboyant signature above some English postage stamps. It was from his Savile Row tailor.

One contact in Petrograd told Reilly that the majority of the population were ready to rise in revolt, but there was no one to lead them.

Bolshevism, he said, "could only be checked by an organization as subterranean, as secret, as mysterious, as ferocious and inhuman as itself". This was a challenge which Reilly was fully prepared to accept. Despite his own partially Jewish origins, Reilly held anti-Semitic views, and inclined to the widely-held belief that the Russian Revolution had been in large measure a Jewish conspiracy. This view fed his belief that its foundations were not solid, and that he could successfully overthrow it.

He soon realized that the nerve centre of the revolution was now Moscow, not Petrograd. Travel was permitted only to officials of the regime, but the same contact (who sold off some public property to finance the requisite bribe) secured passes for both of them to go by rail to Moscow. So far Reilly had been operating under his own name; now it was time to disappear and change identity. He managed to find someone of approximately his own height and stature, who was persuaded to travel, disguised as Reilly, back to Petrograd. Equipped with a fresh identity – Mr Constantine, a Greek merchant – the real Reilly was now loose in Moscow, the Bolshevik power base. There was everything to play for.

Reilly believed that the Latvian regiments in the city were to the Bolsheviks what the Guards regiments had been to the Tsar – a loyal bodyguard of hand-picked troops, and a crucial pillar of support for the regime. He had a valuable contact within the Latvian military: one Colonel Friede, who, though trusted by the Bolsheviks, secretly hated them and what they stood for. Friede used his influence to obtain a new pass for Reilly – yet another alternative identity – this time as "Commissar Relinsky" of the Cheka secret police. With this in his pocket along with his Greek merchant papers, he was well placed to flit between different conspiring groups.

Colonel Friede had a trusted sister who moved in Moscow's artistic circles, mixing with musicians and ballet dancers. The music portfolio she carried on her way around the city came increasingly to be stuffed, not with sheet music and ballet scores, but with military reports which had been extracted by the colonel and passed on to 'Commissar Relinsky'. As he passed these reports on to his intelligence masters in England, Reilly added his own political commentary: the vast majority of the Russian population was only waiting for an opportunity and a leader to rise up and overturn the Bolsheviks. Reilly – never one for modesty – saw himself as providing both the opportunity and the leadership. After all, as he recorded later in his memoirs, "A Corsican lieutenant of artillery trod out the embers of the French Revolution...surely a British espionage agent, with so many factors on his side, could make himself master of Moscow?" This was by no means the only occasion on which Reilly revealed his obsession with Napoleon: throughout his life he accumulated Napoleonic mementos, and indeed spent much more than he could afford on his collection.

The Latvian troops seemed to afford the opportunity Reilly was looking for. Hired as mercenaries by the Bolsheviks but not themselves convinced of the communist credo, they were, he concluded, up for sale to the highest bidder. Reilly intended to be that bidder.

He started to collect funds from the disaffected citizens of Moscow. These were numerous as well as still relatively opulent, and in a surprisingly short time Reilly amassed hundreds of thousands of roubles, which he stored safely in the apartment of a young dancer. He then began to distribute these funds to the commanders of the Latvian regiments.

By this stage Reilly was utterly convinced that it was the Bolsheviks rather than the Germans who were Britain's real enemy. He wrote in his memoirs that the Germans were human beings by whom "we could afford to be beaten" if need be, while the Bolsheviks were "monsters of crime and perversion" with whom there could never be any accommodation.

Reilly's carefully prepared plot was as follows: while Lenin and Trotsky were attending a party meeting in a theatre in Moscow, the Latvian troops, posted on guard duty outside, would surround the building. Meanwhile a special detachment of conspirators, led by Reilly himself, would remain hidden behind the curtains on stage. If all went well, Lenin and Trotsky would be captured by the Latvians and subsequently paraded through the streets of Moscow to show the people that the Bolsheviks were no longer in power. A similar coup against the Cheka leaders would be mounted in Petrograd. Contact would then be made with the White Russian forces still at large in distant parts of the Soviet Union, and these would destroy the leaderless remnants of the Bolshevik army. On the other hand, if things went wrong in the theatre – the Latvians lost their nerve or the party activists resisted – then Reilly and his special detachment would emerge from behind the curtains and throw grenades at Lenin and Trotsky, thus ensuring their death and hopefully triggering the rest of the plot. It was a gamble with the highest possible stakes. Reilly reckoned that he and his band might die, but that at least they could be sure that Lenin and Trotsky – "the tyrants that had made of Russia a charnel-house" – would die with them.

At the last moment Lenin postponed the Moscow theatre meeting. Reilly took advantage of the delay to visit Petrograd again and check how his Latvian accomplices were getting on with their plans there. He got on the train at Moscow as Comrade Relinsky and got off at Petrograd as Mr Massino, a Levantine merchant – the latest of his many undercover identities. In Petrograd he found the population starving: horses which collapsed and died in the street were being cut up for meat. People were even more cowed by the communist terror than they were in Moscow. This helped him evade recognition as he wandered through the streets, since everyone was avoiding everyone else's gaze. Nevertheless, Reilly soon realised that he was being followed by Cheka agents.

Alarmed and confused, he decided to risk calling in at the British embassy. There a shock awaited him: a line of Bolshevik soldiers lay dead on the pavement outside. It transpired that the embassy had been attacked by Red Guards who were searching for the English spy Sidney Reilly. They had battered down the door, and the embassy staff had retaliated – hence the bodies. The Union Jack had been torn down, and the chancery building occupied by the Red Guards. While he stared at the scene and tried to take in what had happened, Reilly was approached by one of the Red Guards, who hailed him in a friendly way as Comrade Relinsky and related with obvious glee what had happened. He learned that when the embassy staff realized they were under attack, some of them burnt the secret papers on an upper floor while the naval attaché stood – an automatic in each hand – and tried to stop the Red horde from mounting the stairs. He had been killed by the mob, "literally riddled with bullets".

Reilly soon discovered the explanation for this sudden violent action against the British embassy – and the renewed search for him. In Moscow there had been an assassination attempt on Lenin, who had been shot and seriously wounded by a woman named Dora Kaplan. Immediately there was a reaction against the British, with Reilly himself suspected of being involved.[5]

In these new circumstances, Reilly felt he had to get back immediately to Moscow to look after his agents and associates there, including the dancers and musicians who had been such faithful fellow conspirators. His friends in Petrograd warned him that he would be walking straight into the lion's den. He was now a wanted man, and the Cheka could be relied upon to use any method available – including torture – to gain information about his whereabouts. Nevertheless, with considerable courage, Reilly stuck to his plan. Travelling as Comrade Relinsky (the "collaborator with the Cheka") he bullied and bluffed his way onto the Moscow train, while keeping a firm hold of his pistol. If he were arrested, he "intended to take some comrades with [him]".

At Kline[6] (a station some forty miles outside Moscow) he got off the train to buy a copy of the communist newspaper *Pravda* on the platform. The news was not good. Reilly's fellow conspirator in the Latvian army – Colonel Friede – had been arrested for alleged complicity in the plot to shoot Lenin, together with his sister and her friends in the musical and ballet worlds. In fact, most of Reilly's

---

5 As described earlier, Bruce Lockhart was arrested and imprisoned following these events. Ironically, the plot in which Reilly was involved – to capture or kill Lenin and Trotsky in the Moscow theatre – was derailed by the unsuccessful shooting of Lenin elsewhere and by another hand.

6 Kline was the nearest point to Moscow reached by Hitler's army in 1942. It is best remembered now as the home of Tchaikovsky. When the author visited it in the 1950s, he was shown the alleged imprint of a German jackboot on the sofa in Tchaikovsky's sitting room. Every shrub in the garden concealed a loudspeaker permanently relaying *Swan Lake* music round the property.

undercover network had been betrayed. Should he return to Petrograd and make a dash for the Finnish border, as his friends had advised? He decided that he would never be able to look himself in the face again if he saved himself at the expense of his remaining Moscow agents.

At that moment he noticed a Red Guard checking documents on the platform. Clearly it was too risky to get back on the train. Without hesitation he jumped off the platform and hid under the train, where he was not greatly surprised to find he was not alone. He crawled to the back of the train and raised himself just high enough to see that the Red Guard on the platform was busy threatening some unfortunate suspect. While he had the chance, Reilly made a dash for a nearby clump of trees and lay hidden there until the train had pulled out on its way to Moscow and the coast was clear. He then walked into Kline and persuaded a peasant to drive him into the next village. From there he used relays of horses to go from one village to another until he reached Moscow, "the city of terror". Tired though he was, he dared not visit any of his friends until he had made a reconnaissance visit to see whether they were under surveillance. Eventually he sought shelter – under one of his pseudonyms – in the apartment of some White Russians he hardly knew, only to discover that this was a most unfortunate choice as they were closely connected with Dora Kaplan and were expecting a call from the Cheka at any moment. He had not so much entered the lion's den as put his head in the lion's mouth.

He left this dangerous address and managed to meet other friends, who brought him up to date. It transpired that Colonel Friede's daughter – who, like her aunt, was in the habit of carrying around secret plans in her music case – had failed to notice a Cheka car outside a house she was visiting, and had been searched as she went up the stairs. The contents of her music case were deeply compromising, and it was for this reason that she and her father together with their artistic friends had been arrested. Reilly knew that Bruce Lockhart was also under arrest, and although Lockhart had known nothing of the theatre plot, seriously considered giving himself up in exchange for Lockhart's release. In the end he decided – rightly as it turned out – that his fellow agent's life was not in any immediate danger.

Reilly himself was now the number one target for the Cheka, who had learnt of his role in masterminding the theatre plot'. They had also learnt his undercover names, including that of Comrade Relinsky – his Cheka cover. His picture was posted up all over town; he was wanted dead or alive. In the public mind he had become a dangerous outlaw, and speculation as to his whereabouts was rife. Some said he was still in Petrograd; others that he had escaped to Finland or to England; still others that he was in Moscow. Some claimed to have sighted him. People, unaware who they were talking to, told him openly how the Cheka were sure to track down Reilly eventually – "they always did".

Reilly responded by never spending two nights in the same place or under the same name. Sometimes he was a Greek merchant with bad debts; sometimes a Tsarist officer on the run; sometimes a Russian merchant dodging military service. He found that people were prepared to help those in difficulties – as long as they did not know that they were helping a prominent enemy of the regime.

Despite these trying circumstances, Reilly somehow managed to trace most of his former agents, and even found ways to help those who had not already been arrested to escape. On one occasion he found himself in a house being searched by the Cheka He boldly walked out, stopping to ask the secret police guard at the door for a light for his cigarette; although he often went without food or a bed at night, he found it was the cigarettes he missed most.

Eventually he found shelter in a brothel, where the *madame* knew who he was, as did some of her charges. But brothels were one of the few places not regularly searched by the Cheka – perhaps out of a desire not to embarrass colleagues. The prostitutes seemed indifferent to the risks they were taking: when Reilly finally came to leave they refused any payment. Perhaps they saw themselves as part of the old regime and were proud of it.

With no more to be done in Moscow, Reilly returned to Petrograd, under yet another false passport. This time he risked the train, having managed to obtain a sleeper berth in a compartment booked by the German embassy. He left the station at Petrograd with a German diplomat he had befriended on the train. The irony of a British secret agent travelling under German protection while the two countries were still at war was not lost on him.[7]

In Petrograd he was little safer than in Moscow. He had by now been formally condemned to death as a spy, and there were more people who knew him by sight here than elsewhere. But having grown a beard – "a really formidable affair" – and donned scruffy, shabby clothes, he felt he was as incognito as he could be. The question now was how to get out of the country.

During this time, while he made his plans, he risked going out in the streets in daylight. It was nearly his undoing. In the Nevsky Prospekt he was overtaken by a man he did not recognize, but who to his horror greeted him by his real name. It turned out to be an acquaintance with a unique interest in beards, and one not easily confused by them – his barber.

Not only did the barber not give Reilly away, he also sheltered him in his own house. He had already been visited by the local "housing committee", who had removed any furniture of value and were therefore unlikely to come back. A couple of weeks later, the barber did Reilly an even greater favour. He introduced him to a Dutch businessman who had his own motor launch, and who – for the consideration of 60,000 roubles – agreed to smuggle him aboard and get him away from Russia.

On the night planned for the escape, Reilly approached the quayside and saw that the pre-arranged warning light in the cabin was switched on. It transpired that the Soviet commissar, who had gone on board to give the vessel clearance to sail, had decided to stay drinking until the moment the ship sailed.

---

7 On another of his many journeys by train between Moscow and Petrograd, he even joined in a hunt for himself –while disguised as a Soviet sailor. He had obtained the costume by knocking the real sailor unconscious in the train lavatory, stripping him of his uniform and (according to some accounts) tipping the unfortunate man out of the train window. Reilly was not fastidious in the pursuit of self-preservation.

At first this looked like being an insoluble problem. But it carried its own solution. The longer the commissar stayed on board, the more he drank. By the time the commissar was taken ashore, he was in no condition to notice the bearded, shabbily clothed man who was ferried out to the waiting motor launch to take his place. At last Reilly was aboard a ship sailing out of Petrograd and out of Russia.

But there was a snag. Amidst the drama of getting on board, he had not asked where the ship was sailing. No doubt he assumed it was to Finland or to some other neutral Baltic port, or perhaps to the owner's homeland of neutral Holland. In fact it was bound for the German naval base at Reval (now Tallinn in Estonia). Not only was Britain still at war with Germany, but Reilly had a track record of espionage there almost as extensive as he had in Russia. He was going from one country where he was a wanted man to another where he was equally liable to arrest on sight. However, his new papers stood the test of the examination by the German authorities, and he even managed to socialize with a group of German naval officers. He then persuaded the Dutch owner of the motor launch to take him as soon as possible to Helsinki, where he really was safe. Before Reilly parted from his Dutch rescuer, he gave him a sealed letter explaining his background and assuring him he would not use any information that he had gleaned while a guest of the German navy at Reval. By way of expressing his gratitude, the letter also promised any help he could ever give him in the future, in Britain or America. Meanwhile Reilly returned to England, where – still holding the rank of a captain in the Royal Flying Corps – he was awarded the Military Cross for his patriotic and daring exploits inside Russia over the previous six months.

Some weeks after his return to England, the armistice of 11 November 1918 was signed with Germany. Reilly might have assumed that he would now have some respite from his perilous overseas activities. But it was not to be. No sooner was the armistice signed than the British government decided – much encouraged by Winston Churchill – that its next overseas venture should be to support the White Russian interventionist forces inside the embryonic Soviet Union. Reilly was duly dispatched to Sevastopol in the Crimea, where he made contact with the various White Russian generals and leaders. He was unimpressed by most of the White Russians he encountered both then and subsequently: he found them vain, talkative and ineffectual. Nor was Reilly a Tsarist at heart: he had seen enough to understand the cruelties and outdated attitudes of the '*ancien régime*'. However, he had no choice but to work with whatever elements of opposition to the Bolsheviks already existed, and he strove hard to coordinate these disparate factions.

When the only White Russian interventionist leader for whom Reilly had any respect – Boris Savinkov – was foolish enough to venture into Soviet territory and be captured, Reilly found himself wholly disillusioned with the intervention task which he had been set, and anxious to find other ways of striking at the Bolsheviks.

The method he chose to do this was typical: it involved forgery, deceit and political calculation. Reilly forged a letter purporting to come from Grigory Zinoviev (the head of the Soviet Comintern) to the British Communist Party. In it, 'Zinoviev' urged the setting up of militant and subversive action groups throughout British society, particularly within the trade unions and the armed forces. It was a cry to arms. Reilly presented it to the head of the British Secret Intelligence Service – Admiral Sir Hugh Sinclair (the celebrated "C") – as a genuine document, and "C" presented it to the foreign secretary and Prime Minister in the same light. Reilly intrigued energetically behind the scenes to ensure that the letter got into the public domain. When it was published – on the eve of the 1924 general election – it caused a sensation. Relations with the Soviet Union plummeted and the Labour government of Ramsay MacDonald (which was perceived by many as being sympathetic towards the communists) was voted out of office. From a technical point of view it was a triumph of deception, but when Reilly's part in it became known he was never trusted again within the British establishment. He also moved right to the top of the Bolshevik's list of targets for revenge.

It might be imagined that – now that he was settled in England – Reilly was out of danger even from the long arm of the Cheka. This proved not to be the case. His wife, who took up the story of his life and completed his memoirs, relates how a stranger once turned up at their house in England with the alarming news that her husband had been involved in a road accident. He offered to drive her to the hospital where Reilly was being treated. She became suspicious when the driver declined to tell her which hospital he was heading, and when she detected a slight chemical smell in the car. All too soon she felt a prick in her right arm from a hypodermic syringe.

She regained consciousness in a chemist's shop and was told that "her husband had gone to fetch a doctor". She quickly realized that the driver who had injected her had passed himself off as her husband to the chemist. She quickly telephoned her husband at home, and found that he too had received a message – this time to the effect that *she* had been injured in an accident and that a driver was coming round to take *him* to the hospital where she was being treated. Reilly, who had a quick mind for detecting sinister plots having hatched so many himself, immediately grasped what was going on. The plan had been to hide his wife away for a few hours, to take him on a wild goose chase to find her, and in the process to kidnap him and somehow bundle him off to Russia, presumably to face interrogation, torture and execution. It was a deeply unnerving experience, and revealed the depth of the Cheka's determination to level their score with him.

Nor was it only in England that the long arm of the Cheka flexed its muscles. When the Reillys went to Paris, they were closely watched. On board an ocean liner bound for the United States, one of the stewards on board turned out to be a Cheka agent. These unwanted attentions were perhaps understandable: even in America, Reilly did not cease from lobbying and plotting against the interests of the Bolsheviks. In public lectures and articles he campaigned against the idea of the Americans extending any loan to the Soviet Union. On discovering that his Russian secretary in New York was secretly feeding copies of his papers to the Soviets, Reilly and his wife spent much time at night devising misleading documents that she could intercept and pass on. Indeed, Mrs Reilly felt at this point that she was a real part of her husband's team, and learnt much of the machinations of the Bolsheviks and of their opponents.

Reilly's continuing one-man war against the Bolsheviks sometimes intruded on their social life. On one occasion her husband quietly slipped out of a restaurant in New York in evening dress to follow a suspicious stranger, who led him to the undercover headquarters of the subversive communist movement in that city. Such sudden unexplained disappearances caused great concern to his wife.

Reilly had always impressed on his wife that under no circumstances – and whatever the pressures or inducements, such as "only you can save somebody" – should she agree to enter Russian territory. The risks of discovery, entrapment or betrayal were too great. It is all the more surprising that in 1925 Reilly himself fell for exactly the kind of trap against which he had warned his wife. He had gone on a mission to Helsinki and was persuaded that a movement called the "Trust" had arisen within the Soviet Union, and was planning to overthrow the Bolshevik regime. All it needed was some strong leadership on the spot from a charismatic figure arriving from the West. Reilly was told he was the only man who could provide this.

Such representations would have fallen on ready ears: was he not the man who – like the young Bonaparte – could stamp out the embers of revolution? Had he not already evaded detection on innumerable occasions? Did he not have unfinished business left behind in Russia: after all, his theatre plot in Moscow had so nearly destroyed the Bolshevik leaders at one stroke. Rashness, bravery and vanity all doubtless played a part in his decision to fly in the face of his own advice, to adopt yet another false identity and to slip across the border from Finland into Russia. This time they were waiting for him. The details of his arrest just over the frontier, his detention and probable torture, and his apparent revelation of at least some British intelligence secrets, remain disputed. What is certain beyond any dispute is that he was shot as a spy. He even features in the KGB museum which has opened in St Petersburg not far from the Hermitage, on the premises of what is believed to have been the Cheka headquarters there in his time.

Sidney Reilly was not the most likeable of the British adventurers who opposed the Bolsheviks, but he was one of the most effective.

Today he is better remembered in the Soviet Union as a villain than in the United Kingdom as a hero. In London, as in Paris, New York and St Petersburg, he was long remembered for his high living as well as for his professional activities, even after he had moved on.[8] Thirty-five years after Reilly's execution, the British ambassador in Moscow (my first chief) felt it necessary to explain from time to time that – despite being called Sir Patrick Reilly – he was in no way related to his notorious namesake.

---

8 During his London years in the 1920s, despite his many wives and mistresses, he had bachelor chambers in Albany off Piccadilly, where the fictional aristocratic rascal Raffles was reputed to have been based. The author also lived in Albany in the 1960s, where Reilly was still occasionally referred to as one of the more colourful former residents.

Stephen Graham

THE RUSSIAN SCHOLAR

Stephen Graham

Robert Bruce Lockhart had become an expert on Russia and the revolution by dint of circumstance: he had been in situ at the British consulate-general in Moscow as events got underway. Stephen Graham, on the other hand, had already made himself an expert on Russia by the time of the revolution.

He was born in Edinburgh in 1884 (three years before Lockhart) leaving school at the age of fourteen and becoming a clerk at Somerset House where, according to W.S. Gilbert, the clerks were

> "like the fountains in Trafalgar Square
> and played all day from ten till four".

In these leisurely surroundings, he early developed two interests: one was in left-wing drama; the other – and more lasting interest – was in Russian literature. In his autobiography he describes how he bought a tattered second-hand copy of *Crime and Punishment* from a wheelbarrow and became immediately hooked on Dostoevsky. This was unusual at the time: hardly anyone in England was reading Dostoevsky, and his name was almost forgotten outside Russia. But the young Graham reckoned that the novel had changed the course of his life. He even began to learn Russian so that he could read it in the original, and in doing so become close friends with his young Russian tutor. The natural next step seemed to be to take a month's holiday in Russia – again, a very unusual thing for a young man to do in the first decade of the 20th century, particularly as the social unrest that would eventually lead to revolution was already becoming apparent – so much so, that one friend lent him a revolver to take with him. Happily – although he was arrested in Poland on the way – he returned home without incident.

Then, quite suddenly, he decided that he would throw up his steady unexciting job and go off to Russia, attempting to earn his living by writing about it. His friends and colleagues tried to dissuade him: he would be throwing away the substance of a career for an idle dream, and would probably starve in the process. But he was undeterred, and resolved to visit as a first port of call his friendly Russian tutor, who had by then returned home.

The journey was fraught with problems and disasters, not the least of which was that he was robbed of his heavy greatcoat (rather like the hero of Gogol's short story, *The Overcoat*) and arrived shivering on his friend's doorstep in winter in Kharkov. He was promptly lent an ancient Siberian cloak made of wolf pelt which enveloped him from ears to ankles. The pair moved to Moscow where they tried to support themselves by playing the guitar and the balalaika and by gambling at cards. Meanwhile Graham's early forays into journalism mostly met with rejection slips. It was at this time that Graham first grew a moustache, noting that it quickly developed icicles on its tips. This was getting to know Tsarist Russia the hard way.

His friend and former tutor began to worry that he was being followed in the streets, and that the Tsarist police were spying on him – although there was no reason why they should since he was in no way a revolutionary. But this was already a country obsessed by secret activities: according to Graham, there were morbid Muscovites who used to follow strangers and play at being spies. Meanwhile, Graham was falling under the spell of Russian Orthodox church services; he felt that he had found a Church underpinned by a deep religious philosophy, consistent with the ideas of Dostoevsky and other thinkers.

By the spring of 1910, Graham felt the need to do something more adventurous than wandering about and contemplating philosophy. He set off for the Caucasus, where he embarked on a series of long walks, or "tramps", as he preferred to call them. Money was still very tight, but his father had sent him a five-pound note, and he was beginning to receive occasional cheques from *Country Life* and the London evening papers for his articles. Poor as he was, he feared that the Georgians or Ossetians would murder him for the sake of his clothes and boots; he even took to sleeping in caves to avoid going into unfriendly villages. Ironically, he felt safest when under arrest, as he was – for no other reason than because he was a stranger in a land where all strangers were suspected of being spies – from the top of the frozen Mamison Pass until he reached the Caucasian town of Vladikavkaz. Here he was briefly imprisoned, and in consequence received gifts – kopecks and bread – from peasants who regarded all prisoners as friends in distress. He sensed the latent hostility to the regime most clearly when he himself – being marched along at pistol point – became temporarily a victim of it.

It was also in Vladikavkaz that he heard the story of a beautiful but cruel Georgian princess called Tamara, who used to lure travellers to her table and to her bed, only to push them over the castle battlements to perish in the fast-flowing waters of the river Terek. (The story haunted me when, as described in the epilogue, I was under the protection of a Georgian princess also called Tamara, in Paris while learning Russian.)

Graham's trek in the Caucasus was no passing whim. He spent a whole year there, having met a young Russian lady to whom – after much reciting of Russian poetry – he became romantically attached. The relationship didn't last, but she told him that the real Russians – those who were not interbred with Tartars – were to be found in the north. Armed with a slender letter of introduction to a Russian painter, Graham traversed the country from south to north, and started to trek around Archangel. Here it was too cold to sleep in caves or in the open, so he was obliged to seek shelter with peasants in their huts. In this way he not only improved his grasp of the language – albeit in a rather vernacular form – but he also discovered that even ordinary, harmless and non-violent people were becoming deeply resentful of the regime. Involuntarily he became involved with potential revolutionaries – young men who had been sent in exile to Archangel and had to report to the local police daily. Graham wrote later that these exiles had "adopted" him.

After these tramps through Russia, Graham returned for a spell to Fleet Street and published his first book, *A Vagabond in the Caucasus*. He also became acquainted with other authorities on Russia – notably Maurice Baring. It was not long, however, before he was off on his travels again. During 1911 and 1912 he walked through the Crimea and along the Black Sea coast: sometimes for days on end along beaches; at other times through dense forests. He often stayed in monasteries. Where he had introductions to Russian friends, he found himself in a Chekhovian world populated with such quirky Russian personalities as the "Slav types who hate themselves all the morning and the whole world for the rest of the day".

He crossed the Black Sea – in steerage class – to Istanbul where he joined Russian pilgrims going by foot to the Holy Land. He was travelling not only with Russian peasants, but travelling as one of them. No one – from Britain, at any rate – had done this before. His next venture was to travel to New York, but – as was his custom – with a group of Russian peasants who were emigrating in the hope of a better life in the New World. When he returned to London, he was taken on by Lord Northcliffe as a regular contributor to *The Times* and his other newspapers. It was his biggest breakthrough yet, and for the first time he was financially independent.

In 1913, Graham published his book *Changing Russia*. Most people in Britain who followed events in Russia – and there were many who did following the 'Bloody Sunday' clashes in 1905 – believed that the greatest danger to the Tsar and his regime came from the intellectual left. Writers (including Dostoevsky) had been sent to Siberia; bourgeois circles were calling for constitutional reform; professors and journalists were viewed with suspicion by the police. Graham was almost alone in predicting otherwise. He was convinced that the greatest danger came from the industrialization of the countryside: "every peasant brought in to a factory," he wrote, "is a man subtracted from the forces of the Tsar." He did not rate highly the effectiveness of the intellectual movement, predicting that the next outbreak against Tsardom would be fired by the passions of the mob. The commercial centres of Russia were "already infested with drunken hooligan mobs only waiting for a chance to murder and pillage". When Kerensky was toppled along with his Provisional Government, and Lenin took over, most observers were astonished; Graham had proved all too right. He could detect no trace of the culture of the intelligentsia in the emerging Bolshevik regime: "Where are the plays of Soviet Russia, the music of it, the novels of it, the philosophy of it, the pictures? What culture has come forth? Zero; that is all." It was a damning indictment.

Meanwhile, his preoccupation with Russia remained as strong as ever. He spent the Russian Christmas (January) of 1913 in Kiev. His journeys grew ever more ambitious: this time he planned to travel diagonally across Russia, through Turkestan and across Siberia, to end in Kamchatka. He had got as far as Siberia when he heard of the assassination of the Austrian archduke Franz Ferdinand at Sarajevo, and very soon "a horseman at the gallop" arrived to declare that Russia was at war – not with Turkey, as many might have assumed, but with Germany and the Austro-Hungarian empire.

Ever one to seek out danger and excitement, Graham immediately took off for the front line, where war was a reality and not merely a series of rumours. There he found that the overweening confidence with which the Tsar's armies had marched out to war had quickly evaporated. Endless fresh regiments from Siberia could not halt the German advance under Hindenburg. Despite being arrested for being a suspicious foreigner too near to the military action, Graham managed to send the first reports from the Russian front to *The Times*. Lord Northcliffe felt his recruitment of this unusual young man had been justified.

After a brief stint in the capital – now renamed Petrograd – Graham returned to London, having survived a U-boat-infested North Sea crossing. When he arrived home, he found himself much in demand as a public speaker about Russia – a country whose politics, war effort and culture seemed fascinatingly mysterious to many British people – and began to be lionized in political society in London as the only person who had any in depth knowledge of Britain's strange and unreliable ally. On one occasion – in 1915 – he found himself sitting between Lord Reading (the Lord Chief Justice) and Lloyd George (the Chancellor of the Exchequer) at a dinner where the merits of extending a loan to Russia were being discussed. He whispered to Lord Reading that "if you treat a Russian generously he will try to outdo you in generosity, but if you haggle you will at once be up against the Tartar in him". This remark was taken seriously by the assembled company: Graham was becoming an important influence on British policies towards Russia. The chaplain of the House of Commons became an influential friend, who shared Graham's respect for the Orthodox Church. Graham was even invited to preach at St Margaret's Westminster, and spoke there of the creative ideas that he had encountered in the writing of Dostoevsky and in the spirit of the Russian people.

The same year – 1915 – he returned to Russia, this time to Odessa, where he witnessed riots against the government. He continued to Moscow, where he saw more riots. He was beginning to sense an impending revolution. He also found a new brand of "defeatists": Russians who felt that a German victory was preferable to a prolonged war and a revolution at home. As the Tsar's armies retreated, their "scorched earth" policy in western Russia left millions of peasants hungry or starving. There was much talk of constitutional changes; Kerensky was emerging as a conspicuous advocate of the benefits of defeatism; the Tsar was felt to be a weak commander-in-chief; the Tsarina was thought to be pro-German and intriguing for a separate peace; the phrase "religion is the opium of the people" began to gain currency.

Back in London, Graham found that he had become even more in demand as an authority on what was going on in the confused country Russia had become. Again he was consulted by Lloyd George, who was in the throes of taking over the government from Herbert Asquith. Graham told Lloyd George that the situation was grave: morale in the Tsar's army was faltering; the soldiers were facing German poison gas without effective masks; there was an unholy revolutionary Russia challenging the traditional Holy Russia. At this time Lloyd George would have liked Lord Kitchener to travel to Russia to see the military state of affairs for himself, but Kitchener did not undertake his disastrous journey to Russia until the following year, at the Tsar's invitation. Lord Sandwich was another statesman who took Graham's views seriously; he also had meetings with the Archbishops of Canterbury and York, during which he discussed the state of the Orthodox Church. And yet – despite Graham's warnings to all those who would listen – London society still tended to regard Russia as the secure, aristocratic and extravagant world of balls and court receptions that it had been before the war: "How do I say, 'Unhand me, Prince!'?" he was asked at one dinner.

Graham soon returned to Russia. Like Lord Kitchener, he went by the northern sea route, but his ship was not sunk and he arrived at Murmansk, going on to the Caucasus and Moscow. By late 1916, he could sense the changed atmosphere. Everywhere his old friends had become more gloomy. Rasputin was hated and feared by many; the Tsar was said to be pale and in dread of assassination; he heard Robert Bruce Lockhart – the consul in Moscow – telling a friend that the city was totally bankrupt and that foreign loans were not forthcoming. Even the British ambassador in Petrograd was downhearted.

In London too, some people in positions of influence were beginning to be nervous about the state of Russia. Although Graham found the Chancellor, Bonar Law, and the Prime Minister, Lloyd George, still fairly unaware of the dangers, Lord Robert Cecil at the Foreign Office was clearly less sanguine, and told him in confidence that he could rely on Foreign Office support if he ever found himself in real danger or difficulty. Meanwhile, the Foreign Office continued to give him the run of their library and other facilities. John Buchan, who was now involved with military intelligence and with whom Graham was in touch at this stage, judged that the current set-up in Petrograd was doomed, but calculated – wrongly, as it turned out – that Russia would be a more effective ally as a democracy than as an autocracy. Buchan told Graham that he should forget "Holy Russia" and work towards a "common-sense reasonable state" with which the West could work. Graham for his part was convinced that the likely alternative to the Tsar was not a moderate government with whom the Allies could work, but something much more dangerous and extreme.

On 16 March 1917 – his birthday – Graham awoke to the news that the Tsar had abdicated and that a "benign" revolution had taken place. But it was not long until his prophecy that the revolution would become an extreme one was fulfilled. There was early shock and disappointment in London when the Bolsheviks signed a separate peace treaty at Brest-Litovsk with the Germans. There was anxiety – particularly in royal circles – about the safety of the Tsar's family, but no practical steps were taken to rescue them or bring them to Britain. Meanwhile, men of Graham's age – he was thirty-three– were being conscripted into the army. He declined an opportunity to go to an officer cadet school and joined the Scots Guards in the ranks as a guardsman. By then the war was nearly over, and he was soon demobilized and brought back to London, where he resumed his role as a consultant on all matters Russian.

Among the people who sought his opinion in the immediate post-war years were such leaders of left-wing opinion as George Lansbury, the Labour MP and prominent pacifist, who thought Bolshevism might prove to be "Christianity by another name"; and H.G. Wells, who hoped that it might be "the nucleus of a comfortable world state". Wells believed that a parliament of the world would eventually bring about a unification of all classes led by some man with good sense – "a practical genius emerging from the masses". Hugh Walpole, another novelist with a sensitive social conscience, spoke to Graham about the need to reach out to "ordinary people". Wickham Steed, the new editor of *The Times*, consulted him about Russian matters.

Graham's apartment in Soho became a salon where intellectuals met and listened to his views. W.H. Davies, the poet and author of *The Autobiography of a Super-Tramp*, who had – like Graham – done much rough walking, was a regular visitor; Sir Edwin Lutyens confided his original thoughts about a cenotaph in Whitehall with a speaker's gallery from which the proletariat might be addressed;

Compton Mackenzie, the bohemian and maverick novelist, who crossed swords on various occasions with the authorities, was a good friend and listened attentively to Graham's views. The roving traveller and writer who had first been taken into the confidence of ministers and statesmen, had now become a guru respected by the intellectual Left. He was to use his influence to powerful effect.

Graham was also in touch with the more active and provocative opponents of the Bolshevik revolution. In Constantinople he met up with many exiled White Russians, including General Baron Wrangel and his aide-de-camp, the young Count Tolstoy. The general was not optimistic about the prospects of starting a military front against the Bolsheviks in the Caucasus, but estimated that two million Russians outside Russia recognized him as a potential leader of counter-revolution: these might be needed to combat similar revolutions in other parts of Europe. Turkey was becoming a haven for disaffected Russians, many of them not aristocrats of the *ancien régime* but Circassian tribesmen who had valued their independence under the Tsars. Graham toured through Europe and found few places – outside Serbia – where there was any sympathy for the new regime in Russia. He was becoming not only a focal point for criticism of the Bolsheviks in England, but a rallying figure for opponents abroad.

By this time Graham's stance on Bolshevism was starting to be well-known inside Lenin's Russia. He had wanted to go back, to retrace some of his earlier "tramps" through the country, to test his views against the evolving reality of the Soviet Union. But it was not to be. He was refused a visa, and there was nothing the Foreign Office in London could do to help him acquire one. Graham's response was to do the next best thing: take a prolonged tour around the frontiers of Russia and see how her neighbours were reacting to the existence of a belligerent new Bolshevik state. He began in Finland, from where he looked across Lake Ladoga (half in Finland and half in Russia) at "the dark mass of forest that veiled the country I loved". It was here that he met the celebrated Russian painter Ilya Repin, who invited Graham to his gallery and showed him many of the pictures he had taken with him when he fled from the Bolsheviks. Among them was a portrait of Kerensky, whose flaws Repin had sought to reveal with "an unmistakable suggestion of the False Dmitriy, the conceited usurper of power".

From Finland, Graham moved on first to Estonia, where he found many Russian refugees – including Baltic barons – who were living in extreme poverty and lucky if they could find jobs in the sawmills. He thought the Estonians had the mentality of ex-serfs, and was glad to move on to Latvia, where he felt much closer to the old Russia that he knew and loved: church bells rang in the streets; the locals sang familiar folk songs; their houses still sported icons on the walls; spoken Russian was everywhere. Next came Lithuania, where – as in Estonia – he found the inhabitants anxious to shake off Russian affiliations and busily trying to be Lithuanians instead.

In Poland, Graham kept as close to Russian frontier as he could. He found that when the Polish police arrested runaway Russians, they tried to return them to the Soviet Union, who then declined to accept them. Some harmless people had been passed like parcels from one side of the frontier and back again repeatedly. One young lady had been reduced to such poverty in Lenin's Russia that she'd had to sell off her clothes one by one, just to get enough money to eat. Eventually, she had agreed to sleep with a Soviet commissar as the price of the wherewithal to travel. She had slipped off a train near the frontier, and made a lonely and frightening trek through the forests towards Poland. But she was attacked by a bunch of armed men – so-called "forest chiefs" – who stole most of her remaining clothes and all of her money. At starvation point, she had slipped across the border into Poland, only to be arrested and dumped back at the Russian border. Graham took pity on her and got her a railway ticket to Serbia and some money to buy clothes, so she should not have to face her husband in her half-naked dishevelled state. He was later to learn that her husband had rejected her on account of her fleeting unfaithfulness with the Soviet commissar. Such unhappy stories only deepened Graham's hatred of the Bolshevik regime. He was not to stay silent on the subject.

He continued his tour round the periphery of the Soviet Union, along the border of the Ukraine and into Romania. Sometimes he was followed by the local police. Sometimes he heard the cries of peasants being flogged for non-payment of taxes; he thought this as uncivilized as the behaviour on the other side – the Bolshevik side – of the border. His travels continued. Everywhere, it seemed, there were miserable refugees and other signs of the harshness of life across the border in Soviet Russia. At the end of his book about his tour – *Russia in Division* – he gives expression to his disgust: there are those, he writes, who think that "Bolsheviks are merely putting baths in working men's homes. Baths, yes, but baths of blood…wave behind wave of hate."

Graham's was an unusual voice. Few argued as forcefully or explicitly as he did against recognizing the legitimacy of the Soviet Union or receiving at court the representatives of "those who killed the kindred of the King". There was a general expectation, shared by the Labour Prime Minister Ramsay MacDonald, that communism would become "respectable" and bring an enlightened form of socialism to every land. Many of the idealistic visitors who visited Russia in the years following the revolution came away starry-eyed about the prospects. When Graham protested otherwise, he was accused of not having been back to Russia since the rise of Lenin – not, it must be said, for want of trying. So strongly did he feel about the unrecognized iniquities of Bolshevism that he contacted Stanley Baldwin (the Conservative leader) and volunteered to tour the country speaking publicly about what he knew. At this period of the 1920s, many members of parliament, the Dean of Canterbury, George Bernard Shaw, the Bloomsbury set and other influential moulders of opinion were convinced that the way ahead lay with communism. Consequently, Graham had a hard time on the hustings; sometimes he was heckled in Russian, and astonished his audience by replying in the same language. In the end, however reluctantly, it was usually recognized by his audiences that – after all – he really did know something of the country he was talking about.

It was acknowledged that the frontier of Russia which Graham had been tracing in his travels was not only a geographical frontier:

it was also a frontier of the mind. He deplored those exiles from Bolshevism who later "would creep back to the Kremlin to have a share in thirty pieces of silver"; but he made a point of meeting as many Russian exiles as he could, and found that most did not believe that Lenin could forever stifle the Church, predicting that "one day there would be a grand escape from the prison of Marxism". Among those he met were "forest priests" who had stayed on in Russia after the revolution and lurked in the woods, where peasant women brought them their children to be secretly baptised.

Graham sought out books about Russia as eagerly as he sought out Russians themselves – especially those written since the revolution. He visited Paris to buy up "armfuls of Soviet novels" to bring back to London. (He was stopped at customs in Folkestone on account of these suspicious activities.) In his public addresses he argued that neither the Orthodox Church nor "the light of Dostoevsky" could be put out. Reviewers of his numerous books[9] recognized that he was "able to write about Russians as Russians" and probably understood the country better than any of his compatriots.

Graham's efforts to expose the contrast between the old Russia which he loved and the new Soviet Union which he detested, were complicated by the somewhat unreal atmosphere of nostalgia that prevailed among the émigré Russian communities in western Europe. Many of the Russians who filled the churches (such as the Alexandre Nevsky cathedral in the Rue Daru in Paris) had seldom been to church in their own country. Rather than trying to engage with their new lands, these expatriates made a point of always talking together in Russian. Pushkin's birthday was celebrated almost as a national day, and literary societies gathered to listen to readings of classical Russian poetry and novels. Russian language publishing houses proliferated. At house-parties in the countryside – both in England and France – Russian émigrés assembled to bathe in a self-consciously

9 Graham was immensely prolific, with no less than eighty-six books attributed to him.

Chekhovian atmosphere.[10] The concentration of highly civilized writers and musicians among the exiles encouraged a disdain for the more commercially-minded bourgeois societies in which they now found themselves living. The émigrés' reconstruction of their own version of Tsarist Russia presented Graham with both opportunities and problems. On the one hand, it helped to bring to life the Russia which he had admired and written about before the revolution; on the other hand, it seemed to many people a world more of imagination than reality – a world that had never quite existed, at least outside the nostalgia-tinted memories of those who believed they had lost it.

Nevertheless, Graham's ability to see and pinpoint the real failings and iniquities of Bolshevism remained a force to be reckoned with. During the Second World War, with Russia was once again Britain's ally, the Foreign Office asked him to refrain from writing anything critical about the Soviet Union in the press. Such criticism was for the moment inappropriate. Stalin had become Uncle Joe – and even that arch-enemy of communism, Winston Churchill, was moved to defend his own more friendly attitude towards his Soviet counterpart: "If Hitler invaded Hell, I would at least make a favourable reference to the Devil in the House of Commons." Meanwhile, many of Graham's earlier friendly writings about Russia were reprinted as if they were current comments.

Graham played a notable role as a clear-sighted early critic of Bolshevism, and over time made himself the leading British expert on Russia and its literature. When people wanted to understand what was happening beneath the surface in that vast, distant and mysterious land, it was often to him that they turned. As late as 1959 Graham was editing a collection of classic Russian short stories, some of which were being translated for the first time. He had seen enough, not only of Moscow and St Petersburg but also of the Caucasus, the Arctic circle and other far-flung corners of Russia, to bear witness to the radical ruthlessness of Lenin's Bolshevik revolution. He was not

---

10 In his scholarly history of Russian culture, *Natasha's Dance*, Orlando Figes explains this movement in detail.

hypnotized by the egalitarian rhetoric. He was aware that a philosophy that reduced the value of each individual soul to a mere part of the state to which it belonged was in no way compatible with the teaching of the Russian Orthodox Church – or indeed of any Christian church. He understood – before others did – how this collectivized philosophy would lead (in Stalin's time) to a justification for starving out minorities who did not fit into the communist master plan. As he circulated in London among the great and the good (whose names he drops with sickening regularity in his memoirs), he enlightened those who would listen. He did not confront the Bolsheviks with cloak and dagger in hidden places, as did MacDonell, Noel and Teague-Jones, but with wit and wisdom across fashionable dinner tables.

Frederick Bailey

IN DISGUISE IN CENTRAL ASIA

Frederick Bailey

As the Russian Revolution developed through 1917–18, the British government grew increasingly confused as to how it should react. Would the revolutionary regime remain allies against Germany? Would the Bolshevik takeover turn Russia from an ally into a new hostile threat to western society as a whole? Would a communist Russia join with the Central Powers (Germany and Austria) to threaten British India? It was to find answers to these questions – as well as to influence the new regime – that Bruce Lockhart had been sent to Moscow, and that Ranald MacDonell had been dispatched along with his undercover colleagues to the Caucasus. But there were other parts of the Tsar's former domains equally unknown in their affiliations and just as unpredictable in their likely actions. Among these were the traditionally Muslim parts of Russian Central Asia.

It was for these reasons that Lieutenant Colonel Frederick Bailey was sent to Tashkent in 1918. In the course of the Tsarist conquest of Central Asia, Tashkent – formerly part of the emirate of Kokand – had fallen to the armies of Tsar Alexander II in 1855. A decade later, the city (which would later become capital of the Soviet Socialist Republic of Uzbekistan) was decreed the capital of Turkestan, an amorphous region of Central Asia largely inhabited by Turkic-speaking nomadic tribes.

By the early 20th century, Tashkent had grown into a more substantial city than its more romantic-sounding neighbours – Samarkand, Bokhara and Khiva – and lay at the heart of a prosperous cotton industry. As a centre of population and trade, it was more than just a junction of interweaving caravan routes. It was a strategic and political objective in its own right.

Bailey, unlike so many of the British adventurers who challenged the early Bolsheviks, was not a born Scotsman. His father, after a career in India, had ended his working life as a lecturer at Edinburgh University, and the young Frederick had been sent to school at Edinburgh Academy. There he had developed a strong affection for Scotland, and when his exploring exploits won him fame, it was the Royal Scottish Geographical Society that awarded him the prized Livingstone Gold Medal.

His father was anxious that he should join the army, and Bailey was moved from Edinburgh Academy to school in England at Wellington College (a school with a strong military orientation). He completed his education at Sandhurst and as a member of Francis Younghusband's mission to Lhasa in 1903, had extensively explored the frontiers of Tibet and China. For this reason, like many other explorers, he had gravitated towards the Indian political and secret service.

In 1918 Bailey was personally selected by the Viceroy of India, Lord Chelmsford, to lead a reporting mission from India to Tashkent, and to try and influence those in charge to work in sympathy with British foreign policy.

This was always going to be a difficult task, and as it began several unpredictable events lengthened the odds of success. There had been an armed clash between General Malleson's British intervention force and the Bolsheviks at Ashkabad just before Bailey arrived. Meanwhile, King George V's cousin, Tsar Nicholas II had been murdered together with his wife and children by the Bolsheviks in July 1918. The following month, an assassination attempt was made on Lenin's life (the so-called Lockhart plot); British troops landed at Archangel to oppose the Bolshevik takeover and as September 1918 dawned, twenty-six Communist commissars in Baku were murdered, allegedly on British instructions .

When Bailey left India, Britain's relations with the Bolsheviks were largely undefined. By the time he reached Russia, his country was well on the way to becoming the Bolsheviks' enemy. This was hardly an easy environment in which to make sensitive inquiries and exercise influence.

One thing, however, worked in favour of Bailey and his mission. The Bolsheviks had virtually no international recognition, and were eager to be recognized as a legitimate state by Great Britain, in the hope that such recognition would sway the decision of other countries. Perhaps, it was reasoned in the revolutionary corridors of power, a formal acknowledgement, or at least not too unfriendly a reception of Bailey might go some way toward acceptance on the world stage. This was an advantage, but it could have been more of one if Bailey had had official credentials. The American representative at Tashkent, by contrast, was officially registered as the Consul-General of his country. With Britain still uncertain about how to treat the Bolsheviks, however, the Viceroy had felt reluctant to issue Bailey with any similarly helpful documentation.

The first Russian settlement of any size Bailey reached was the town of Osh. It had been a hot and exhausting march, and Bailey decided to spend a day resting there "to get ourselves straight and tidy after our journey". He wanted to arrive in Tashkent in a condition to make a good impression as a serious envoy. In Osh, though he was neither arrested nor detained, Bailey was treated with grave suspicion.

There were rumours that the party was the vanguard of a British army advancing from India to occupy Russian Central Asia before the revolutionaries had established themselves. His Indian servants were thought to be sepoys (native Indian troops) in civilian clothes. They were, however, allowed to proceed on their journey, and Bailey hired some tarantasses (spring-less four-wheeled carriages on long flexible wooden chassis), in which they bumped over the steppes for nearly forty miles the following day.

During the year before Bailey arrived, Tashkent had been the scene of numerous disturbances and attempted coups. The predominantly Muslim inhabitants (95 per cent of the population) had risen up against the European minority and the Bolsheviks had clashed with the Socialist Revolutionaries. Unemployment was rife and food was in short supply. Nonetheless, Bailey found the Bolsheviks definitely – if not altogether securely – in control. He wasted no time in seeking an audience with the commissar for foreign affairs and, after a somewhat impolite delay, was eventually received.

It was not a propitious moment for a first contact. The developments mentioned above had soured the atmosphere between Britain and Bolshevik Russia. Bailey – who was unaware of many of these events – tried to present himself as a viable interlocutor between two governments yet to take a formal view of each other. At the same time, he repeatedly tried to point out the dangers of allowing German agents a free rein in Tashkent. He also did his best to persuade the commissar that allowing cotton and other strategic stocks to fall into German hands would be unfortunate.

Despite his diplomatic endeavours, Bailey sensed he was being regarded more as a spy than as an envoy, and that he might at any moment be interned or arrested. The jail – where parties of drunken Bolshevik troops regularly showed up and shot the inmates - would hardly have been a safe billet at that juncture. Bizarrely, the authorities justified the prison shooting sprees on humanitarian grounds, claiming that the jail was dangerously overcrowded, and that the men they murdered had been so badly beaten up that shooting was an act of mercy.

Bailey survived his first interview with the commissar and was able to spend some weeks in the late summer of 1918, under surveillance but happily still at large, discovering what was happening in Tashkent. It was not an encouraging picture. Although the Bolsheviks had professed to support freedom of the press, freedom of assembly and other civil rights, all were being systematically and brutally suppressed. Those suspected of being "unreliable" supporters of the regime – the staff of a radio station were a case in point – were not brought to trial but summarily executed. Neither were material conditions much better than the political: even the delightful avenues of poplars lining the broad streets were being cut down for firewood.

In such circumstances, everyone, especially Bailey and his American colleague, had to be continually on their guard against *agents provocateurs*, who might trick them into some expression of opposition to the regime. The rank and file of the Bolshevik army was largely made up of conscripted Austrian prisoners of war, who could be seen roaming the streets in their tattered grey uniforms. The atmosphere of revolutionary excess reminded Bailey of the course of the French Revolution: young people – intoxicated by a sudden experience of power – committing appalling atrocities, before they, in turn, were overtaken and eliminated by their successors. He learned that many residents of Tashkent believed the whole aberration would be over quickly. After all, the Paris Commune had lasted only for seventy days – perhaps the Bolshevik experiment would last no longer.

Amidst the general gloom and despondency, Bailey made some promising contacts. One of these was a young Irish girl[11] who, despite the dangers, and having had a chance to leave safely, had stayed on as the governess to a Russian aristocratic family's children. She was to give Bailey every possible assistance, and her knowledge of the city, its expatriate community, and who could be trusted proved invaluable to him. Eventually, this spirited young woman was prevented from teaching or associating with the children of her former employers, since all "private tuition" had been forbidden by the Bolshevik authorities, and transferred to a state job teaching at a Soviet military academy. The one advantage of this was that, as a "state worker", she was permitted to travel on the railway and was thus able, though not without difficulty, to get herself to Ashkabad. There she went into hiding before finally convincing some armed smugglers to take her with them on horseback to the nearby Persian frontier. She must have been a remarkable young woman to persuade the smugglers, who were all "wanted men" by the Persian frontier guards, to entrust their fates to her. Encounters with such people as this Irish governess encouraged Bailey to believe something useful could be achieved in Tashkent, despite the omnipresent secret "inquiry commission" agents.

---

11 Miss Houston, the governess in question, was by no means unique. For a delightful account of English, Scottish and Irish governesses who stayed behind to look after their charges throughout the revolution, one should read *When Miss Emmie was in Russia* (Eland Press, London, 2011).

However, his time as a free agent was to prove much shorter than that of the governess. In the middle of October, Bailey was tipped off that he was about to be arrested. He took immediate precautionary steps, destroying his more compromising correspondence and acquiring – from one of the many prisoners of war in the city – a grey Austrian military uniform complete with cap and boots, which he kept ready to use as a disguise. He was indeed to make good use of it, and he had not long to wait.

The next day the secret police arrived and informed him that he was under arrest. His papers were confiscated and all his possessions searched. A pistol was found, and they took this away – unaware that he was concealing a second one. Worse, a police agent announced he was going to sleep in Bailey's room to ensure that he did not try to escape in the night.

Although he had no diplomatic immunity, Bailey protested strongly at the impropriety of his arrest. He said that "he would not care to be the people who had ordered it" when news of his detention reached the House of Commons in London. This was a worthwhile punt on Bailey's part. He knew that the Bolsheviks, innocently ignorant of British institutions, imagined the House of Commons to be a proletarian assembly of anti-establishment activists bent on upsetting the capitalist regime and natural allies of the revolutionary extremists in Lenin's Russia. Rather than flinging him into jail, the nervous local authorities kept him under virtual, but not total house arrest with six guards, awaiting a decision from Moscow.

Prompted by a further warning, as well as by articles in the Soviet press decrying British military intervention in support of the Whites, Bailey decided Moscow's decision probably wasn't going to go his way, and made plans to flee. His original idea had been to escape from Tashkent and head for India, but he was advised that he was unlikely to get away from the city once the secret police noticed him missing. As a 'Plan B' he decided to lie low in the city until the initial furore had died down and the heat was off. That strategy, of course, carried its own demands, not least a safe place to hole up and allies to assist him.

In the event, Bailey's disappearance was greatly aided by his possession of the Austrian uniform. Dressed in a light overcoat and hat, and followed as always by his six secret policemen, he entered a terraced house where he had stowed the uniform, except for the high boots that he was wearing concealed inside his trousers. The minders dutifully waited outside the house.

Bailey changed briskly into his Austrian uniform, tucking his grey trousers into his high boots and putting his kepi on his head to shade his face from observation. He then raced out of the back door of the house and into the garden, which adjoined a series of further gardens behind a row of semi-detached houses. He dashed through the gardens, kicking open a locked gate between two of them. When he reached the garden of the house at the far end of the terrace, he entered it through the back door, as previously agreed with the occupant, and shortly thereafter emerged from the front door as an Austrian prisoner of war. He walked briskly away, while his minders kept their eyes on the front door of the house they had their prisoner entering. He even took the trouble to carry his original overcoat, wrapped round his original hat, so that if any subsequent search occurred there would be no incriminating evidence of his having changed there. He had effectively disappeared.

The next step was to reach the safe house which Bailey had arranged and where he could lie low until it was safe to try and leave Tashkent. He doubled and redoubled back on his tracks to ensure that he was not being followed, before entering the modest residence that had been chosen. The Irish governess, one of the few people who knew he was there, had at some risk to herself collected and brought to him his riding boots and breeches, which were irreplaceable in Tashkent and would later be of great use.

The first thing Bailey did the next day was shave his head and cut off his traditional British military moustache. From now on he would sport a beard and short hair in keeping with his new, Austrian personality. Having read John Buchan's *The Thirty-Nine Steps*, published just three years before, he followed the hero Richard Hannay's techniques in avoiding detection: adopting alien habits like clicking his heels and bowing formally when introduced to anyone.

Luckily for Bailey, the man-hunt was not all that determined. Several of his Bolshevik contacts surmised that he had been murdered by one of the German agents in Tashkent, who would have been well aware of his plotting against them. Others thought he had already escaped to Samarkand. There was a price on his head, but it was – as Bailey himself remarked –an embarrassingly small one. The Bolsheviks might have expended more energy on searching for Bailey, if they hadn't been so insecure about their own fortunes. Many shared the view on the streets, that the regime might be as short-lived as the Terror in the French Revolution, and were looking ahead to their own survival in the aftermath. The foreign affairs commissar had even made discreet inquiries about seeking asylum in England.

After waiting a week or two for the novelty of his disappearance to have subsided, Bailey headed for the hills outside Tashkent, planning to stay with a friend who kept bees. He made the escape journey from the city, still dressed as an Austrian prisoner of war, on the back of a hay cart. There were many anxious moments. Some villages were full of Austrians, whom he feared might engage him in conversation and become suspicious. At other times, just when he wanted to move on before too many people saw his face, his unsuspecting hosts would delay him with a long tea-drinking session around the samovar.

When he reached the bee-keeper's establishment, Bailey found a White Russian general and another refugee from the Bolsheviks also sheltering there. After bumping into a number of curious locals on boar-hunting trips, the trio realized it was only a matter of time before some peasant gossiped about their presence and a party was sent to investigate. Should this happen, they planned to resist capture with the few rifles they had obtained, then set off in different directions towards a cave rendezvous deeper in the hills, where further firearms and provisions had been stowed.

Then disaster struck. Unable to report on the political goings-on from his mountain retreat, Bailey decided to smuggle himself back into Tashkent. Before he could leave, however, he slipped on some snow whilst out boar-hunting, badly dislocating one leg and injuring the other.

A pony was fetched and Bailey was carried back to their hideaway, where he had to retire to bed and soon developed a fever. The White Russian general looked after him, but all plans to defend themselves with their rifles, or to make off to caves in the mountains, were clearly now out of the question. After a fortnight of convalescence in bed, Bailey got up to find that their retreat was four-foot deep in snow. Nevertheless, by the New Year of 1920, he was determined to move on by pony, sledge, or whatever means were available. He knew he was achieving nothing at so great a distance from Tashkent, and all the time the danger of discovery was increasing.

Returning to the city was not easy. Not only were Bailey's legs still severely hampering his movement, but as the party approached the city, they met a stream of refugees who reported an uprising against the Bolsheviks. According to some reports, later proved false, the Bolsheviks had been overthrown. At the time Bailey was disappointed that he had not been in the city to influence the outcome. Later on, he realised he'd have been unlikely to survive the shootings and recriminations that followed the attempted coup. Altogether some 4,000 suspected participants in the rebellion were shot, and Bailey later recorded that anyone even wearing a collar was taken to be bourgeois, and summarily murdered.

Once he was sure the worst of the reprisals were over, Bailey re-established contact with the Irish governess and other supporters. He found that Bolshevik social structures had been further established in the city. The few surviving upper-class or bourgeois residents were moving in to share houses with one other, and so avoid having peasants quartered on them, or having to accommodate Bolshevik spies.

The situation was similar to the one described by Boris Pasternak in his novel *Dr Zhivago* (1957) about the years immediately after the revolution in other parts of Russia. Indeed, many of the social experiments of the early Communist years had their first airing in

Central Asia. Wages were abolished or frozen; hoarding goods or cash was prohibited; barter replaced a free economy and shorter hours were worked in farms and factories. This latter move was because, so the Bolsheviks explained, most of the profits from a full eight- or ten-hour day's work had gone to line the pockets of the bourgeois landowners or industrialists.

Bailey was unable to risk leaving his safe house in Tashkent in daylight, even though he had changed his cover and his disguise. Thus confined, and forced to await developments he could either influence or report back to his seniors, he had time on his hands. He embarked on Tolstoy's stories in the original Russian, read the Bible (now a subversive text) from beginning to end in English and devoured Dickens's *The Old Curiosity Shop* (the only English novel he could find) twice. On one occasion the house was raided, not by members of the secret police, but by the officious Quartering Commission, tasked with making sure no accommodation space was wasted. Bailey, now a master of deception, reverted to his role as an Austrian prisoner of war who was giving French lessons to his landlady.

He also had a narrow squeak when he arranged for someone to act as a courier and take his latest set of false papers, made out in the name of a dead man, to obtain a residence permit. With an irony Dickens might have enjoyed, the official in charge of the permits recognised the name, and claimed that the man in question owed him money. "If he wants his permit, tell him to come himself and pay me back what he owes me!" he said. The courier was lucky to get away without being arrested herself, and Bailey's papers were retained by the official.

Bailey's next set of false papers belonged to a citizen of the Baltic States. These had the advantage that a Baltic citizen might be expected not to speak good Russian (just like Bailey...), but were marred somewhat by the birth-date. According to Bailey's papers, he was seventy-five years old, until some careful tampering changed the seven to a four. Even so, he changed the papers as soon as he could – this time for those of a Romanian prisoner of war. Obtaining credible documentation was part of the continual struggle for survival.

Shelter presented a further problem. Bailey's fall-back plan was that if found at night in the house where he was staying (a billet again found for him by his Irish governess friend), he would claim that he had only come there for a cup of tea, had left it too late to get home before the curfew, so had been obliged to overnight there. The Bolsheviks were now actively looking for him, so he started rumours, by telling indiscreet friends that he was preparing to escape from Tashkent to Bokhara.

He also found it almost impossible to get news of what was happening in the outside world. It was long after General Dunsterville's intervention in the Caucasus (see chapter 2) that Bailey learnt anything of this development. One thing he did learn, and later report to the government in India, was the extent of plotting and propaganda against the British Raj in India in communist Central Asia.

This plotting was activated and encouraged by Indian revolutionaries who had left India expressly to stir up trouble abroad. It was also encouraged by the Bolsheviks, who as early as 1919 were beginning to realize that Lenin's dream of a simultaneous revolution throughout the western world might not be fulfilled. They had therefore turned to inciting revolution in India and other eastern countries, with the aim of ending British rule. Like the Kaiser before them, the Bolsheviks saw the presence of a large Muslim population in India (particularly in the north-western area now Pakistan) as usefully susceptible to influence by the Muslims of Central Asia. The Great Game was continuing under a new guise, and Bailey's intelligence about this proved vital to the authorities in Delhi and Simla, as well as in London.

Meanwhile, he was finding it harder and harder to stay concealed. Whatever it said on his new papers, he was able to speak not a single word of Romanian, and was therefore in constant fear of being addressed by imagined compatriots. One day he found himself sitting in a barber's shop alongside a secret police agent he knew was looking for him. He even discovered that for several weeks the secret police had monitored the movements of his dog, whose company he had been obliged to do without, in the hope it would lead them to Bailey.

On one occasion, he spotted this faithful animal on the street, and rapidly walked away before there could be any encounter. The net was tightening: it was becoming necessary to change his address every night.

Again Bailey left Tashkent for the mountains, where he spent some time sheltering in yurts among the semi-nomadic Kirgiz peoples. When suddenly confronted with Red Army soldiers here, he claimed to be a geologist and a member of a survey team looking for iron ore in the mountains. He was beginning to find it difficult to remember what his latest cover story was. What little news percolated through to his mountain fastness was not encouraging. The British intervention forces had mostly been withdrawn and Ashkabad, a key station on the railway between Tashkent and the Caspian Sea, had fallen to the Bolsheviks. Anxious to know more, he returned to Tashkent where the situation was becoming increasingly oppressive. Anyone unemployed was being rounded up and sent off for forced labour. The city was filling up with soldiers who had deserted from the intervention forces in Siberia. Some of these wore looted British uniforms: "Tommies from Tomsk!" was the local joke.

At this point, Bailey made his most daring and imaginative gambit of all. Through a contact he got himself recruited into the Bolshevik counter-espionage service – a branch of the dreaded Cheka. In pre-revolutionary days, the head of this service had been a wealthy member of the bourgeoisie. Now, having converted or defected to the Bolsheviks, the Cheka boss had become a particularly savage executioner of his former class.

Yet another cover story and nationality were deemed necessary before facing an interview with this alarming man. This time, the nationality chosen was Albanian, for two reasons. First, because – although Bailey himself spoke no Albanian – he was fairly convinced no one else in Tashkent did either. Second, his contact had managed to acquire a rubber stamp and some stationery belonging to the Serbian volunteer corps – a body which included some Albanians and which had sent some individuals to Russia to help with organisational tasks. An outstanding snag was that the Serbian pass required a photograph. Luckily, Bailey's old Austrian uniform, with its epaulettes cut off and its standard-issue kepi worn back to front, bore a passable resemblance to that of a Serbian volunteer.

The circumstances that gave Bailey a chance to be recruited were bizarre. The head of counter-espionage was convinced that there were British officers in Bokhara – the neighbouring Central Asian city, which had been an independent emirate before the Russians took over – and that these officers were actively training local Muslims to fight against the Bolsheviks. He had sent no less than fifteen separate agents into Bokhara to investigate. None had returned, and he concluded that they had all been strangled by supporters of the former emir, who wanted Bokhara to regain its independence or at least avoid becoming part of a Soviet Union.

Understandably, no-one was exactly volunteering to be the sixteenth agent sent, but here Bailey spied his chance. The prospect of a formal interview with the Cheka boss in an office stuffed with agents, many of them specifically looking for Bailey, was of course not an appealing one, though. Various plans were devised, but in the end, by sheer good luck, Bailey and a friend encountered the departmental head in the street and the conversation took place informally, without the presence of other agents. Bailey was accepted for what he was pretending to be – an Albanian with the Serbian volunteers - and issued with genuine secret police documentation.

Thus equipped, he set off for Bokhara by train, passing through Samarkand and even doing some innocent sight-seeing. His intention was to slip away from Bokhara then head across country to the Persian frontier and from there to Mashad, where he could report all that he had discovered during his long on-and-off mission, to the British representatives in Persia. But when Bailey reached Kagan, the railway station for Bokhara, he and his travelling companion received explicit instructions to track down one "Anglo-Indian Service Colonel Bailey". He was being instructed to spy on himself! Suitably misleading replies were sent, suggesting that Bailey had been spotted heading off in an altogether different direction.

In a further surprise, Bailey found himself sharing a hotel with one of the leading Indian anti-British agitators. This man – Mahendra Pratap – explained in detail to Bailey (believing all the while that Bailey was a former Austrian soldier and ally of the Germans) that the Indians had not mutinied against the British during the First World War solely because they'd been afraid of the Turks taking over from Britain and – as Muslims – making conditions worse for the Hindu population. Now, he said, he was working hard to unite Muslims and Hindus against the Raj. Although all this was, by 1919, in a sense history, it provided Bailey with useful insight into the anti-British and republican elements in India.

Bailey spent some time in Bokhara, and at one point suggested to the British mission in Mashad that he should remain there as a link between Mashad and Tashkent. But it seemed his message did not get through, and he decided it was time to leave Bokhara, making the hazardous desert-crossing into Persia and on to Mashad. He feared that the longer he remained in Bokhara, the more liable he was to be kidnapped by those suspicious of his identity.

He set about making preparations for his departure – buying horses, leather water bags, saddles and other equipment, as well as selecting five companions. Four White Russian officers insisted on joining his expedition, one of them the son of a Grand Duke, who wanted to get away from the Bolsheviks as fast as he could. Another was a much-decorated Turkoman officer; all were armed. Although Bailey was keen to remain a small party (large travelling bands could be refused access to the wells in the desert) he reckoned he would be glad of some armed and tested officers if there were any altercations. Just before they were due to leave, seven further Russians attached themselves to the party.

Bailey and his entourage decided to wear Turkoman khalats (robes) over their normal clothes, and large black sheepskin hats, so that from a distance they would resemble a Turkoman caravan and attract less attention. Bailey was also glad of the breeches and riding boots his governess-friend had rescued for him prior to his departure.

They had planned to start their journey on ponies and switch to camels when they reached the Oxus. The desert-crossing beyond the river was punctuated only by occasional, very deep wells, accessible only by long ropes, which in turn could only be carried on the backs of sturdy camels. But in the end, reasoning that camel travel was too slow and risky, they decided to stick with the ponies. A long rope could be strung together, Bailey reckoned, out of the horses' bridles, girths and all the other straps and strings they had. It was destined to be a hasty trip. Away from Bokhara, the well-worn routes between the wells were controlled by roving bands of Bolsheviks, who might all too easily spot and intercept a caravan.

Reaching the Oxus on Christmas Day 1919, it took the party nearly four hours to cross the river. There was now a long, bleak desert passage until they reached the next river – the Murghab –near the Persian frontier. More than once, they only just reached a well before they collapsed due to thirst, and almost always they were lucky enough to find people with ropes who could help them reach the deep water. At one well, they encountered an armed party of robbers, whom the White Russian officers were inclined to attack immediately. Bailey prudently negotiated with them instead, persuading them to share access to the well. In the process, they discovered a Persian agent, who had been sent on a mission to report to the Bolsheviks any caravans such as theirs. They took this informer with them – his feet tied together under his pony's girth – to avoid his riding off with any reports of their whereabouts. No one could be trusted.

When they reached the Murghab River, they were able to hire or bribe the only boatman to take them across in shifts, while the ponies swam the twenty yards of fast-flowing water. They considered themselves lucky to have avoided encounters with the Bolshevik bands known to patrol the river banks. By now they were starving, all the more so after having purchased food parcels from the Turkomans at the last oasis-stop and discovering many miles down the road, that they had been seriously short-changed. Sometimes they lost the track in the sands of the steppes, or failed to extract water from a well. At other points on the journey, they were reduced to eating the fodder for the ponies or shooting in vain at distant gazelles, and bickering about the waste of ammunition for hours afterwards.

When they reached the next and final river, forming the border with Persia, there was one last drama. The only lady in the party fell from her horse and had to be rescued by the Grand Duke's son. While this operation was going on, some Bolshevik border guards, hidden in the long reeds along the river bank, opened fire. The fire was returned, and none of Bailey's party was injured, though they later heard that some of the Bolshevik snipers, who were foolishly sporting enormous fur hats, had been hit. Having survived this last encounter, Russia with all its dangers and difficulties was behind them: they had arrived in Persia. The Russians announced that Bailey had been killed and given a military funeral. The British press and public, meanwhile, as addicted to John Buchan-type adventures as Bailey himself was, rejoiced in the reappearance of a hero who had outsmarted the Russian bear for so long.

Colonel Bailey had been on the run for such a time, adopted so many disguises and false personalities, and made up so many rapidly changing stories about his mission and roles, that at one stage he remarked "it felt quite strange to tell a true story again".

He also felt aggrieved to have been left incommunicado by his masters in India or Mashad: "They might have done more to keep in touch with me," he complained. Of course this had been tricky: some of the messages from him and most of the messages to him had either gone astray or been destroyed to avoid compromising the carriers. On one occasion a carrier pigeon had been shot by one of his companions before it could deliver its message. Bailey felt nonetheless that greater efforts might have been made to send him advice, instructions or even encouragement. His had been a lonely mission, conducted largely in the dark as to events in the world outside. And there'd been many events: the First World War had ended; Allied intervention in Russia had foundered; Britain was in direct confrontation with the Bolsheviks to whom Bailey was unofficial envoy. Most significantly, the Bolsheviks had established themselves through the length and breadth of Russia much faster and more firmly than anticipated.

There is no question that Bailey underwent much discomfort and much danger over the course of his activities in central Asia. But what had he achieved?

The Viceroy of India had sent him to Tashkent to find out what was happening there and influence the new regime in favour of British interests. However, he'd soon found out that the Bolshevik regime was not open to useful negotiation, and Britain and Russia were already at loggerheads. He failed to undermine or overthrow the Bolshevik leadership, although it is possible he would have had more success had he not been hiding in the mountains in January 1919 when the attempted coup took place.

What Bailey did do was record and report to his masters in London and Delhi the true nature of this new regime in Central Asia. Britain now became fully aware of what rule by Russia meant. In no particular order, this comprised: the denial of personal liberty and press freedom, the seizure of private property, the collective housing conditions inflicted on the bourgeoisie, the destruction of the natural resources of the countryside, the enforced labour imposed on large numbers and – worst of all – the indiscriminate killing of any who considered opponents of the regime. Bailey was too late to alter the course of events in Central Asia, but he was the first to reveal what was happening there in the years following Lenin's takeover. His courage and his efforts were not in vain.

A NOVELIST'S VIEW FROM THE FRONT

Hugh Walpole

Arthur Ransome was not quite Robert Bruce Lockhart's only companionable compatriot as he played his lonely and controversial role at the British Consulate in Moscow during the early years of the First World War. There was also Hugh Walpole, already an established novelist himself and a friend of such leading literary figures as Henry James, Arnold Bennett and Joseph Conrad. Walpole had been unable to join the armed forces in England because of his poor eyesight, but he was determined to do something useful for the Allied cause, at a time when non-combatant young men – particularly if they were practising homosexuals, as he was – were liable to receive white feathers through the post and abuse in pubs and clubs. He had started learning Russian at Cambridge, and was fast falling under the spell of that country and its literature. The answer seemed to be to go to Russia and volunteer as a Red Cross worker on the eastern front.

His efforts were not in vain: so conspicuous was his dedication to rescuing the wounded that he was awarded the Russian Cross of St George. Nobody could now accuse him of chickening-out of the war effort. His social contacts and literary talents were not, however, used to full advantage as a stretcher-bearer, and by 1916 he had been redeployed to Petrograd to head up the Anglo-Russian propaganda bureau – an organization whose aim was to encourage the Russians to maintain a vigorous campaign on the eastern front, while at the same time trying to explode the myth – widely believed in Russia – that England was preserving its navy too carefully and solely for its own protection, and that the British army was happy to fight the Germans "to the last drop of Russian blood". (Such suspicions were to resurface – equally unjustifiably – in the Second World War.)

Bruce Lockhart found Walpole a cheerful companion, who helped him to overcome his periodical bouts of depression. Walpole was an incorrigible optimist: he was thrilled to be living in Russia and was an unqualified admirer of virtually everything Russian – the poetry, the novels, the patriotic peasantry, the sophisticated aristocracy, the balalaika music, the free-flowing vodka. He and Lockhart had much in common, despite their widely diverging sexual interests.

Walpole used his experience on the eastern front to provide the background to one of his bestselling novels – *The Dark Forest* (1916). In this, he reveals his own complex attitudes towards a Russia that was already on the brink of revolution. To some of his characters, Russia was "Holy Russia" – a world of kremlins, monasteries and icons; to others it was Petrograd, with its cafés and literary gossip; but – most significantly – to the student generation it was "a platform for frantic speeches, incipient revolution, little untidy hysterical meetings in a dirty room in a back street, newspapers, the incapacities of the Duma, the robberies and villainies of the government". Despite his own love affair with all things Russian, Walpole could see that all was not well: his time in the Red Cross field stations and the hospitals behind the lines on the eastern front had shown him that the Tsar was out of touch with his government, that the government was out of touch with the army's officer corps, and that the officers were out of touch with the rank and file of their soldiery. Always in the background, and sometimes in the foreground, of his tale of suffering and distress in the field dressing stations is the inadequacy of the Tsarist government's support of its own troops in the front line, in particular the shortage of ammunition. As early as 1915, Walpole saw that an explosion of anger and frustration was waiting to happen.

After his move from the eastern front to Petrograd, Walpole

wrote a second Russian novel, *The Secret City* (1919), in which his characters – some of them the same as in his earlier novel – get to grips with the realities and horrors of the revolution, just as before they had confronted the fatal inadequacies and corruption of the old regime. Some of the incidents portrayed are merely distressing, as when a servant goes to a revolutionary meeting and arrives at the house of her bourgeois employers the next morning declaring that she will no longer work for them on the grounds that "everyone is equal now, and they must do things for themselves". But as the revolution moves on and the Bolsheviks tighten their grip, things become more frightening. At one point Walpole's heroine has her flat in Petrograd invaded by some soldiers, commanded by a young student. They burst into her dining room with their rifles, demanding to search the flat and claiming that a renegade Tsarist policeman has been firing at them from a window. They threaten to burn the house down if they can't find him. Later, after the soldiers have left, the policeman in question turns up at he door and begs for somewhere to hide. He denies having fired at anyone and pleads convincingly that "they are going to kill me…I've done nothing…I've done no one any harm…only my duty". The girls in the flat believe him; they hide him in a cupboard in a bedroom. When the Bolsheviks come again to search the flat, one soldier – "a large dirty fellow, who quite frankly terrified her…stared at her, as it were licking his lips over her" – insists they open the bedroom cupboard, but the policeman has already slipped into another hiding place, and they get away with their daring concealment of him. The incident gives a very vivid impression of the fear which has been loosed into society. This was not just regime change, but the reincarnation of the worst aspects of the French Revolution.

In *The Secret City* Walpole reveals to his English-speaking readers not only the radicalism of the new Bolshevik movement – "the greatest war the world has ever seen, the war of the proletariat against the bourgeoisie" – but also the depth of its anti-British feeling. The English are portrayed as "hidebound with prejudices and conventions", and the First World War as a struggle between capitalists to secure ever greater extortions from the colonial peoples they dominate. He maintains that in the weeks between the first revolution (the abdication of the Tsar) and Easter 1917, "all the seeds of the later crop of horrors were sown"; the change from the illusion of Utopia to "the worst sort of Communism" was so rapid that those who did not experience it first-hand – as Walpole did – could hardly be aware of what was happening. In this revolutionary atmosphere anti-Semitic sentiment is as rife as ever, even though many of the early communist leaders were Jewish. Walpole was writing fiction and not reportage, but the message that comes across in his two Russian novels is as effective a piece of anti-Bolshevik propaganda as anything which he produced in the course of his more conventional office duties at the Anglo-Russian Bureau.

A more reflective and studied view of the events which had unrolled before his eyes during those wartime years in Petrograd and Moscow is contained in his autobiographical book, *The Crystal Box*, which he published privately (in an edition of only 150 signed copies) in 1924 after his return to England. The book paints a vivid portrait of the literary circles in which Walpole moved: he describes, for instance, his friendship with H.G. Wells. As we have seen, Wells was an enthusiastic supporter of the revolution in Russia; it was all the more noteworthy that Walpole reached his own – much less favourable – verdict on the Bolshevik takeover.

Walpole certainly had a ringside view of the revolution as it unfurled: he recounts how when he arrived in Petrograd in 1917 "the Cossacks were clearing the Nevsky [Prospekt], women were fighting for bread on the other side of the Neva, Kerensky was standing on a tub in the Duma screaming – and the old world tumbled through a hole into limbo". He concluded – in contrast to most observers – that there was nothing inevitable about the Bolshevik coup: if the Cossack General Kornilov and Kerensky had managed to pull off their own *coup d'état* three months after the abdication of the Tsar, then Lenin would have been pre-empted and Bolshevism stopped dead in its tracks. All that the Russian people needed was a strong and determined leadership for their new, post-imperial regime. Kerensky on his own had failed to provide this, and Kornilov was to fall out with him and lead his own – unsuccessful – White Russian resistance to the Bolsheviks. It had been – according to Walpole – a close run thing.

Walpole's views and impressions carry a special validity because he had first-hand experience of two different worlds: he had been an adventurer on the eastern front – albeit a civilian paramedic and not a soldier – when he was collecting his material for *The Dark Forest*, and he had been one of the few foreigners in Petrograd when he was collecting material for *The Secret City*. He had seen for himself what was happening, and he had heard for himself "that flood of talk that swept the country" during the first uncertain months of revolution. He had witnessed and recorded how this pessimistic talk had brought about the very conditions that the chattering classes (as we would now call them) had most wanted to avoid: "When those grim presences Lenin, Trotsky and the others rose out of the dust, they had only to lift their long hands over the landscape and the country was like a dead man."

Bruce Lockhart was not the only fellow Englishman who enjoyed Walpole's company in Russia in 1917. A far more distinguished novelist than Walpole – Willie Somerset Maugham (the subject of a later chapter) – was also there. The two men had been acquainted before their Russian assignments, and were happy to spend time in the lonely surroundings of revolutionary St Petersburg chatting together about the literary world. They had somewhat different motivations: Walpole was anxious to ingratiate himself with an eminent novelist and playwright; Maugham, on the other hand, while relishing literary and social gossip with a compatriot, found Walpole a conceited and sycophantic companion, whom he closely observed and parodied mercilessly in one of his later novels – *Cakes and Ale* (1930). Walpole was never to forgive this betrayal.

On leaving Russia, Walpole missed the freedom of debate which he had found there, and the sense that all was still to play for in a world that was in the melting pot. Yet he remained convinced that Russia had a great and significant future ahead of her, and that in another hundred years she would be the most powerful country in the world. Had he known how soon communism would come to dominate large tracts of the world, how it would roll up Eastern Europe and be the first to penetrate (with its 'Sputnik') outer space, he might have reduced his estimate to half that time. He concludes the chapter about Russia in his autobiography by declaring that he was glad to have been able to share in the crisis of her history. He certainly had.

But how far had he influenced western opinion about these events? Probably more than we realize. Although Walpole is now hardly remembered as a writer, in his day his fiction was widely read and admired. He was to write some three dozen novels as well as half-a-dozen volumes of short stories and several plays and Hollywood film scripts, winning praise from Henry James and becoming a respected friend of Virginia Woolf. Soon after returning from Russia, he joined John Buchan at the Ministry of Information, where he helped form Buchan's view of Bolshevism (as evidenced by the sinister and aggressive Bolshevik anarchists portrayed in *Huntingtower*). He toured the United States as a lecturer in the years immediately following the Russian Revolution, always attracting large audiences.

Almost uniquely, Walpole had first-hand and front-line experience of the events which he was describing. People knew that his warnings about the horrors of Bolshevism – so different from the reaction of such starry-eyed observers as Bernard Shaw and H.G. Wells – were based on direct observation on the ground. Readers identified with the dilemma of the ladies who had been forced into sheltering the fugitive policeman who had harmed no one.

Walpole was awarded a CBE in 1918 and went on to be knighted for his services to literature in 1937. This sensitive, short-sighted, gay stretcher-bearer had become a Cold Warrior long before the Cold War was even recognized as existing.

George Hill

THE AFFABLE KILLER

George Hill

Just as Shakespeare said that some are born great, some achieve greatness and some have greatness thrust upon them, so it is with espionage. Captain George Hill was born in 1892 into espionage. His father was a merchant whose business ranged across Russia – not just across European Russia, but across Siberia, Central Asia and the Caucasus. The young George grew up travelling – by carriage, on horseback and by camel sledge – across vast swathes of the Tsar's domains. He spoke Russian with his Russian nurse, Tartar with the family handyman, Persian with the coachman and grooms, Armenian with his childhood friend, and French and German with his governesses. From an early age he was the eyes and ears of his monoglot parents.

Spies and agents provocateurs were part of Hill's experience from childhood. During the unsettled years between the 1905 uprisings and the outbreak of revolution in 1917, one of his schoolmates was found to be reporting to the police on any politically controversial conversations by his fellow pupils or their parents. On one occasion Hill witnessed the shooting of two Nihilist would-be assassins; another time, he watched the lynching of a suspected police *provocateur*. As a schoolboy he himself smuggled secret photographs out of the country in the lining of his top hat (presumably this was part of his school uniform).

Later he became involved – almost involuntarily – in ever more exciting ventures. When the daughter of some Jewish friends was implicated in Socialist Revolutionary activities at her university and faced the prospect of a lengthy exile to Siberia, Hill was asked by her family to smuggle her out of Russia via Riga. He duly arranged for her – she turned out to be a beautiful girl called Sonia – to be among the party seeing him off on a ship from Riga bound for Stettin. When his other friends left the ship, he concealed Sonia behind a cupboard in the bathroom-lavatory of his cabin; and when the Russian search party arrived, checking the ship for stowaways before departure, he left the cabin door open and retired to the lavatory. The searchers were so embarrassed at having disturbed him in a half-dressed state that they withdrew with abject apologies. Once they had set sail, the ship's captain – who would never have dared to take a political refugee as a stowaway – was convinced by Hill that Sonia was his lover, and cheerfully acquiesced in her brief presence on board. Hill was learning the arts of deceit with remarkable speed.

When the First World War began, Hill – now in his twenties, of age for military service, and living in Canada – joined up in the Canadian light infantry and served on the western front in France. He was soon seconded to the intelligence staff on account of his remarkable command of languages, and he was given formal training in the skills of espionage – how to use codes and invisible inks, how to shadow people and how to detect those who were shadowing him. He also became familiar with the latest professional techniques and devices, such as tiny cameras "the size of a half-crown", film concealed in cigarettes, and messages written on linen rather than paper so that they did not crackle if sewn into the lining of a jacket. He learnt that there were various modest but useful potential presents that an agent should always have to hand – good plain chocolate, ladies' silk stockings, expensive Parisian soaps – which "would unlock doors which neither wine nor gold could open".

His first formal assignment was to Bulgaria to monitor the aid that the Bulgarians were giving to the German and Turkish forces in the early stages of the First World War. He joined the Royal Flying Corps (RFC) and qualified as a pilot, and was mainly involved in dropping other spies into enemy territory. But it was not long before he was redeployed to the land he knew best, and where his linguistic abilities could be put to the most effective use: Russia. In July 1917 he was ordered to join the RFC mission to Petrograd (as St Petersburg had been renamed). He travelled by train through Swedish Lapland –the only route open – into northern Russia, where the chaos following the Tsar's abdication was already all too apparent.

At this stage Hill's mission was entirely in the open. He wore his RFC uniform and even gave advice to Trotsky and others about the Russian air force. In particular, he advised on how to clear up the railway grid-lock in order to get food into beleaguered Petrograd and to the front line in southern Russia, where there was still desultory fighting against the Germans. Even after the flight of Kerensky (whom he had met), he had hopes that "Russia might still be turned to the advantage of the Allies".

Even before his clandestine mission had begun, Hill's life in Russia was not without its dangers. He had spoken out strongly on several occasions against Russians with pro-German sympathies, and had been warned that he might be a target for some violent response. He was therefore not altogether surprised when he found himself followed one evening down an ill-lit street by two thugs, who then closed in to attack him. Hill brandished his walking stick at them. One of the thugs made the mistake of grabbing it, only to find that it was a sword stick ("specially designed by Messrs Wilkinson, the swordmakers of Pall Mall") and that he was left with the scabbard in his hand while Hill held the rapier-like blade of the sword. Without hesitation, Hill lunged at his attacker and ran him through. With a scream, the thug collapsed in a heap on the road, while his companion took flight. Hill calmly picked up the scabbard from the pavement and, having checked that his revolver was still safely in his pocket, continued on his way.

This incident illustrates a fundamental fact about Hill which was to resurface regularly during his time in Russia: he was quick on the draw and in no way averse to violence. On another occasion, he smashed in the head of an assailant with a brick. His revolver was seldom far from his hand, and frequently in use. Later he would express surprise and disappointment on learning that most White Russian officers were reluctant to assassinate their enemies. His readiness to engage in lethal conflict seemed all the more remarkable on account of his outward appearance. Unlike most of the fit, agile and sharp-looking operatives in this field, Hill was distinctly plump and immensely affable in manner. His friends called him "Podge", and he had great difficulty fitting his ample dimensions into disguises and uniforms, or indeed into any clothes that were not generously tailored for him. But those who viewed him as a soft touch because of his appearance were frequently to experience a rude shock. In his *Writer's Notebook*, Somerset Maugham writes about a secret agent in Russia who "though ruthless, was good-humoured, and was capable of killing a fellow-creature without a trace of ill-feeling". The pair were in Russia at the same time, and it seems all too likely that Maugham had Hill in mind.

In late 1917 Hill's relations with the Bolsheviks were still friendly, on account of the help he had given in easing the railway blockages. He took advantage of the situation to undertake a most unusual and potentially perilous venture. Early in the war, the Romanian government had thought it prudent to remove the national treasure to Moscow (a city apparently far from the German threat) as a safe haven. Not only the crown jewels, but also the country's gold reserves and a very large quantity of paper money had been transferred to the vaults of the Kremlin. Now, with Russia in revolution and a deal with the Germans in the offing, the Romanians wanted their treasure back. Hill and his colleague Colonel Joe Boyle seemed the most promising adventurers with whom to entrust this unusual mission.

Initially Hill had felt a degree of sympathy with the revolutionaries in Russia, having seen the shortcomings of the Tsar's regime. But now he was convinced that any treasure left in Bolshevik hands would be used to further causes opposed not only to Romanian interests but to British interests too. On no account, he felt, should the Bolsheviks be allowed to get their hands on such valuable assets. So, without instructions and in defiance of all caution and considerations of personal safety, Hill accepted the invitation, as did Boyle.

It took all their powers of persuasion – and all the credit they had gained through their previous co-operation with the regime – to obtain the permission of the Kremlin's military governor to remove the chests of treasure and return them to their acknowledged owners. They decided that camouflage rather than armed protection was the best way to safeguard their cargo; they would never have been able to acquire a large enough escort to defend such a lucrative haul if word got out of what they were carrying. They therefore decanted the jewels and gold from steel chests into wicker picnic baskets and transported them by sledges to a post train. This was said to take ten days to make the journey from Moscow to Romania via Odessa. Only with great difficulty did they manage to shake off a proffered but inadequate armed guard, which would only have attracted attention to their precious cargo.

While they were en route, the Soviet commissar in charge gave the sudden and unexplained order to uncouple the wagon carrying the treasure from the rest of the post train. Hill and Boyle found "a ruffianly figure" in the act of doing this. They knocked him out with a single blow to the chin and he "went down like a log" – neither Hill nor Boyle were squeamish – whereupon they reconnected the wagon. Worse problems lay ahead. They were going through a war zone – Soviet troops fought against nationalist Ukrainians – and the train regularly came under fire. Hill and Boyle took it in turns to sleep while the other kept watch. At every station they had to be on their guard against fresh attempts at uncoupling the wagon.

On one occasion they passed a blazing vodka factory. It had been set on fire and stripped of its products by drunken looters – many of whom, alarmingly, boarded the train. Various official search parties tried to probe their cargo. Hill fended them off with the claim that they had diplomatic immunity and that any such action would violate the diplomatic relations between their country and Russia. Of course, he knew full well that at this stage no diplomatic relations existed between Britain and the Bolshevik regime. When questioned about his nationality, Hill claimed to be Canadian – he had realised that "British" was not a popular label – which both baffled and mollified the commissars. A lavish distribution of "Canadian" cigarettes helped to ease the tension.

There were other, more practical problems. The train ran out of fuel and came to a halt in the middle of a snowbound forest. Hill discovered a clearing a few hundred yards away; it was stacked with sawn logs. With considerable presence of mind and force of personality, he and Boyle organized the passengers – some still drunk on vodka – into a human chain, passing logs from the stack in the clearing to the engine on the train. Many of the chain were standing above their waists in snow, but they entered into the spirit of the challenge. In a short time the timber-fuelled train was underway.

As they neared the Romanian frontier, a Bolshevik general intervened to stop the train. He was convinced – had there been a telegraph message? – that Hill was stealing something important from Russia. He informed them they were under arrest, that they would not be allowed to proceed across the frontier and that he had trained guns on their wagon. If they attempted to move they would be shelled.

The two Englishmen realised their trip had reached its crisis point. They began to plot a way forward. In the station yard there was one engine which was kept permanently with steam up, ready to perform any shunting duties required. Hill set about chatting up the engine driver and his stoker; further cigarettes were distributed. Commandeering the shunting engine seemed the answer to their problem. The Bolshevik general had allocated a detachment of troops to watch Hill and Boyle; these soldiers were similarly courted: a sing-song was arranged, and they were softened up with a samovar of tea laced with rum and brandy.

The escape plan was now ready for implementation. Hill and Boyle boarded the engine with their revolvers pointing at the driver and stoker. They delivered a mix of threats and promises: a fat bribe and asylum in Romania if they drove them across the frontier; death if they refused. The frightened driver and stoker agreed. Hill told the driver that at "the slightest sign of treachery [he] would fill him with lead"; we may surmise it was no idle threat. He then studied the driver's actions closely, so that if necessary he would be able to take over the controls.

To start with all went according to plan. In the darkness, the gun crew did not see the departing engine and wagon, and the soldiers on guard were too tired or sozzled to react. After ten miles, they stopped to lasso with a rope the overhead telegraph wires in an attempt – too late, as it turned out – to prevent news of their escape from getting through to the frontier station.

Twenty minutes later, red flashing lights warned them that a level-crossing gate had been shut across the line and was blocking their progress. Hill ordered the driver to crash through the gates, but he refused to do so on the grounds that it was too dangerous. A prod with the revolver failed to make the driver change his mind, so Hill butted him in the stomach with his knee, reducing the driver to a groaning heap on the floor of the engine. He then took over the controls himself, got up speed and crashed through the barrier himself. Shortly afterwards, the driver – terrified at the speed at which Hill was driving – recovered sufficiently to retake control.

At the frontier the Romanian border guard at first opened fire on them, but Hill – from his position crouched on the floor of the engine – managed to call out messages of friendship, which were accepted. An escort of local cavalry was provided, and the heroes were received by the Romanian foreign minister and Prime Minister in the provisional capital of Jassy. Later they were decorated for gallantry by the king and queen of that country. Hill had not acted out of any great affection for Romania, but his extraordinary expedition had successfully deprived the Bolsheviks in Russia of a fortune that would have financed their operations.

By 1918, Hill had lost all illusions about the methods and intentions of the Bolsheviks. He had witnessed and been deeply shocked by the lynching in late 1917 of General Dukhonin, who had been the commander of the Russian forces on the German front. Dukhonin had refused to step down from his command when the Bolsheviks had wanted to replace him with a junior and inexperienced officer who was prepared to negotiate an immediate ceasefire with the Germans.

He was then betrayed by his own guards, and held as a prisoner by the Bolsheviks. At the provincial railway station of Mogilev that Hill had encountered "a howling mob of armed men who kept baying like hungry wolves" for Dukhonin to be handed over to them. When this was done, the general was thrown into the air and impaled on a mass of bayonets. His body was mutilated while the crowd cheered; it had not been an edifying sight.

Other high-handed and violent actions contributed to Hill's disillusionment. The Romanian ambassador (with whom, after his recent escapade, Hill felt some kinship) was imprisoned in the grim St Peter and Paul Fortress in Petrograd, in defiance of all the rules of diplomatic immunity. Various former ministers in Kerensky's government were murdered – some while in bed in hospital. While on a visit to Odessa and the Black Sea ports, Hill was well aware that the very sailors who entertained him had only a few days before thrown their own officers into the sea with their ankles weighted down with anchor chains.

He was later to be even more horrified by the indiscriminate revenge taken after the assassination attempt on Lenin in August of 1918. He reported that the Cheka had rounded up some 500 prominent citizens of the former regime in Moscow and shot them summarily. The secret police had reacted similarly after the assassination of their own leader in Petrograd, Moisei Uritsky. Hill was far from averse to using violence himself when he felt that the circumstances justified it, but even he was shocked at the wanton cruelty and terror of the Bolsheviks.

By early 1918, Hill was living a double life: part of the time he was in uniform, in the role of a British officer attached to an erstwhile ally; the rest of the time he was in mufti, recruiting and running a network of agents – mostly, but not exclusively, still working against German interests in the Ukraine, where the Kaiser's army was resting and recuperating after its front-line activities. Hill's agents – many of whom were White Russian ex-officers – harried and raided these German camps. But by the summer of that year, the Allies had landed their – totally inadequate – intervention force at Archangel and everything changed.

Trotsky, deciding that British officers could no longer be viewed as allies or friends, ordered the arrest of Hill. Just before the arrest party arrived, Hill got news of the decision, and had to decide rapidly which of his possessions he could take with him as he went undercover. He concluded that he could not risk carrying a revolver, and abandoned the two he owned. He did however keep his sword-stick with him, though his uniform, his personal photographs, his books, and even his much-prized Romanian decorations, all had to be left behind. He left his apartment by the servants' stairs, travelling to the other end of Moscow by cab and tram, all the while covering his tracks as best he could. He then rented rooms in a flat belonging to a prostitute, who was a patriot of the old school and who did not ask any awkward questions. The great advantage of this arrangement was that, since the lady's profession was well known to her neighbours, the comings and goings of strange men at all times of day and night did not arouse any undue attention. This was ideal for Hill, who was planning to run his network of agents and couriers from there.

Hill had been anticipating the necessity to go underground for a while. He already had available a complete outfit of Russian clothes; these were second-hand, well-used, inexpensive and of the sort which might have been bought in any peasant market. He burnt his well-cut English suit, shoes and clothing. He also acquired through one of his agents a forged passport whose details tallied with his own age and ample build; this had even been tried out on a journey to Petrograd and so had collected some convincing official stamps. The name on the passport was Bergmann, which with its slightly Germanic flavour would help explain any lapses in his – near perfect – Russian. But it was not enough to change his dress and documentation: he also had to change his personal appearance. He put it about that he had suffered an attack of malaria, stayed indoors for several days and grew a beard. This turned out to be red (although his hair was dark brown), but had the compensation that – when trimmed – it made him look "utterly foreign". Nevertheless, shortly after this, he was disconcerted to be hailed by name in the Moscow street. However, his interlocutor quickly apologized for his mistake. It later transpired that he had mistaken Hill for his father, who had worn a beard during his time in Russia thirty years before. The most difficult part of his disguise was dropping his habit of walking like an English officer on parade: his friends had told him that no Russian ever walked like that, so he was forced to develop a non-military slouch.

Hill's preparations for an undercover existence had led him to establish no fewer than eight secret flats or sets of rooms – safe houses – in Moscow alone, as well as a dacha forty miles outside the city if life within became too hot for him. He was supported by a group of trusted assistants, mostly girls. Some of these were English by birth, but even among themselves they were careful always to speak Russian: if they lapsed inadvertently into English they would penalize themselves by going without sugar for twenty-four hours! Hill was also in contact with Sidney Reilly during this period, but they were sensible enough to keep fairly clear of each other.

As the First World War drew to a close, Hill devoted more and more of his time and energies to countering Bolshevik rather than German activities. He started to run a clandestine courier service between Moscow and the Allied intervention forces around Murmansk. However, the Cheka and other Bolshevik intelligence services were closing in on him. One day he found that the Cheka had put a chain around the street where he was living and were systematically checking all the houses for suspicious and undeclared residents. He was saved on this occasion as a direct result of his earlier, typically affable behaviour towards all those whom he came across. It happened like this: one day he had given an apple (all food was scarce) to the daughter of a sweet-shop owner whom he regularly passed in the street. A few days later he was disturbed to see her sobbing as she sat outside her shop, and asked her what was the trouble. It turned out that her father had been arrested on charges of illegally hoarding sugar to make his sweets, and imprisoned. She had no money either to buy food for herself or to take to her father in prison. Hill helped her out. While his street was being searched, he turned to the girl for help: "Hide me. I must not be caught." She promptly took him into the back of her shop and hid him in a large cauldron where the sweets were made, covering him in old sacking and putting the wooden lid back on the cauldron just in time.

When the Cheka agents came and searched the shop, they were so busy stealing sweets that she was able to deflect their interest from the cauldron. When they had gone, the girl smilingly released Hill. She had now repaid him for the apple, she said. He promptly recruited her to his team. "Podge" was someone who liked to help everyone and whom everyone liked to help.

All the while the Red Terror was getting worse. Hill considered that its horrors surpassed those of the Spanish Inquisition. Anyone with a grudge against a neighbour only had to whisper a few words to the Cheka to ensure their victim's arrest. Twelve of Hill's couriers were executed during this period, and he reckoned that some could have saved themselves if they had been prepared to give him away. That the German intelligence services were now working hand-in-glove with the Bolsheviks, made his situation still more dangerous, on account of his anti-German activities during the last months of the war.

One night the block of houses where he was staying was surrounded by the Cheka. One of his couriers was lodging with him in the house, without any legitimate papers and with a pile of code books and other compromising material in his possession. It seemed their number was up at last. One of the girls who assisted Hill said to him that, whatever was to become of them, she was glad to have been part of the operation: "We have done good, and no matter what happens now it has been well worth it." Hill was deeply moved by her commitment and courage, which was further evidence of his gift for inspiring affection and devotion in others. In the event, the Cheka operation turned out to be part of a more general manhunt, in which others were arrested and shot, but Hill and his team once again talked and bluffed their way out of trouble.

In his memoirs, Hill is coyly reserved about the specific nature of much of his anti-Bolshevik activity at this time. Understandably he was more prepared to give the details of anti-German operations, which were carried out at a time when we were formally at war with

Germany.[12] However, we do know that he was a key connection between the various abortive attempts to intervene in different parts of Russia against the Bolshevik regime in its early days; and his network of couriers – which suffered such heavy casualties – provided a vital link between the various fronts opposing Trotsky and his embryonic Red Army.

At first Robert Bruce Lockhart was reluctant to include Hill in the evacuation plans for the British mission in Moscow, having been advised by his companions that Hill – as an undercover agent – might compromise the diplomatic case for allowing such an evacuation. In the end Hill was included in the party who were permitted to leave by train through Finland. Hill became an unqualified admirer of Lockhart after this episode: he describes in his book the dignity with which Lockhart played his part as head of the British mission, despite the fact that he had just emerged from his dire imprisonment in the Kremlin. "He was always ready to assume responsibility, to protect and forward his countrymen's rights and interests", Hill records.

Far from being relieved of his espionage duties on arrival in England, Hill was promptly instructed to return to Russia for a further assignment. This time there was no diplomatic train: he had to make his own way back, wading and swimming through the freezing river which formed the frontier between Finland and Russia. In three weeks he had accomplished this additional (and mysteriously undefined) mission, and he finally returned to England on Armistice Day 1918. It was only then that he met "C", the chief of MI6, and was formally recruited into the British secret service which he had already served so well.

The chief was complimentary about Hill's work – and asked him to go back to Russia with Sidney Reilly to report back, for the benefit of the British delegates to the Paris Peace Conference, on political developments along Black Sea coast and in southern Russia.

---

12 Hill is more communicative about his anti-Bolshevik activities after he left Russia than he is about those activities during his time there.

The easygoing Hill was overwhelmed by the impetuous Reilly, who insisted that they make a dash via Paris to Marseilles to catch an RN cruiser to Athens, then a Greek destroyer to the Black Sea – all the while disguised as two English commercial travellers. At one stage on the journey, the pair found themselves sharing a cabin with Paderewski (the concert pianist who was about to become Prime Minister of his native Poland). They spent most of the night discussing the menace of Bolshevism, not only to Poland but to the whole of Europe. Increasingly, Hill was becoming not just an active agent operating against the Bolsheviks, but a thoughtful opponent of their philosophy and ideas.

On occasion, however, he reverted to his old, more controversial activities. In Odessa a group of Cossacks approached him with a proposal to blow up a treacherous White Russian colonel who was selling information to the Bolsheviks. Hill pointed out the dangers to passing civilians of using high explosive in a public area, but did not appear in the least perturbed – or surprised – to hear shortly afterwards that the Cossacks had found another, more effective way of assassinating their target. Violence was still part of the foreground as well as the background to his life.

In the years immediately following the First World War, Hill spent much time travelling around eastern Europe and southern Russia, always with a brief from MI6, and frequently involved with the various interventionist activities designed to undermine the new Bolshevik regime. Arguably, however, the most severe damage he ever inflicted on the Bolsheviks was during his time at the Paris Peace Conference in 1919. He had already made friends with Lord Northcliffe (the owner of *The Times*) and had an even closer friendship with Wickham Steed (the foreign editor of *The Times*). He persuaded these contacts to argue in the columns of that newspaper against any recognition of the newly set-up Soviet Union. While at Versailles, he also had long talks with Harold Nicolson (then a young diplomat who was much engaged in the negotiations). He explained to all these influential interlocutors his own experiences of the Red Terror in revolutionary Russia, and pointed out the "madness" of granting formal recognition to a regime that was intent on spreading revolution throughout Europe and was "rabidly hostile to all that western civilization stood for". He argued forcefully that not only Poland, Czechoslovakia and the Baltic Republics, but also the defeated and vulnerable Germany, were at risk of being swallowed up by a brutal and sinister force. His protestations met with ready listeners and had a considerable – possibly decisive – influence.

If Lenin and Trotsky had known what harm the affable but ruthless "Podge" would do to their cause, they might have made even more determined efforts than they did to rid themselves of this tiresome Englishman.

Percy Etherton

KEEPING THE BOLSHEVIKS OUT OF SINKIANG

Percy Etherton

Unlike Bruce Lockhart in Moscow, Ranald MacDonell in the Caucasus and Frederick Bailey in Central Asia, who had all tried to establish a useful working relationship with the Bolsheviks before finally turning to confrontation, Major Percy Etherton had no doubts from the start that the Bolsheviks were an enemy who must be confronted. The scene for his activity was Kashgar, the capital of the western Chinese province of Sinkiang, where he was the British Consul-General from 1918 until 1922.

Before he was sent to Kashgar, originally in an unofficial capacity, Etherton had reached the rank of major in the Indian army, but unlike most of his fellow officers he had not had the traditional education at Wellington and Sandhurst; his background was more exotic. He had chosen to go to Australia and try his luck as a gold prospector. Having joined the army with this unconventional background, he had experienced active service as a scout in the Boer War in South Africa, and had moved on to take part in the continual skirmishing on the north-west frontiers of India. Later he had travelled extensively across the Pamirs and other parts of the Himalayan "roof of the world". So by the time he arrived in a consular capacity in Kashgar, he was already a proven adventurer.

Normally the duties of a Consul-General would be mainly focused on protecting the commercial interests of the British community –

in the case of Kashgar, a commercial community that was mostly comprised of Indians under the protection of the British Raj. But Etherton, with his Indian army background and first-hand awareness of the long-standing Russian ambitions in Central Asia, was more interested in the political aspects of the job. He realized that his new Russian neighbours – whom he described as "Bolsheviks and revolutionary scum" – were even more of a threat to British interests in Kashgar than were the traditional Tsarist Russians. They were trying to infiltrate the province, indoctrinate its leaders with their subversive Bolshevik ideas and cut off trade with British India. There were other unsavoury elements who often overlapped with the revolutionaries – gun runners and opium smugglers.

This was a tense situation which required the Consul-General to meet the threats with rather more than a staff of commercial consuls and vice-consuls: Etherton set about recruiting his own network of secret agents. So effective was this network, that he reckoned that no move of any importance could be made by subversive elements in Sinkiang without his quickly becoming aware of it. His agents often operated at some risk to their own safety, and the Consul-General himself was likely to be a target for personal attack; for this reason, he was protected by an escort of some thirty Indian cavalrymen, under command of a British officer, who possibly added more to his prestige than to his security.

With the fall of the Tsar in 1917, there was initially a feeling in Kashgar that pressure from Russia had been lifted; some even regarded the Bolsheviks as the potential champions of liberty. But they were soon disillusioned. Brutal behaviour in those parts of Russian Turkestan under the domination of the Bolsheviks was a warning to Kashgar of what the Chinese might expect if Russian influence were to spread further east. By the summer of 1918, Lenin was beginning to recognize that there would be no instant world revolution, and to concentrate his efforts on spreading a generalized class warfare and terminating British rule in India by Muslim revolt from within.

Etherton was quick to react. He secured a prohibition on the export of cotton to prevent the Russians increasing their munitions manufacture; Chinese cotton was a significant ingredient in the making of explosives. He also negotiated a new set of passport regulations which put a brake on the influx of suspected Russian communists into Kashgaria. All persons crossing the frontier were in future to be searched, and suspicious characters turned back. Getting such regulations enforced was no easy task with "so lethargic a nation and such a vast land frontier". He also persuaded the authorities to make it compulsory for everyone to register any firearms and ammunition in their possession; arrests followed and, even if not all those arrested were prosecuted in the end, "undesirables" were prevented from fermenting violent disorder. In effect, Etherton was managing to convince the rulers of Kashgar that China and British India shared a common interest in frustrating the spread of Bolshevism.

Unusually for a Consul-General, Etherton also launched a news-sheet providing accurate information about developments in the First World War, which was at last beginning to reach its final stages and indicate an eventual Allied victory in the West. The material for the news-sheet was mostly received at the consulate via the newly installed radio station, and was widely disseminated in various local languages. One of the many false rumours which his news-sheet discounted was that the Afghans were successfully infiltrating British India and had already occupied Peshawar; another was that the British had designs on Tibet (a recurring theme after Younghusband's military expedition from India in 1904, dispatched by Lord Curzon).

When he travelled around the country, Etherton became ever more aware of the ramifications of the opium-smuggling business. It was always difficult to persuade the authorities to stop this, in part because – in a country where corruption was rife – so many people were taking a slice of the profits. Each pony-load of the drugs was worth some £165 – a substantial sum at the time. One reason he took unusually vigorous action against this was that he realised that opium was a regular source of income for the neighbouring Bolsheviks. If smuggled out of Turkestan, it could be paid for in silver or other hard currencies. As always, Etherton gave his political agenda priority.

Although (unlike Bailey) Etherton was never in Tashkent himself, he was well aware that it was the centre of Bolshevik activity in Turkestan. He considered that the Bolsheviks had done more active Russification in Turkestan than the Tsarists had ever achieved: they viewed the region as an essential granary for the rest of Russia and had no intention of allowing the predominantly Muslim population to have any real say in the running of the region. It was also a natural headquarters for generating subversive propaganda against the British in India; the Bolsheviks had even imported Russians from other parts – as far away as Siberia – to add to the number of activists promoting their cause, as well as large numbers of prisoners of war – mostly Austrians and Czechs – some of whom desecrated the mosques and Muslim shrines. A great many of the local population were massacred and more still (some 900,000 it was calculated) allowed to starve. Bolshevik bullying took many odious forms, including raids on private houses. The inhabitants would be made to hand over their money, their furniture and other possessions; if they resisted, they were rounded up outside and one or two people singled out and taken off out of sight; a few rifle shots would then be heard and the frightened people would assume that the unfortunate few selected had been shot; the rest would quickly offer up their savings and possessions to avoid a similar fate. Anarchy, chaos and brutality were the hallmarks of the regime. Turkestan had not been so devastated since the Mongol conquests of Genghis Khan and Tamerlane.

But if the Bolsheviks thought that such drastic measures would open the way to establishing an equal domination of neighbouring Kashgaria, they had not reckoned with an adversary of Etherton's calibre. He encouraged local Islamic leaders to publicly state that the doctrines of Bolshevism were totally opposed to the teaching of Islam. So incensed were the communists by Etherton's role in such denunciations, that they officially declared him an obstacle to their dream of universal freedom; they even invented an improbable story that the British had desecrated the holy places at Medina by "casting the Koran before swine". The Bolsheviks were trying to cultivate Islamic allies to join with them in a jihad against the British. As part of that campaign, they declared it was essential "to put to death the bloodthirsty British Consul in Kashgar". Etherton had no illusions about the possibility of being able to do business with the Bolsheviks. Indeed, in his subsequent account of all these events, he wistfully remarks that if "the British Labour party [were not] so lamentably ignorant of what goes on in Russia" they might not have been so starry-eyed about the regime at that date.

The Chinese authorities, perhaps unsurprisingly, offered little support to Etherton, but he was not entirely without allies in Kashgar. Aided by the superannuated Tsarist Russian Consul-General, who had maintained his office and continued to fly the Tsarist flag, he arranged a night raid on the house of some Indian revolutionary activists. His agents drew a cordon around the house, but the bird had flown before they got there. It was – to say the least – a cavalier way for a consul to behave in someone else's country. But Etherton was not squeamish about such things.

Nor was he bothered by considerations of social equality. Strenuously as he had opposed the efforts of the Russians before the revolution to influence events in Kashgar, he felt that at least their representatives were gentlemen who knew how to behave and what they were talking about. After the revolution, his hostility to the Russians who were trying to infiltrate Kashgar was enhanced by his scorn for their ill-educated ignorance of everything around them: the Bolshevik governor of Turkestan was a former non-commissioned officer in the Russian army who had "amassed a degree of affluence strangely out of harmony with communist ideals"; the commissar for foreign affairs was a clerk who had been given his new job for no better reason than he knew how to read a map; another commissar had been a railway porter, and others had been cab-drivers or peasants. Doubtless, to his diplomatic superiors in 1920, such derogatory remarks about the social and professional background of his opponents were acceptable; they would hardly be so now.

When the Bolsheviks eventually succeeded in taking over Bokhara in 1920 (which was after the exploits of Colonel Bailey there), it was to Etherton in Kashgar that the emir first turned for help. He even

N
NW
NE
W
E
SW
SE
S
RUSSIA
Astrakhan
Caspian Sea
TURKESTAN
River Oxus
Khiva
Bokhara
Samarka
Ashkabad
Elburz Range
Astrabad
Mashad
Tehran
Herat
PERSIA
AFGHANISTAN
Kandahar
Persian Gulf
BALUCHISTAN
Arabian Sea

Central Asia
CHINA
Alma Ata
TIEN SHAN MOUNTAINS
SINKIANG
Kashgar
Yarkand
KASHMIR
Peshawar
PUNJAB
TIBET
Lahore
Simla
River Indus
INDIA
0 100 200 300 400 miles

suggested that the emirate of Bokhara might be incorporated into the British empire. For all his anti-Bolshevik ambitions, this was not a commitment that Etherton felt able to recommend to the Viceroy; but he did try to assist the emir to escape to Kashgar. (In the event, the emir went to Afghanistan.)

One specific achievement of Etherton in Kashgar related to his campaign against those he regarded as Indian revolutionaries. Mahendra Pratab was a man wanted by the Indian government. Now he was at large in Central Asia stirring up trouble for the British – and had even given himself the title of Raja, to which he was in no way entitled (as Etherton was quick to point out). He had demonstrated his hostility during the war by trying to curry favour in Berlin, and later – after the revolution – in Moscow. With an escort of some fifty armed and disgruntled Afghans, Pratab attempted to gain access to Kashgar, where he planned to agitate against British India. He had little difficulty in blustering and threatening his way through the ineffective Kashgarian frontier security forces. Once inside Kashgaria, Pratab had the effrontery to call on a British consular agent, who was so disconcerted by his unexpected appearance that he failed to detain or arrest him – much to the Consul-General's annoyance. Nevertheless, Etherton did manage to get Pratab and his escort expelled from the country with reasonable promptness; an Indian troublemaker and a friend of the Bolsheviks was not likely to evade his attentions for long.

Percy Etherton did not have the personal adventures which enlivened the careers of such British agents as Ranald MacDonell or Frederick Bailey. He did not have to live for months in disguise, nor was he smuggled across frontiers and dogged by sinister communist minders. But his actions did entail great risk to his personal safety. Many times he received death threats from gangs and organizations who had shown themselves more than capable of carrying out such threats. His was not, therefore, an altogether sheltered life.

Bailey, though he had undeniably lived the more dangerously of the two, often wondered whether he had achieved any of his objectives. He had failed to exert meaningful influence over the Bolsheviks in

Tashkent, and he had often been in the dark about what was happening both in Turkestan and further afield. Etherton, on the other hand, had persuaded the authorities in Kashgar to comply with his requests on a whole range of issues: they had stoutly resisted Bolshevik incursions and they had cooperated in suppressing the subversive activities aimed at British India. It was no wonder that for several years after he left, Kashgar remained a bastion of anti-Bolshevik sentiment and endeavour. And no wonder that Etherton remained on the Bolshevik hit list.

NOT-SO-SILENT WITNESSES

The English-Speaking Governesses

Before the revolution, the Russian aristocracy spoke French among their family and friends, and Russian to their servants and estate staff. Some, particularly around the court where the German-born Tsarina's influence was great, also spoke German. Increasingly, though, English was thought to be the language of the future. More and more of the best families sought to employ an "English governess"[13] to educate their children, and having one in the household became a status symbol.

English governesses were considered less flirtatious than their French counterparts – Tolstoy's *Anna Karenina* famously opens with Oblonsky's wife discovering that their former French governess was her husband's mistress – and more wholesome and outdoorsy than their German counterparts. Most importantly, the English girls from respectable family backgrounds (many were clergymen's daughters) who came out to Russia were viewed as totally reliable. They could be counted upon in bad times as well as good to act loyally and sensibly.

For a middle-class British girl to take up an appointment in far-

---

13 "English" really meant "English-speaking", many of the best governesses being either Scottish or Irish.

away Russia in the early 20th century was a considerable adventure. Indeed, it seemed to some that an English girl going as a governess to Russia was renouncing her future prospects as finally as if entering a nunnery. But most saw it as an opportunity rather than a retreat. Very few had ever been abroad, some had never been outside their own counties. They had heard, however, good things from a few pioneers in the field.

To start with, the pay better than in England. The market for governesses in England was overcrowded: a single advertisement for a place in the personal column of *The Times* would receive scores of applications. Equally, if not more importantly, the status of a governess in an upper-class Russian family was far higher than in a middle-class British family. She not only had her meals at the table with the family, but a footman would stand behind, ministering to her every need. She was treated as a member of the family, rather than as a servant. She would have her own room, and her laundry done for her.

In summers, the governess would accompany the family to their country estate. In a life played out to the sleepy rhythms of a Chekhov play, long sunny days would be spent on broad verandahs overlooking meadows and forests, punctuated by expeditions to distant neighbours by horse and pony-trap. In winter, the family would return to their mansions in Moscow or St Petersburg. Here there would be additional excitements: governesses were often invited to balls and receptions in the palaces of family friends. They could hope, if not expect, to be invited to dance by dashing young officers, even receive proposals of marriage - which were, in a number of cases, accepted. Needless to say, the more tales of ordinary English, Irish or Scottish girls marrying Russian princes percolated back to the British Isles, the more girls were keen to follow the trail.

As Harvey Pitcher explains in his delightful book entitled *When Miss Emmie was in Russia* (first published in 1977), the adventures for these young women started before they reached Russia. Most travelled by sea to St Petersburg and, if necessary, by rail on to Moscow[14], and the passage could be rough. Others went the whole way by rail from Charing Cross at a cost of £15 18s 6d, taking fifty-one hours in 1911. The majority travelled alone, in itself a novel experience for girls who might have never left home before. Once across the frontier into Russia, the forest-lined journey would have been punctuated with endless visits to the samovar to collect cups of tea, and games of chess with fellow passengers.

The earliest and grandest of the English-speaking governesses to record her experiences was Miss Margaretta Eager (at the time she did not disclose her first name, writing as Miss M. Eager), an Irish girl who went to St Petersburg in 1899 to "take charge of the little Grand Duchesses of Russia". She was to stay for nearly six years, leaving soon after the birth of the ill-fated Tsarevitch and before the beginning of the 1905 uprisings.

Her impressions vividly illuminate the precarious state of Russia during the last years of the Tsar. She recorded peasants kneeling in the road as the carriage bearing the young grand duchesses passed by and women yoked to ploughs alongside farm animals. Her memoirs mentioned the universal censorship of mail, the brutality of the Cossacks charging and lashing out with their knouts at student demonstrators. They also described assassination attempts by anarchists against the Tsar and his family, endemic hatred of the Jews and handsome young officers regularly dying or acquiring life-changing injuries from duelling.

From her ringside seat, Miss M. Eager perceived more clearly than most the fatal flaws of the pre-revolutionary social scene. Despite these unsettling experiences, she was – reading between the lines of her memoirs – an excellent, sensible, trusted and good-natured help to the imperial family. But in spite of her best efforts, the behaviour

---

14 This was still the normal method of travel to Moscow for British diplomats – like the author – in the 1950s. It was hoped that travelling on a Russian ship (renamed the *Baltica*, but still showing beneath the paint its former name of the fallen-from-grace foreign minister, *Molotov*) would provide an opportunity to practice one's Russian language skills before arriving *en poste*.

of her regal young charges occasionally left something to be desired. On one occasion the five-year-old grand duchess Tatiana was asked by the Empress to shake hands with the visiting Prince of Siam, and (to Miss Eager's horror) replied, "That's not a gentleman, Mama, that's only a monkey."

During my years in Moscow I became personally acquainted with a Scottish governess whom I will call Heather. Heather, who had taught her young charges to speak English with a distinctly Scots brogue, was an impartial observer of both the pre-revolutionary scene and the excesses of the revolution. In her letters home at the time, as well as in later conversations, she reported on both to an audience who had been blissfully unaware of the failings of the former regime and the brutalities and iniquities of the later one. In their quiet way, such English governesses blew the whistle on the excesses of the revolution as accurately – if less influentially – as the captains and the consuls who are the subject of other chapters.

Heather was in Russia between 1913 and 1918, when in her late teens and early twenties. In the 1950s, post-Stalin era, she returned in her early sixties, which was when we became acquainted. Heather had so many happy memories of the pre-revolutionary period, and so many exciting stories of the immediate revolutionary times, that she wanted to revisit the scenes of her experiences while still active enough to do so. She loved to talk about her adventures, and I – a newcomer to Russia – relished her first-hand accounts of an era so rich in literary associations and yet so distant in terms of the reality of everyday life. She told me not only about her own experiences, but those of her fellow English-speaking governesses. Some of these were more nannies than governesses; others were "companions" to Russian ladies of good family, many of whom were kept on as retainers after their charges had grown up, married and moved away.

Some governesses were employed by affluent Moscow merchants, but several worked for grand aristocrats in St Petersburg. Doughty, hard-working Scots, Irish and English girls were often disturbed by the idleness and ostentatious lifestyles of their employers, many of whom had never even dressed themselves. Even when some of these grandees volunteered for work as nurses in field hospitals during World War One, they were attended by maids who got them into their uniforms and ministered to their every requirement. Such high-ranking families seemed unaware of the problems of those they employed in their town house, let alone those of the peasants who toiled on their rural estates. One governess was horrified to observe her mistress tossing sweets and biscuits out of her carriage window to the peasant families who were begging for bread –much like Marie Antoinette on the eve of the French Revolution.

On another, perhaps prophetic occasion, a governess was passing through the potato fields in a comfortable pony-trap with her well-dressed aristocratic family, when a drunk peasant attempted to overturn their trap. Violence and resentment were bubbling below the surface, it seemed. And it was hardly surprising. Baffled by the number of pig sheds she saw on the family's country estate, a further new arrival was disconcerted to discover that they were not pig sheds but the cabins in which the farm workers and their families lived all year round.

Heather's family had a dacha and a modest estate some hundred miles north of Moscow on the banks of the Volga River. She recalled coming down to dinner one evening wearing a modest, but much-prized necklace made of malachite. The wife of one of the guests commented to her, "What a pretty little necklace, my dear!" Heather had replied proudly, "Yes, and it's real malachite." Which earned the response: "I know that, my dear, we have a staircase made of it in St Petersburg."

Edith Kerby had not come to Russia to work as a governess, but been living there at the time of the 1905 revolution due to her father's business. In January 1917 she left for Shanghai and, although she heard from her mother, who had remained in Petrograd, that life was not easy and there was a shortage of flour, she had no idea of the violence and upheaval that had taken place since she left. Pleased by the reports that reached her of a more "liberal" regime and society emerging in Russia, she decided in May of the same year to return overland by the Trans-Siberian express.. At the Chinese-Russian frontier, she had a foretaste of how much things had changed when she asked where she could find the First Class coach. "There is no first class now," she was abruptly told. "Get in where you can."

Edith spent the next two weeks on a bunk in an overcrowded compartment, clutching a bag of flour she had bought for her mother, and talking to the soldiers – all of them deserters – who were quarrelling and scuffling among themselves for places, some even travelling on the roof. She heard for the first time of the dark face of the revolution. Soon she would experience it at first hand.

When Edith left the station at Petrograd, the surly cab driver declined to help her with her heavy bag of flour; shortly afterwards, a man informed her of his intention to steal half of it, threatening to shoot her with his revolver if she resisted. This was not the safe, well-mannered country she had left. She stayed on nonetheless, working for Paul Dukes and Hugh Walpole (both the subjects of other chapters) at the Anglo-Russian Commission in Petrograd, where she compiled summaries of the news from the local press.

However, before the Bolshevik October revolution broke out, the British ambassador, Sir George Buchanan decided it was too dangerous for her to remain, and arranged her transfer to the Foreign Office in London. Her tales of the chaos and violence were almost the first private notice the Foreign Office had received from this newly-troubled Russia.

Governesses were not politically active, but they could not help observing and often describing – in letters and conversations –the highly political scenes they witnessed. One had stumbled with her charges into a crowd in St Petersburg in 1905, only to find that she and the children were on the fringe of the march to the Winter Palace. This would, in a few hours, result in the 'Bloody Sunday' shootings that triggered riots across the country. She hastily steered her charges away from the crowd, which was just as well, as many innocent bystanders, including children, would be among those injured.

Another had encountered the sinister Rasputin and found him smelly and "rather greasy" – just the sort of person she wanted to keep the children well away from. Another governess had been sufficiently intrigued to join the crowd at a public meeting and had heard Lenin speak. To do so without risking drawing hostile attention to herself, she had borrowed the dress of one of the housemaids. She subsequently commented that Lenin "had a way of rubbing in his message" – which was either a compliment or a considerable understatement. One of her colleagues, meanwhile, fell under the charm of the dashing Prince Youssoupoff, who was later to murder Rasputin.

When Heather went to a country estate north of Moscow with her employers, she found them keen to enjoy the country and sporting activities of other landowners. She would take the children on long walks through the forests bordering the Volga, hunting for mushrooms while their parents went duck-shooting at dawn and twilight on the river. In those days, there were still bears in the forests, and the ghillies who took her employers out shooting or fishing would often tell Heather of their adventures. The brown bears, which she always feared encountering when she was out with the children or on her own, were considered by one and all as a menace. They enjoyed no protection, and the ghillies were encouraged to hunt them down and kill them. If they did so, they were allowed to keep and sell the valuable skins – the largest source of income any of them ever experienced. But the ghillies could not afford guns, so they hunted the bears with long spears. This was highly dangerous, as they had to approach the bears so closely that sometimes the latter would strike out at them with fatal results. The risk to life and limb, for the sake of the bear skin, was all too real. Heather was shocked that the poverty of the ghillies should make it impossible for them afford a gun even when hunting was their business, and that they should be so hard-up that such life-threatening risks seemed worthwhile.

In Moscow, she was equally shocked that so many people, including those in employment, were unable to afford a warm overcoat for the long winter months. She herself had viewed her fur-lined winter coat as her biggest investment, and when she had read Gogol's short story *The Overcoat* (sometimes called in translation *The Cloak*) she had realized what a significant part such a garment could play in people's lives in Russia, both for its comfort and for its prestige. As Russia entered the First World War, she became aware that things could not go on as they were. When the hospitals began filling up with wounded soldiers, and stories filtered back from the Front about how ill-equipped and badly led the army was, Heather and her Russian family became increasingly worried about the fate of their country and their class.

When the first stage of the revolution occurred in early 1917 and Kerensky's government took over from the Tsar, most of the English-speaking governesses saw no immediate reason to return to Britain. They had rejected the idea of doing so at the outbreak of war in 1914, partly because the voyage home, via a Baltic Sea infested with German U-boats and mines, was far from safe. It was even less safe in early 1917, and Russian families had become ever more dependent on their governesses.

When Lenin returned and the Bolsheviks took over in October 1917, however, things looked very different. If anyone looking well-dressed was seen collecting firewood or even carrying their own luggage in the streets – something they would never have done before – they would be mocked as "bourgeois horses". More alarmingly, fatal street fighting broke out in Moscow between the different factions, often for the most spurious of reasons. Governess Helen Clarke saw a man shot in cold blood because he had opened a door on a train to get some fresh air when the Red Guards had ordered him not to.

Many families decided Moscow was too dangerous for them to stay on. "Bourgeois" properties were being taken over and packed with the families of workers. In the meantime, assets and bank accounts were being seized or frozen and upper-class families were being forced into manual work to survive. Heather's family, like many others, evacuated to Yalta in the Crimea, where many of their friends had gone and where the horrors of the revolution were not yet in full swing.

When eventually the Bolsheviks occupied the Crimea, the family who employed Emma Dashwood as a governess had their house searched by a hostile mob. Often, in such cases, another member of the family would have already hidden weapons without telling anyone else where they were. In a search, revolvers were likely to turn up stuffed down the sides of sofas, daggers in sock drawers, boxes of ammunition above the tanks in water closets, and – in one particularly foolish case – a package of gunpowder on top of a porcelain-tiled corner stove. The only really safe hiding place was the pond or lake in the grounds of the country house.

Emma herself had managed to stop Bolshevik search parties from entering her room only by producing her British passport and insisting that this gave her immunity from intrusion. Her fear was that if they entered her room they would find her Bible – an object that evoked reprisals as surely as weapons or undeclared jewellery.

With the arrival of the western intervention forces, however, British citizenship – the protection of the "Onion Jack" as it was known – was not to remain an asset for long. One girl was advised to take out Russian nationality, to give her more anonymity, but promptly rejected the idea as "too silly". After the October revolution, any foreigner was liable to be considered as a potential spy: many were, of course, as other chapters reveal, but not the English-speaking governesses.

Like several of her compatriots, Heather was asked to carry some of the family jewellery concealed in the sewn-up hems of her clothing for the journey south. It was considered that – as a foreigner – she was less likely to be searched than members of the family. Nonetheless it was a request that, if accepted, put her in some danger. Her foreign passport would not have protected her had she been discovered secreting treasures the Bolsheviks considered fair loot.

Another request was to follow: could she find room for some silver candlesticks among the clothes in her suitcase? She agreed to do both these things, but insisted that the children's clothing and luggage were kept free of any compromising items. In complying with the suggestion, she went far beyond the call of duty for any governess, and earned her place as just as much of an adventurer as anyone else in this book, putting her freedom at risk for the sake, not of her country but of her adopted Russian family.

The journey south passed uneventfully and Heather felt more

comfortable in Yalta than in Moscow. Her Russian family had a dacha there, which they used as a summer holiday house, and Heather had been there with them before. Pre-war life in Yalta had been socially active and, from the viewpoint of a Scottish girl unsure of the niceties of Russian etiquette, quite demanding. The Tsar had a summer palace at Livadia, a few miles outside Yalta, and many of the smart set from St Petersburg congregated there in summer to enjoy the climate and the proximity to the imperial family. Heather learnt how to preside over the samovar and dispense tea as a hostess should. She learnt how to address her elders and betters, with the politeness expected but without the subservience appropriate from domestic staff. And she found herself wearing her smartest clothes and her malachite necklace most evenings, while the children enjoyed the warmer weather and the seaside life.

Heather and her Russian family did not stay long in Yalta, though. The Crimea was in danger of being overrun by the Red Army before the Allied intervention forces could arrive to save the White Russians. It was felt that a return to Moscow was necessary, and then another move further north to Archangel where the western intervention forces were expected to make their landing. Heather's family, like many other upper-class and bourgeois families, were convinced that once the Allies (British, French and American troops) arrived, all would be well; the Bolshevik army would be driven back from the cities and countryside and Russia restored to its pre-revolutionary, if not Tsarist, character.

Archangel, when they got there, was little more secure than Yalta and much less fun. During 1918, some intervention forces did arrive; there were moments of elation among the White Russian community; there were also moments of despair and apprehension that the winter sea ice would cut Archangel off before the Bolsheviks were overthrown. Some people brought shotguns out of hiding, in the expectation of using them in support of the interventionist army. Others hid their arms fearing they would be shot if they were found with them when the Red Army invaded. Heather played her part in the hiding of these weapons, because her family were afraid of asking their Russian servants to do so.

While all this was going on in Archangel, stories reached them of even worse things happening in Moscow and Petrograd. Gangs of hooligans – claiming to be "representatives of the people" – were looting and raping; property was being seized, houses ransacked for objects of value. The people faced food shortages of starvation proportions; they had no fuel (even in this heavily forested land) to stave off the oncoming winter. There had been breakdown of all public services, including transport and post; hospitals were deprived of power and nurses and people were being arrested or simply disappearing off the streets without explanation. The "dictatorship of the proletariat" was becoming revealed for what it was: a reign of terror. It would soon spread to Archangel and all other centres of population in Russia.

Heather herself, in her conversations with me some forty years later, was disconcertingly vague about the specifics of her final months in Russia in 1918. Possibly she still felt some guilt about her own escape. The youngest of the children entrusted to her charge, now not only for tuition but also for comfort and protection, had contracted some unspecified disease and, just when Heather thought she had nursed him back to health, he died. Although she felt the loss almost as keenly as the boy's parents, this did relieve her of a large part of her responsibilities. The older children (I believe there were two) were nearly self-sufficient by this stage, and there were still ships leaving Murmansk for England, Scotland and Finland. Some ships' captains could be persuaded to take on board British nationals who needed evacuation. Heather's Russian family, she maintained, did not try to persuade her to stay on, and the few letters that got through to her from home desperately urged her to jump on any ship heading out of revolutionary Russia. Her circumstances were not unlike those described so vividly by Eugenie Fraser (herself half-Scottish and half-Russian) in her moving book *The House by the Dvina* (1984).

In the event, more governesses – like Emma Dashwood and Helen Clarke – eventually escaped in 1919 from the southern Crimean ports than from the northern ports, as did a number of the Tsar's and other noblemen's families. In all cases, there had been a succession of rumours, counter-rumours and disappointments concerning the arrival of British warships. Some did not appear; some could take no passengers (it is hard to understand why); some arrived at different times and different ports – Yalta, Sevastopol or Theodosia – to those expected. Even the boldest and most tenacious of the governesses were relieved when eventually they stepped on board a Royal Naval vessel and headed away from the now troubled country.

Many such English-speaking girls – including my friend Heather – had stayed on caring for their charges far beyond the call of duty. They had seen for themselves the full cycle of revolution far more closely, or at least much more from the viewpoint of a Russian family, than the captains and the consuls, the spies and the itinerant writers had been able to. And in the months and years they had spent in Russia before the revolution, few had been indifferent to the need – the necessity, even – for change. They'd had no illusions about the inequalities of the Tsarist regime. They had seen for themselves the shoeless peasants on the country estates and the extravagant lifestyles of the booted-and-spurred cavalry officers surrounding the Tsar's court at St Petersburg. They had travelled themselves in comfortable carriages while their hosts tossed kopecks out of the windows to placate hungry children who needed food, not patronage. And they had seen their landowner hosts evicting struggling tenant farmers from their lands. Even the least observant of them had sensed they were living through the twilight of a fading era.

Later they had seen in reality the alternative: the horrors of the so-called "dictatorship of the proletariat". They had felt the chill blast of the people's revolution sweeping through homes and schools, through streets and empty markets. They had been living in bourgeois households when the "accommodation committees" and the less-official freelance looters had stripped the houses of their furniture and everything removable. They had known as friends people who, for no reason, had been whisked away to incarceration or to firing squads. They had felt – not as observers but as participants – the atmosphere of fear, chaos and confusion that characterized the *Dr Zhivago* years.

And they had not kept their impressions to themselves. While the consuls had been reporting to governments, and while the spies had been reporting to influential secret circles, and while the erudite travellers had been reporting to literate and sophisticated readers, they – the governesses – had been reporting to a less definable but equally important audience: their own families, their own friends, and a wide circle of unsophisticated but impressionable people. Peter Fleming's travel books might have reached a wide and influential readership. Stephen Graham's after-dinner stories might have been heard by many well-placed ears, just as Sidney Reilly's confidential reports might be have been pondered over by many shrewd observers. But the governesses' first-hand accounts had a ring of natural truth hard to refute, and a simple, undeniable message. Bolshevism was bad news for those who wanted to lead normal, dignified lives.

Somerset Maugham

A SPY TOO FAMOUS

Somerset Maugham

Somerset Maugham was, you might assume, far from your average choice of secret agent. He had published his bestselling novel *Liza of Lambeth* as early as 1897, and eight other novels before the outbreak of the First World War. His popular play *Lady Frederick* had first appeared on stage in 1911, meanwhile, and had, along with some nine other of his plays, been a West End success prior to the outbreak of hostilities. When the secret intelligence service (later to be known as MI6) sent him to Russia, in 1917, there seem to have been few qualms about sending a minor celebrity off to do dangerous, undercover work. Maugham was given a new name – Somerville – and the cover role of a simple, undistinguished journalist, following post-revolutionary developments for a London paper.

He had been recruited, much to his own surprise by Sir William Wiseman, MI6 station chief in the United States, where Maugham was living at the time having just married his wife, Syrie in New Jersey. The purpose of the mission, Wiseman explained, was two-fold. First, Maugham was to encourage those elements in Russia who wanted to continue the fight against the Kaiser's Germany. Since the Bolsheviks wanted a truce – 'Peace' was a basic plan of their platform, along with 'Land' and 'Bread' – this effectively meant supporting everyone who stood against Bolshevism. These were a mixed bag: Kerensky's Provisional Government, factions of the Socialist Revolutionaries,

White Russian activists, elements of the Cossacks and indeed anyone who hated communism, whether or not they felt any loyalty to Britain.

Maugham's second objective was more cerebral: to report accurately and impartially on the power struggle within Russia, and help London and Washington answer some key questions. Could Kerensky hold on? How likely was a Bolshevik takeover? Would it possible to exert any influence over the Bolsheviks if they did come to power? Ironically, Maugham might have had more success if he gone to Russia under his own name. Russians, then and now, revere authors - famous writer would have found it easier, therefore, than an unknown journalist to obtain the ear of the key influencers. Then again, he would also have attracted more unwelcome attention, too.

Although surprised to be handed the job, Maugham was no newcomer to intelligence work. He had grown up in an Embassy, and undertaken his first mission for MI6 two years previously. In Switzerland, he had lured people out of the protection of the neutral mountain steadfast to regions where they could be arrested and where their lives would be at risk, demonstrating himself to be discreet, efficient and certainly not squeamish.

The British and US embassies in Petrograd were informed in confidence of Maugham's impending arrival, but not given details of his assignment. He was to operate, as Somerville, on his own. If he achieved success, it would go unrecognized; if he failed or got into trouble he would face the dire consequences alone.

Distanced in this way from the diplomatic missions, Maugham was sceptical and not well disposed towards them. The feeling seems to have been mutual. When he called on the British ambassador, Sir George Buchanan, Maugham found an aloof figure who, in his view, was out of touch with the realities of the ever-changing situation. Buchanan, for his part, understandably resented Maugham using the embassy's cypher facilities to send messages which he – the ambassador – wasn't allowed to read.

Maugham had a working knowledge of the Russian language. At least, he could read it and carry on a simple conversation with some hesitation – he stuttered in any language. He took an interpreter with him to all important meetings. His knowledge of Russia and indeed his mission strategy was informed very much by his professional interest in the country's literature.

He wrote thoughtfully about Dostoevsky and others in his notebook at the time (publishing thirty years later as *A Writer's Notebook*), but he concluded that all the classics of Russian literature – Gogol, Lermontov, Turgenev and Tolstoy – were concentrated into one, relatively short period during the 19th century between Pushkin and Chekhov. He saw Russia as a nation which had been trying, since the time of Peter the Great and the founding of St Petersburg, to turn westwards towards Europe and away from its own Tartar and Mongol roots.

He tried to build on this sentiment in encouraging the leaders of the Provisional Government to consolidate their links with the western allies – notably with France, a country prominent in the affections of many Russians and Maugham himself. He sensed, however that, as the Russian army became ever more disenchanted with its officers and its equipment, it was turning in on itself. The common soldiers, like the peasants and factory workers, saw western European culture as effete, elite, belonging to the officer-landowner classes towards whom they felt growing resentment. They had begun looking instead towards a more distinctively folkic, Slav identity. Lenin was capitalizing on this growing sentiment and Maugham, reluctantly, had to report this to his masters in London.

As well as a genuine interest in Russia, Maugham had another strong qualification for undertaking secret work. Due to the laws and mores current in the Britain of the time, he risked constantly, as a practising homosexual, the ruination of his career and the loss of his liberty. Like a great many men of the period (and a fair number of those drawn into intelligence work), necessity had made him a master of deceit. His marriage to Syrie had been a cover-story of a different kind, giving him social legitimacy whilst allowing him privately to continue his long-term affair with his private secretary, Gerald Haxton.

His true sexuality, within the circles of power and influence in which he moved in London and the USA, was something of a 'known unknown', acknowledged, unspoken yet still, to Maugham's thinking, keeping him on the margins. Until his death, it rankled with the great man that he had never received, for his literary or espionage activities, a Knighthood or an Order of Merit. He may have been right in believing that his private life was to blame. In 1954, as attitudes were beginning to soften and Maugham was turning eighty, he finally received the lesser compliment of Companion of Honour.

Having been recruited in the United States, and seeking a less conspicuous way of entering the revolutionary state, Maugham travelled west to Petrograd, crossing the Pacific to Vladivostok, and traversing the whole of Russian via the Trans-Siberian railway. His collection of spy stories, *Ashenden*, published in 1928, drew heavily on that journey and his later experiences in Russia.

The story 'Mr Harington's Washing' describes an American businessman journeying across Russia by train. Its superficially comical crux is the man's reluctance to leave his laundry behind in an increasingly dangerous Petrograd, but it hints at an alarming episode Maugham experienced on his own journey on the Trans-Siberian. Revolutionaries had attempted to blow up a bridge over a river and the train came to a halt. Realising that he might be turned out of his berth, perhaps even taken prisoner on the freezing steppes, Maugham hurriedly emptied his suitcase, putting on his warmest clothes. It was a false alarm, he arrived in Petrograd safely, where his frosty encounter with the ambassador, Sir George Buchanan, would inspire the story 'His Excellency'.

In Petrograd, Maugham turned his mind towards helping the faltering Provisional Government of Kerensky. His first strategy was propaganda, but he very soon realized he was too late for a war of words. He met Kerensky several times, and although he was an effective public speaker, Maugham failed to see in the man any of the Napoleonic qualities ascribed to the leader by his supporters. He found Kerensky's face set in "an anxious immobility" and thought he had a "strangely hunted look". He seemed unwell, and even spoke of himself as a dying man.

Maugham concluded that Kerensky was more a man of words

than a man of deeds, who had surrounded himself with sycophants who never challenged his opinions. He appeared more afraid of doing the wrong thing than anxious to do the right, and so tended to do nothing. Kerensky asked Maugham to carry a message – memorized rather than written down – to Prime Minister Lloyd George. This was a plea, to offer the Germans peace terms they would be certain to refuse. Kerensky's rather desperate logic was that this would inspire the restive and rebellious Russian troops into fighting on, because they'd have no choice.

Maugham, for his part, duly took the message to Lloyd George. Perhaps he was especially anxious that day, perhaps he had grave misgivings about how the Prime Minister would react. At any rate, Maugham stammered so badly that, in the end, he was required to put the message in writing. It received a crisp refusal.[15]

On the other hand, Maugham, while following up his contacts in Moscow, had been very impressed by Boris Savinkov, minister of war in Kerensky's cabinet. Although an active revolutionary, who had personally assassinated both the Grand Duke Sergius and the Tsar's police chief, Plehve, Savinkov was always neatly – indeed, formally – dressed in a stiff collar and frock coat. He looked more like a quiet provincial lawyer than a dangerous plotter and killer. Imprisoned under the Tsar's regime, he had escaped with the help of a prison officer, who was a secret convert to communism. Maugham concluded that Savinkov had that capacity to inspire, influence and lead sadly so lacking in Kerensky. But it was not enough to prop up the Provisional Government in the face of the impending Bolshevik threat. He reported back that the Provisional Government was a broken reed.

Maugham also understood the momentum and force of the Bolsheviks, who, once Lenin had reappeared on the scene, were unstoppable in their bid for power. Perhaps vainly, Maugham surmised that he could have changed the fate of Russia, if only he'd been sent there six months earlier. He couldn't blame a lack of

---

15 By this time it would have been too late to help Kerensky in any case.

funding: he carried more than $20,000 in a concealed belt. With it, he could have arranged the distribution of popular literature supporting Kerensky, organized the appearance of popular speakers at political meetings, workers' assemblies, religious gatherings and even military events. By the time he showed up, though, it was too late, and in his own eyes, his mission had consequently failed.

He was, perhaps, overly pessimistic in this summary though. As a result of Maugham's reports, Washington and London were better informed about, and better prepared for Lenin's takeover. His experience of intelligence work, his sensitivity to human weaknesses, ability to set out his findings in a convincing form and his inherent scepticism all made him an ideal agent for the task.

No agent can stay secret forever, though. As the Kerensky regime tottered towards its fall, the Bolsheviks identified Maugham as someone working against them. He might only, to them, have been some foreign agent called Somerville, but he was nonetheless a marked man. His handlers managed to smuggle him onto a train from Petrograd to Oslo just a few days before the October revolution (which in fact took place in November 1917) reached its decisive point. Maugham would remember, relish and revisit his Russian adventures for the rest of his life. Although he was generally fond of retracing his steps, he thought it prudent never to return to Russia after it had become the Soviet Union..

For Maugham, the revisiting would have to be in written form. Since he was barred, by the Official Secrets Act, from recounting his time in Russia as memoirs, he turned it into a loosely-linked set of stories, based around a character called Ashenden, a playwright, recruited into working for the intelligence services. Entertaining rather than strictly informative, *Ashenden* perhaps tells us more about Maugham and his attitude towards authority than Russia in 1917.

Somerset Maugham confronted the Bolsheviks and warned his masters about their seemingly inevitable rise to power. In spite of his status as a popular and much-loved writer, though, he did not expose wickedness of the new regime to a wider public. It is ironic that, of all the agents sent into Russia during the formative years of the revolution, none was so well equipped by talent, connections and reputation to tell the world what was going wrong; and none in the event told the world so little. The private, stuttering Maugham was better as an observer and reporter than a spokesman.

John Buchan

Paul Dukes

THE VELVET GLOVE AND THE IRON HAND

John Buchan & Paul Dukes

John Buchan was a great inspirer of wild exploits in others, but by the time of the Russian Revolution his own adventuring days were largely over. As a young man, and a member of Lord Milner's "kindergarten" in South Africa, he had travelled widely and carried out tasks that were not only enterprising but sometimes dangerous. Following that, the "Middle Years" (as he describes the decade before the First World War in his autobiography) had seen him practising at the Bar and entering the House of Commons. But by the outbreak of war in 1914 his health had become a problem: he records that a combination of family anxieties and public activities had played havoc with his digestion, and he had to go into hospital and then to rest for a long period. He was already thirty-nine and beyond the age when he would have been conscripted, but many men of that age were volunteering for active service, as he would doubtless have liked to have done. A high proportion of his closest friends were killed in the early months of the war. Later in the war, Buchan found a role for himself as a liaison and intelligence officer; but it was a back-room role compared to that played by other protagonists in this book.

Buchan's early Richard Hannay novels – *The Thirty-Nine Steps* (1915) and *Greenmantle* (1916) – concentrated on the Kaiser's Germany as the natural enemy of Britain, but by the time of *Mr Standfast* (1919) he was already becoming increasingly aware that another menace was looming on the horizon – the Bolsheviks in Russia who had murdered their own Tsar and his family the previous year. On two occasions in that book he refers to Russia as "heading straight for the devil" and having "gone head-long to the devil". While much opinion in Britain was still undecided about the merits of the communist revolution, Buchan was firmly seeing it as a disaster and a threat to the British way of life.

His views about this had found full expression by 1924 in his novel *Huntingtower*. This opens with a romantic scene at a society ball in the green marble ballroom of the Nirski Palace in St Petersburg in January 1916, where a young and beautiful Russian princess sits out a dance with a young Scottish officer whose leg has been too badly injured in the war for him to dance. The girl has no forebodings about the coming disasters for her class and her country; after all, she says, Russia is winning the war and she looks forward to being able to be a volunteer nurse in a military hospital. The young officer is privately less optimistic, and tells her he wishes she was still in Paris (where they had first met) because she would be safer there. "What nonsense!" she says. "Where should I be safe if not in my own Russia…it is France and England that are unsafe with the German guns rumbling at their doors…my complaint is I am too secure." Before Princess Saskia is swept off for the next dance by a Russian guards officer, the wounded Scotsman – Quentin Kennedy – makes her promise that if ever she is in deep trouble she will turn to him for help: "Now I can do no more for you than the mouse for the lion – at the beginning of the story…but some day it may be in my power to help you." Although he does not say so, he has in mind that his castle in Scotland could be a safe haven should she ever need one.

The main story of *Huntingtower* centres around a retired Glasgow grocer – Dickson McCunn – and a group of ragamuffin boys from the Gorbals. McCunn takes off on holiday to Carrick, a west-coast region of Scotland, and finds himself at Huntingtower Castle on the coast, the ancestral home of Quentin Kennedy – the young Scottish officer who had befriended Princess Saskia in St Petersburg. He hears that Kennedy died of his wounds and that, there being no heir to take it over, the castle is now lying semi-derelict and empty. McCunn and a friend he has met on his travels resolve to try to walk around the castle, but are repelled by an unfriendly caretaker. When eventually they approach the castle from the seaward side, McCunn's friend declares that he can hear a girl's voice from within singing a Russian song. The voice turns out to belong to Princess Saskia, who had managed to escape from Russia but had been betrayed and was in fact now being held prisoner in the very castle Kennedy had once offered as a refuge.

John Buchan puts into the mouth of the princess a savage denunciation of the Bolsheviks: "You good people in England think they are well-meaning dreamers who are forced into violence...but the power lies with madmen and degenerates, and they have for allies the special devil that dwells in each country." The novel goes on to tell at length of a Bolshevik plot to come by sea and carry off the princess and force her to give up the hidden jewels. Most readers of Buchan's book remember the story best for its vivid description of the Gorbals gang and their distinctive language and indomitable spirits. Readers who had hitherto associated Buchan's heroes with the club land of London's West End now saw a different, more socially aware and more democratic side of his interests. But what *Huntingtower* also did in a forceful way was to denounce the revolutionaries in Russia and portray them as international gangsters. These were not the liberal descendants of Tolstoy, or the pioneers of a new utopia, as many in Britain were still inclined to think. Princess Saskia makes a damning indictment of the international effects of what has happened in her country: "There is crime everywhere in the world, and the unfettered crime in Russia is so powerful that it stretches its hand to crime throughout the globe and there is a great mobilizing everywhere of wicked men."

John Buchan was also directly responsible for the recruitment of others who confronted the Bolsheviks in their early days. During the First World War he served in the Intelligence Corps and later (1917–18) as a director of the Ministry of Information. His initial responsibilities were to undermine and expose the machinations of the Germans, and later – as the Russian Revolution entered its second phase – of the Bolshevik regime. It was in connection with the latter period that he employed a young man called Paul Dukes, who had acquired an unusual insider knowledge of Russia and Russian thinking.

Dukes had been brought up as a "son of the manse" in Scotland, where his father was a somewhat unconventional minister in the congregational church. Young Dukes showed considerable musical talent and his father was directing him towards a career as an organist. But Dukes wanted to do something more exciting, and ran away from home, working his way across Europe by teaching English until he reached St Petersburg, where he enrolled as a musical scholar in the *conservatoire* and where his tutor introduced him to the circle of the imperial family at their summer residence of Tsarskoe Selo. When the war broke out in 1914 he felt he should do something more patriotic, and he enlisted at the British embassy as a translator. But when Kerensky's revolution took place in February 1917, Dukes – despite or because of his exposure to the Romanovs – found himself in active sympathy with the revolutionaries; he was disinclined to stay longer in St Petersburg, so he returned to England and – doubtless with recommendations from the British embassy in Russia – started working for John Buchan.

Buchan, though now ostensibly concerned with information (material in the public domain) rather than intelligence (more secretive) work, still had a keen eye open for likely British agents who could help him in his new-found antagonism to the Bolsheviks. Dukes was someone who not only spoke good Russian but knew the scene in depth. Buchan dispatched him to Paris to liaise with the French intelligence service in their anti-Bolshevik researches. He then sent him back to Russia under cover of a job with – of all things – the Boy Scout movement. When he distinguished himself in these tasks, Buchan thought Dukes should be passed on to the British Secret Intelligence Service for more long-term and possibly dangerous clandestine missions.

Dukes returned to St Petersburg with the task of gathering

information about the likely durability and the popularity or unpopularity of the new Bolshevik regime. Would it survive long enough to make it worth negotiating with? Were the Russian troops and people just waiting for an opportunity to revert to a more normal social system? Were the Germans stirring up revolutionary sentiment inside Russia? Was the Red Terror succeeding in cowing the population? By now, the western intervention against the communists was getting under way, and entry into what was shortly to become the Soviet Union was far less easy than slipping into the old Russia. Having failed to reach St Petersburg from Murmansk, Dukes eventually succeeded in slipping across the frontier from Helsinki. He was not spying in any conventional sense – not measuring bridges, recruiting agents, estimating troop strengths. His remit was more general and vague: he was going from place to place – Smolensk (behind the western front), Samara (a Socialist Revolutionary/pro-Kerensky stronghold), Vologda (a retreat for those hoping to escape abroad) – and in all of these he took the temperature of local opinion. In his own words, he went to Russia not to conspire, but to inquire. Were people becoming restive with Lenin's regime, or could they be induced to be so? He returned to London and, as well as reporting his findings to MI6, he also passed on his impressions to his former mentor John Buchan.

More assignments to Russia followed. Dukes was now operating on the direct instructions of "C" – the chief of MI6 – who, at the conclusion of his briefing, impressed on him the risks he was taking by admonishing him: "Don't go and get killed!" "C" had enlarged on the questions – those enumerated above – on which he hoped Dukes could provide enlightenment, but had not given him any idea of how he was to achieve this, or even on how he was to penetrate as far as Petrograd.

The next time he tried – in 1918 – he failed to get to Petrograd from Archangel, because "the roads were closely watched" and therefore most of the six-hundred-mile route would have had to be done "on foot through unknown moorland and forest…and impassable marshes".

The frontier with Finland proved a more possible route, although not without its own difficulties: the border river was fringed with ice and – "having taken a pull at my little bottle of whisky" – he had to punt his way across and "midstream had the sort of feeling I should imagine a man has as he walks his last walk to the gallows". Although he noisily cracked the ice on landing, Dukes managed to evade the awakened frontier guards, "blessing the man who invented whisky, for I was very cold". He had grown a beard and moustache, donned a fur hat and thick spectacles, and altogether transformed himself into a Dostoevsky-like radical intellectual.

As the intervention forces in 1918 became increasingly mired in the confusion of a country trying to define its new character and role, Dukes found himself acting as a paymaster to dissident (counter-revolutionary) elements. This was extremely dangerous territory: one of his couriers was caught by the Cheka and shot, and he himself had to resort to ever more elaborate disguises. He was continually either growing or shaving off his beard. He was mixing with avowed enemies of the Bolshevik regime, but always uncertain as to how many of them were agents provocateurs. Some dubious figures were undoubtedly being paid by both sides. He was appalled at the degree of hunger and poverty, especially among those who had led comfortable lives before the revolution: "people were selling sugar by the lump". Some categories of people seemed still to enjoy a degree of privileged access to food and housing; among these were the actors and dancers of the theatres and ballet which still – surprisingly – continued to perform. There was widespread expectation of Allied intervention against the Red Army, and the latter was now largely commanded by ex-officers from the Tsarist army; Trotsky's ruthless command of the Red Army saw every unit that was engaged against the Poles or the White Russian forces having a contingent in its rear whose job it was to shoot defectors, or even to shoot those inclined to retreat rather than advance. All the time, Dukes was trying to piece together an accurate picture of the likely durability of the new Communist order. Both Lenin and Trotsky impressed him with their eloquence, but he felt that the regime could not endure by words alone.

Like Bailey, who in Tashkent was recruited by the secret police to search for himself, Dukes found that the best and safest cover was that of being an agent of the Bolshevik security forces. He managed to get forged documents, with the help of the same Finns who had smuggled him across the border and who had copies of stolen genuine identification papers from which they transcribed signatures and reproduced rubber stamps. These carefully fabricated documents presented him as a member of the All-Russian Extraordinary Commission for the Suppression of the Counter-Revolution, Speculation and Sabotage ("speculation" in this context being a euphemism for indulgence in private commerce). This was the body charged with uprooting – by means of terror and inquisition – all anti-Bolshevik activity in any walk of life. His false papers helped to get him into places he could not otherwise have penetrated, and to get him out of scrapes – usually searches of cafés or other premises frequented by anti-Bolsheviks – where he might otherwise have been arrested or trapped.

It was during this phase of Duke's activities that he became involved in arranging the escape of various fellow agents or would-be refugees. Having bribed the guards, he organized an ingenious escape for the wife of one fellow agent from the most dreaded Cheka prison. This involved buying "a warm [green] cloak which had seen better days…from an impoverished refined lady", smuggling this disguise into the Petrograd prison, and finally himself making a rendezvous with the escaped lady inside St Isaac's Cathedral: "How interminably the minutes passed…then the green shawl appeared…I walked up to this shrouded figure and said, 'I am the person you are to meet.' He then accompanied her on a dramatic crossing of the frozen northern frontier into Finland, at one stage throwing himself on the ground as a human bridge across a snowdrift which would have otherwise collapsed when walked over. On this particular crossing he was also accompanying two attractive young Russian girls who were determined to escape to Finland; only later did he discover that they were the daughters of the Grand Duke Paul Alexandrovitch, the Tsar's uncle, who had just been imprisoned and was about to be shot by his custodians and executioners. On yet another trip across the frozen frontier, he donned dark clothes and had to lie on a patch of black ice while the horses of his pursuers nearly galloped right over him. Getting back into Russia was often as difficult as getting out; once Dukes skied across the frontier at night, finding to his relief that – although he had not skied for four years – he had not lost the knack of doing so. Despite having been away in Finland for a while, he was disturbed to find on his return to Russia that the Cheka still had a full description of him and he remained on their wanted list.

His task was not over and – later in 1918 – he adopted a completely new persona. Having spent some time previously avoiding being conscripted into the Red Army, he now volunteered to join it. He found this easier than he expected and was soon registered as an artillery commander ("officer" was no longer an acceptable word in the Red Army) named Piotrovski. Apart from the cover and access that his new personality provided, Dukes was greatly attracted by the fact that he could now draw army rations, and would no longer be on the edge of starvation, like so many Russians were during these troubled years. He had to sign a declaration recording that he accepted that if he displayed any "disloyalty to the soviet government" his relatives would be arrested and deported. There were so many desertions from the army that this threat was considered a necessary deterrent, and Dukes knew of a number of cases where the threats had been implemented. Most towns and villages behind the lines had special commissions for combating desertion: these bodies manned crossroads and other key points, prodding every passing wagon with their bayonets to seek out deserters hidden under bales of straw or other camouflage.

He also noted – by their absence from the ranks of the army – that one of the groups which consistently avoided military service was the Jewish community. Even when Jews were conscripted, Dukes noted that they invariably managed to be employed in the rear echelons, as political commissars or in jobs concerned with food, propaganda or transport. He commented that this, together with the arrogance which the Jews showed towards the Russians generally, contributed to widespread anti-Semitism and to the popular belief in Russia that "Bolshevism is a Jewish 'put-up job' ". From his position inside the army, he also observed at first hand both the cordiality and the ruthlessness of Trotsky (still commanding the Red Army), who "casts off friends as he would clothing, the moment they have served his purpose". He was not surprised that Trotsky had shed his original Jewish name of Bronstein in favour of his adopted one.

He felt that the army would remain under Trotsky's direction "as long as he can feed it", or until a charismatic leader emerged from the Bolshevik ranks who could rally the entire peasantry as well as the soldiery behind him. Unlike the vain and self-centred Sidney Reilly, Dukes did not see himself as that man.

One of the most significant trends in military thinking that Dukes detected was a tendency to believe that the Bolshevik regime would be short-lived. It was this conviction that persuaded many former Tsarist officers to join the Red Army since – they felt – it would not be a long-term commitment; by the end of 1919, Dukes reckoned that most of the senior posts – such as divisional or brigade commanders – were occupied by such former Tsarist officers; but it remained the case that any conspicuously useful service by ex-Tsarists was never forgiven by the remaining White Russian activists.[16]

While he was studying the morale and effectiveness of the Red Army from his vantage point within it, it was not always easy to preserve his cover. He relates that he was considered to be an invalid, suffering in body and mind from the ill-treatment received at the hands of a capitalist government. He explained his occasionally observed "English" manners by maintaining that his father had been a musician who was expelled for being too bourgeois and who had taken temporary refuge in England and America. His alleged ill-treatment was supposed to have followed his refusal in England to fight in the war, after which he had been deported to his native land as an undesirable alien. This story accounted not only for

---

16 As an aside, one of the strengths of the Red Army in Dukes's opinion was that, unlike in the Tsarist army, promotion was on merit and not on account of social standing or land ownership.

his foreign mannerisms but also for the unavoidable lapses in his Russian speech.

As he circulated around Petrograd, trying to find answers to all the questions that "C" and Buchan posed, Dukes found it essential to have some safe houses where he could hide and from which he could contact his agents. He always approached such addresses with great circumspection, never being sure that they had not been identified by the Cheka, or that he might not be walking into some trap. On one occasion he recounts how he found his safe house inhabited only by a simple-minded boy, who told him that the Cheka had indeed been looking for him there twice and had searched the house; they even knew one of his more obscure pseudonyms. He asked the lad how they had described him and was told "tall, sort of ...black beard...long hair...one front tooth missing...speaks not quite our way...walks quickly". He immediately took measures to alter all these characteristics with the help of barbers and tailors, and even in the case of the most difficult feature he had an answer: "Cutting open the lapel of the jacket I was discarding, I extracted a tiny paper packet and, unwrapping it, took out the contents – my missing tooth, carefully preserved for this emergency. I inserted it in the gaping aperture." Dukes was ready for most exigencies.

Useful as was Dukes's insider view of the Red Army, he was not always accurate in his forecasts of how the wider scene in Russia would pan out. He could not believe that a "government of workers and peasants" could be an enduring reality, and attached undue importance to various pieces of evidence showing the frailty of the regime, whose leadership were predominantly middle-class intellectuals. When he encountered a demonstration carrying banners saying "Down with Lenin and horseflesh, give us a Tsar and pork!", he thought it was representative of a wider movement than was the case. He was aware of other demonstrations against the regime which were never reported in the press or elsewhere. And he was aware that brutal measures, against not only the demonstrators but also against their families, further served to suppress news of dissent. In Petrograd, Communist Party membership was much reduced, and Trotsky declared that its ranks should be purged of those he described as "radishes" – those who were red only on the outside.

Dukes may have been wrong in his forecast of the transitory nature of the Bolshevik regime, but he gave an in-depth picture of life under that regime in Russia, both in civilian and military circles, which no one had been able to provide before. When eventually he escaped for the final time it was via Latvia – wading through bogs and finally rowing across the border river in a leaking boat propelled by oars made from the branches of overhanging trees. He returned to debrief in London. His accounts of the brutality of Communist government went some way towards enlightening the British Labour party about the realities of a regime about which they had been hitherto rather starry-eyed. For their part – according to Dukes – the Bolsheviks regarded the Labour party as a collection of "radishes". His campaign to expose the truth about the Bolshevik regime was not limited to the Labour party; he wrote to the editor of the *Manchester Guardian* in 1919 warning him of being too naive in his approach to communism; he also felt it necessary to write to the editor of *The Times* which had never been uncritical of the Bolsheviks. In 1921, Dukes set off on a lecture tour of the United States, being one of the few people who could speak there from personal experience of actually living in post-revolutionary Russia. It was no wonder that the Bolshevik supporters in London tried to retaliate: they caused uproars at meetings where he was speaking and did all they could to undermine his efforts. Dukes's reporting also included giving a full account of his adventures and conclusions to his original mentor – John Buchan. This proved to be a major factor in turning Buchan against the people whom he was to demonize in *Huntingtower*.

As Director of Information at the end of the war, Buchan's interests had moved on from specific intelligence to the broader picture, and it was this broader picture which Dukes fleshed out. Dukes had achieved some feats of outstanding courage as well as of broader interpretation. On return, he received a knighthood for his services (an honour which Buchan had hoped for but failed to achieve for his own First World War services) and it was said that when King George V heard the details of some of Dukes's more heroic exploits – notably in helping other people escape – he had suggested that a Victoria Cross had been deserved; but the chiefs of staff of the armed forces pointed out that the VC was an award reserved for military gallantry in the face of a declared and armed enemy. The personal risks and adventures had been Dukes's, while the political use of his reporting and the interpretation of it to a wider political public had been the role of Buchan.

Indeed, John Buchan's confrontation of Bolshevism was not of the same order as that of other adventurers like Bruce Lockhart and Ranald MacDonell; nor did he explore the confines of the Soviet Union and report his perceptive and critical findings as did travellers Stephen Graham, Peter Fleming and Fitzroy Maclean. But there is no doubt that he awakened and alerted a generation of young adventurers to the reality of the far-flung and destructive ambitions of those who embraced the Bolshevik creed. His thrillers had a huge following among those setting out on the more exciting paths of life – and to a certain extent still do. It was given to some to use a dagger as well as a cloak in their efforts to unmask the evil they perceived; it was given to Buchan to use a pen, with nib well sharpened, for the same purpose.

Alfred Gough

A CLERGYMAN BLOWS THE WHISTLE

Alfred Gough

One might have expected that, even if there was reluctance – for political, social or financial reasons – for parliamentarians, diplomats and scholars to expose and denounce the Bolshevik revolution, there would have been no constraints on churchmen. But it was not only inside Russia that the Church was strangely silent. Protestant, Catholic and even Orthodox clergy were slow to realize and even slower to reveal the incompatibility of communism and Christianity.

In England, this was in part because the greatest authority on the Russian Orthodox Church was a mild-mannered theologian called Canon John Douglas, who devoted much time and energy to exploring the possibilities of some working union – or at least mutual recognition and respect – between the Anglican and Russian churches. He travelled extensively in those countries formerly part of the Byzantine Church and empire, and he visited Russia after the 1917 revolutions. The motivation for his visits, however, was the exploration of theological common ground rather than anxiety about the persecution of a church and it followers. Latterly – in 1923 – he returned to Russia to receive from Patriarch Tikhon of the Russian

Church the much-prized Protopresbyter's Cross of the Russian Synod; the acceptance of this order by an Anglican clergyman possibly implied to others that nothing was too seriously amiss. It was only much later that he wrote pamphlets expressing concern about the Russian Church and its ability to survive the onslaught of communism. These pamphlets did not receive very wide attention, and most people – both inside and outside the Church – continued to think of him (if they thought of him at all) as an intellectual absorbed in liturgical rather than survival issues.

It was left to a more dynamic priest – Prebendary Alfred Gough, the vicar of Holy Trinity Brompton in London – to focus on the life and death issues of Christian survival in Russia, and he only got round to addressing this question at the very end of the 1920s. But before examining how and why he did this, it is necessary to see the wider context of Church –communist relations. Were the two belief systems at loggerheads, or were they mutually compatible aspects of the quest for a fairer world?

From the start, there was plenty to confuse Christians about their reaction to communism. There was even, some would argue, a scriptural basis for the abolition of private property. In the book of The Acts of the Apostles in the New Testament, communism (without the capital C it was often to acquire in Russia) appears to be consistent with the passage reading "neither said any of them [the multitude of believers] that ought of the things which he possessed was his own; but they all had all things common".

Sir Thomas More, a martyr to his faith in the reign of Henry VIII, hinted in his *Utopia* in 1516 at a world in which effectively all things were communally shared. In the wake of the French Revolution, the Comte de Saint-Simon explored the idea of requiring a contribution from everyone according to their ability, and rewarding everyone according to their needs.

Although Marx seems to have dismissed these utopian concepts as unrealistic, and to have favoured a much more confrontational form of class struggle, the idea persisted that communism had its roots in Christian ideas of sharing, and was promoted by such prominent

Anglican figures as Hewlett Johnson (Dean of Canterbury) as late as the 1960s.[17]

Some explanation has already been given, in the introductory chapter of this book, for the reluctance of Christians – both inside and outside Russia – to denounce the atheist nature of the Bolshevik regime. But the reaction of churchmen everywhere was further complicated by the divisions within the Orthodox Church itself.

As so often in political and social matters, Moscow and St Petersburg represented different approaches. Moscow was the spiritual home of Holy Russia, of the traditionally independent church descended from Kievan Rus, where Russian Christianity had been born in the 10th century. In St Petersburg, meanwhile, Peter the Great had abolished the traditional patriarchate in favour of a new Holy Synod, headed by a Prokurator, who in effect acknowledged the supremacy of the Tsar and the virtual incorporation of the Church into the state. As Edward Crankshaw has pointed out in his *The Shadow of the Winter Palace*, with only slight exaggeration, in Moscow almost every other building was a church, while by contrast in St Petersburg almost every other building was a palace or a barracks.

The contrast between these two aspects of the Orthodox Church was vividly illustrated in the works and careers of the writers Leo Tolstoy and Fyodor Dostoevsky. No one could have been more imbued with the essence of Christianity – the spirit of the Sermon on the Mount – than Tolstoy. He embraced the simplicity of peasant life; he denounced cruelty, exploitation and oppression wherever he encountered them; he believed that "the kingdom of God is within you" and not externalized in the Church; on his deathbed, he declared he wanted to "die as the peasants die" trusting in a simple faith. Yet the Orthodox Church excommunicated him in 1901, largely because they interpreted his novel *Resurrection* (written two years previously and eventually to become the most popular of all his novels in his own

17 When the author was at the British embassy in Moscow in the late 1950s, and Hewlett Johnson was a not-infrequent visitor and recipient of the Stalin Peace Prize, it was necessary to explain to his enthusiastic Soviet hosts that the role of Dean of Canterbury was not the equivalent of Patriarch of the Anglican Church, as they appeared to believe.

lifetime) as an attack on the established church, on the Tsarist judicial system and on a system of land tenure which even after the abolition of serfdom subjugated the peasants to the will of the landowners. The Tsar and the Church both tried to deny him a Christian burial in consecrated ground, although in the event even the policemen sent to enforce the ban found themselves kneeling round his grave in involuntary silent tribute.

Similarly Dostoevsky, although advocating the coexistence of the Church with the concept of social change, managed to get on the wrong side of the authorities. In his case it was not excommunication by the Orthodox Church which he suffered, but (as has been recounted earlier) arrest by the Tsarist police and exile to hard labour in Siberia.

Dostoevsky looked forward to a future in which the state was absorbed into the wider spiritual orbit of the Church, rather than the other way round – as had been the case in Russia progressively since the time of Peter the Great. He saw life as an effort to reconcile the teachings of the Gospels with the urgent need for social justice on earth. The two ideals were not, in his view, incompatible. Punishment in the form of prison and exile were not the answers to crime; atonement and redemption were. Innocent as such ideas may seem today, in Tsarist Russia thinking for oneself about political and social ideas in this way was subversion. Indeed, the Tsarist authorities found it almost impossible to distinguish between reforming liberals and bomb-building revolutionaries. This blindness was to be their ultimate undoing, but in the meantime, this unfortunate mind-set dispatched Dostoevsky to a Siberian salt mine.

A further complication for churchmen trying to evaluate the Church's relationship to communism was Grigoriy Rasputin, the professional pilgrim and reprobate "Holy Man". The influence of this figure on the Tsarina – and indeed on Tsar Nicholas II himself – was a constant source of embarrassment for the last six years of the Tsar's reign, based as it was on Rasputin's apparently supernatural ability to stem the Tsarevich's haemophiliac attacks of internal bleeding. Rasputin was not representative of the Orthodox church and, although he frequently dressed as a monk, was not in fact a priest at all. As early as 1912, Rasputin's support for an even more scurrilous monk called Iliodor had brought him into direct conflict with the Prokurator of the Holy Synod. However, the Siberian's apparent association with the church did no good to its already compromised reputation. The Russian Church was not only mistrusted because of its uncritical allegiance to the Tsar, but it was also seen to be divided internally over a whole range of issues. It was therefore in no way a natural bastion against the Bolsheviks.

It was not until the Stalinist purges in the 1920s and 1930s that the outside world realised the full horror of what was happening to Christians in Russia.[18] There had long been a brisk trade in timber from northern Russia to Europe, especially to England. Widespread business interests were involved in this trade, and Ramsay MacDonald's new Labour government in England had just re-established diplomatic relations with the Soviet Union. There was a strong desire therefore, in commercial quarters as well as in socialist and government circles, not to provoke a quarrel with Russia. Bernard Shaw and the other left-wing intellectuals remained apologists for the Bolshevik regime; all evidence of anti-religious activities was dismissed as "fabrications of the bourgeois classes" intent on undermining the compelling message of communism.

But as British ships and their crews made the voyage to Archangel and other White Sea ports such as Kem to collect the felled tree trunks from the Arctic forests, the evidence was accumulating. The sailors and timber merchants on board became aware that the Russians supplying this timber were not a normal and paid work force, but *de facto* slaves. Many members of this workforce, who had been transported in cattle trucks from other parts of Russia to the frozen north – estimates ran

18 British governments and the Anglican and Roman Catholic Churches in England have traditionally been slow to react to the problems of fellow Christians in other parts of the world. It was not until the publication in 1997 of William Dalrymple's *From the Holy Mountain* that the plight of Christian monastic and other communities throughout the Islamic Middle East was clearly brought to the attention of general readers in England. Since then, the position has notably deteriorated in Syria, Egypt and elsewhere.

at more than a million of them – were the kulaks (yeoman farmers) so hated by Stalin. Many of the rest were merely churchgoing Christians condemned because the former seminary student Stalin had defined their faith as incompatible with his own.

The essential disparity was over the status of individual souls: for Stalin, each person only had value as part of the nation they comprised. For all true Christians, of course, each individual soul was an entity of infinite value, not to be trafficked in some government-defined national interest. Stalin could justify starving millions of his fellow citizens in the interests of fulfilling a five-year plan; the Christian Church could not. What had been a disagreement of beliefs was fast becoming a violent clash. Where previously religion had been dismissed as "the opium of the people", now any adherence to Christianity – churchgoing or openly professed faith – was a criminal activity which threatened the state.

But for the reports coming back from the Arctic timber convoys, though, in the few ice-free months of the year when the ships could pass unhindered, no one would have heard about the Soviet persecution of Christians. Once the seas froze over again, a total silence about conditions in these labour camps was re-imposed. Gradually, though, the initial rumours became confirmed reports. A large proportion of the Russian forest workers turned out to be displaced Christians. They were dying of cold and under-nourishment in large numbers. Their camps were little more than self-constructed hovels in the snow; frostbite and diseases were taking a constant toll, particularly on the children. It was (in Solzhenitsyn's later words) "an ethnic catastrophe". In the prisoners' home villages, from which they had been so brutally removed, their churches had been burnt down; icons were being defaced; altars were being desecrated; priests were being shot.

A few victims of Stalin's oppression managed to escape on the ships which had come from Britain to fetch the timber. They revealed that the labour camps from which they had fled were in fact prison settlements The British Labour party refused to recognize this, because, had they done so, they would have had to refuse to accept goods "manufactured" (even felled trees) in prison.

Britain reacted, though – and some accounts suggest that it was the *Morning Post* (a predecessor of the *Daily Telegraph*) that first fastened on the story and invited the Reverend Alfred Gough to take up the cause. Certainly Gough's reputation as a magnetic preacher was well known; he had been compared to John Donne, and his sermons were more like a rousing call to the crusades than a soporific Sunday morning lecture; on occasions there were queues to hear him outside his church. Other accounts suggest it was Gough who persuaded the *Morning Post* to run the story.

At any rate, Gough was quick to launch a Christian protest movement and to instigate a popular public meeting in the Albert Hall in London. Christian churchmen from all denominations attended, along with religious leaders from other faiths. Giles Udy, who has made an in-depth study of the subject, calculates that by early 1930 Gough was speaking almost every other day at some public gathering or other, denouncing the persecution of Christians in Russia, and that his organization had distributed almost a quarter of a million pamphlets devoted to the same theme.

Gough also enlisted the support of the Archbishop of Canterbury – Cosmo Lang – who took to preaching against Stalin's anti-Church policies and actions, and (albeit whilst on a Mediterranean cruise) to seeking out Orthodox bishops to commiserate with them about what was happening to their flocks inside Russia.

An international day of prayer for the beleaguered Christians in Russia was proposed by Gough and supported by the archbishop; Catholics joined with Copts, Americans with Armenians, and Serbs with South Africans in gathering to protest at Stalin's efforts to extinguish the light of Christianity within the ever-darkening frontiers of Russia. The Bishop of Durham – Hensley Henson – who had spoken against slavery in other contexts and was to be one of the first Anglican church leaders to denounce fascism in the early 1930s, now intervened in the House of Lords to expose and protest about the forced labour practices in Russia.

The archbishop also lobbied the government at home to take a firmer stand, but Ramsay MacDonald himself and most of his senior cabinet ministers preferred to make excuses. "Excessive severity" was the worst charge levelled at the Bolsheviks by those in the House of Commons, where further debate on the matter was blocked. The day of prayer for the victims of the persecution was boycotted by the government and in consequence by the armed forces, despite the chaplain-general's reluctance to be associated with any such move. Even British diplomats abroad were discouraged from attending protests in the Vatican and elsewhere against these Soviet activities, although – to their credit – a number did so anyway. Cosmo Lang was lampooned in the Soviet press for his remarks and interventions, and criticized by his own Prime Minister for his alleged meddling in political affairs.[19]

Some British diplomats serving in the Soviet Union joined in Gough's efforts to expose the forced labour and anti-Christian activities of the Bolsheviks . It was difficult and usually impossible for British diplomatic or consular officers to visit the "frozen north" of Russia where the timber forests were, although a number of them tried to do so; already the clamp-down on foreign diplomats having access to "controversial" regions was in place – and was to remain so throughout the Cold War period. But a young diplomat called Reader Bullard, who was consul in Leningrad at the time (and would later host the Tehran conference at which Stalin, Churchill and Roosevelt met in 1943), had already recorded reports of what was going on; he also tended to think – rightly – that his own ambassador in Moscow was too sanguine about the situation. William Strang, who was acting as *chargé d'affaires* during the ambassador's absences

---

19 The attacks on Archbishop Lang over this issue were later to be surpassed by the criticism of his stance against the Duke of Windsor over the abdication issue, when the Sitwell family were thought to be behind the much-quoted lines:

> "Oh my archbishop, what a scold you are,
> And when your man is down, how very bold you are;
> Of Christian charity how scant you are;
> Oh my Lord Lang, how full of cant you are."

(and who would go on to be head of the Diplomatic Service), did his best to correct the ambassador's blindness to the horrors of the timber camps.

These more alarming reports were received by the head of the Northern Department, the relevant section in the Foreign Office in London, Sir Robert Vansittart, another senior British diplomat (he would later sacrifice his job by standing out against the Munich Agreement with Hitler in 1938), who also went on record condemning the Soviet labour camps. In other words, the high-flyers in the British diplomatic service were not only aware of the atrocities but were also explicit in their denunciation of them.

Despite all this, it was the anodyne and reassuring reports that were picked up and quoted by the Labour ministers in London, who, for their own reasons – innate sympathy for the Bolshevik experiment and reluctance to rock the commercial boat – did not want to provoke a breach with the Soviet Union. Other embassies – notably the nearby Scandinavian ones – were also reporting on the plight of the timber workers and of the Christians. But because of the government's attitude in London, and because British diplomats could not press their case without seeming disloyal, the issue could not receive the attention it deserved until after the 1935 General Election. With a new government in place, and Anthony Eden (who visited Moscow in 1935) eventually becoming Foreign Secretary, the Foreign Office's critical and revealing reports were finally heard in Westminster. Meanwhile, it was left to the clergymen – and particularly to the vicar of Holy Trinity Brompton – to take the truth to the nation.

Alfred Gough was not a physical adventurer like MacDonell or Bailey, or like Hill or Dukes, but he was a moral adventurer who stood up in his pulpit in Brompton and spoke truth to power. He toured the country talking at town halls and theatres and facing fierce barracking, threatening remarks and false accusations that he was supporting a dying world order and the protest he inspired was the largest and most vocal religious response so far to the aggressive atheism of communism.

Many of the other adventurers who confronted and exposed Bolshevism in the 1920s and 1930s risked their lives in so doing. Arguably, Gough did not so much risk his life as sacrifice it: he suffered a fatal heart attack while on the platform campaigning against the persecution of Christians. It could be claimed he was a martyr to the cause in which he so passionately believed.

Peter Fleming

AN EXPLORER WITH HIS OWN AGENDA

Peter Fleming

Peter Fleming, despite being the brother of James Bond's creator, Ian, and much involved with secret operations during the Second World War, was never involved in any undercover activities against the Bolsheviks. He was, instead, a publicist for the cause. His ceaseless travelling, and his fluent, perceptive and critical writing alerted millions to the iniquities of Soviet communism through the printed word.

Fleming was born into a strongly Scottish tradition. His family had long-standing connections with Glen Etive, Black Mount and Rannoch Moor in the western Highlands, and although he was born and educated in England – conventionally at Eton and Oxford – he always found time to return to his native roots. His grandfather, Robert Fleming, had come south from Scotland and founded the merchant bank that bore his name, and there was a strong family expectation that the promisingly bright and charming young Peter would pursue a financial career, consolidating the family's interests. He was duly dispatched to New York to learn something about the world of finance and – perhaps because he arrived there just as the Wall Street crash of 1929 was taking place – he loathed both his work and the city itself. He found New York everything that Oxford was not: ugly to look at, noisy to live in and an expensive environment in which to try to enjoy oneself. As soon as he could, he resigned and returned home, beginning to earn small sums of money by writing for the *Spectator*, and securing a job as assistant literary editor there. But he was soon planning to set off on distant travels.

Unimpressed by his first taste of the New World, Fleming now decided to discover the East. On the slightly flimsy excuse of attending a conference in China on behalf of Chatham House, he set off in 1931 across the Soviet Union by the Trans-Siberian Express. So began (in the words of his admirable biographer Duff Hart-Davis) "a kind of masochistic affection for the Russians which he retained ever afterwards". But even before Fleming embarked on the long train journey, he was becoming aware of the stifling bureaucracy of the communist regime and the run-down and decrepit nature of the amenities and services such a regime fostered.

He later described his existence during the week-long rail trip across Russia: the endless tea-drinking and chess-playing; the long hours spent looking through the compartment window at the empty, pine-forested landscape; the sensation of living in a vacuum; and the infinite opportunity to read for undisturbed hours on end.[20] Having survived the long journey across Russia, Fleming spent some months in China and the Far East, in his own words, "swanning around". But his first big adventure was to come after his return to London, and as a result of responding to an advertisement in the agony column of *The Times*. He joined a highly amateur expedition into the Amazon rainforests of Brazil, in part an attempt to discover the fate of Colonel Fawcett who had disappeared there some years before. The book that resulted from this trip – *Brazilian Adventure* – was an instant best-seller and indeed started a whole new genre of light-hearted travel writing. With the success of this book, his future career – about which he had been uncertain for so long – was determined: he was to be a professional writer.

---

20 Little has changed in Russian rail travel. Fleming's description of his journey could have equally applied to several made by the author more than twenty years later. When travelling south (to Central Asia rather than Siberia) it was the custom to change into pyjamas on the first night and stay in them for the duration of the trip. If so dressed one wandered off the platform at station stops, friendly Russians would approach and warn, "Comrade, your train is about to leave."

1933 found Fleming setting off again eastwards on the Trans-Siberian Express, and the experience merged in his mind with his previous journey. But this time there was a dramatic difference: the train's brakes failed and it crashed off the line and – although no one was seriously hurt – he was glad when he transferred to a Chinese train for the final part of his trip. The incident had provided him with early evidence of the Bolshevik propensity to suppress all news that was not good news. He had been spotted photographing the crashed coaches, and the police and railway officials were determined to find his film and confiscate it. They did not succeed; Fleming was already becoming an expert at concealment. This second excursion to the East resulted in another bestseller – *One's Company*; he found himself now being acclaimed as "a modern Elizabethan".

It was in 1934 that he conceived his most ambitious plan of all. He would return to China and then set out overland to India – walking, hitching lifts on trucks, riding, taking whatever mode of transport came to hand. He travelled out in a leisurely manner, exploring the Caucasus, crossing the Caspian Sea, taking a train to Samarkand, and eventually linking up with the Trans-Siberian Express again at Novosibirsk. As he travelled yet further east across these little-penetrated regions of Russia, he found that his genuine enthusiasm for shooting often gave him access to places which would otherwise have been out of bounds. He seldom missed an opportunity to do a little close observation of strategic targets – some would have called it spying – such as charting the railway line around Lake Baikal, whose tunnels, flyovers and culverts were all assessed for their vulnerability to air attack.

The most difficult section of the whole proposed trek from China to India was likely to be the western province of China, variously known as Sinkiang, Chinese Turkestan or Kashgaria (Etherton's former territory). But this was also the region Fleming was most anxious to visit. In Peking there was little hard information about what was happening in this distant province; the one thing everyone agreed on was that the normal caravan routes were closed. The state of this province, and the extent and nature of Russian activities there, were likely to make compelling copy for *The Times*, who were funding Fleming's trip in return for regular despatches. It was a case of Kashgaria at any cost. After many doubts on both sides, Fleming had agreed to travel with an intrepid Swiss lady called Ella 'Kini' Maillart, who had already made some notably adventurous journeys. The party also comprised a White Russian couple called Smigunov, who were anxious to return home and who offered to act as both interpreters and guides. Fleming's knowledge of both the route and of the languages – including Turki – to be encountered on that route was at this juncture fairly rudimentary, so such an offer was too good to be turned down. The excitements and hardships of the trip included physically agonizing passages – clinging onto the luggage on top of overcrowded trucks – and also emotionally agonizing experiences, such as abandoning an exhausted camel in the desert. This last was a particularly painful event: "I decided not to shoot the camel; for all I knew he might recover his strength… but it was horrible to leave him there, hunched, apathetic, and somehow shrunken, with the snow plastering his inexpressive face."

At Lanchow they were detained for six days, partly because all travel westward was considered inadvisable on account of the suspected Russian incursions from the north; but partly because the Lanchow authorities thought Fleming and his travelling companions might be Russian agents smuggling communist literature into the region. They could hardly have arrived at a less accurate assessment of their visitors! The whole journey from China to India is a dramatic story in itself, and most memorably told in Fleming's book *News from Tartary*. His confrontation with Bolshevism however, was more narrowly focused on his discoveries in Sinkiang.

Fleming set out his stall rather when he wrote in his account: "This book is called *News from Tartary* and the news we brought back was political news". He devoted four chapters of his book to revealing for the first time the nature and extent of Bolshevik Russian intervention in Sinkiang. In his promised articles for *The Times,* meanwhile, he concentrated even more on this aspect of his travels and discoveries. He had after all been sent out and, to a large extent, financed by *The*

Times as a political correspondent, and he was committed to exposing the disturbing political scene he encountered.

When Fleming set off for Sinkiang, it was widely believed that the province was undergoing a civil war and that the White Russians were dominating the scene. He found quite the reverse: the province was at peace, but the so-called White Russians who had escaped there had almost all abandoned their resistance to the Bolshevik regime and had thrown in their hand with the extremist communist elements now in control. Those "agents of a Certain Power" were now revealed unequivocally as agents of Bolshevism.

Fleming was concerned with the economic as well as the political implications of this takeover. For centuries traders from India had crossed the mountain passes into this neighbouring market; now, they were being squeezed out by Russian traders and merchants. Not only was this going on in a legitimate and open way, but there were also undercover trade negotiations in hand. The Russians, it seemed, had granted a secret loan of half-a-million gold roubles to the Sinkiang authorities, as well as arms, ammunition and military aircraft, in return for a monopoly on the products of the province, including Persian unborn lamb skins.

But inevitably it was the political threat that was uppermost in Fleming's mind and in his reporting. The Russians had built their Trans-Caspian railway, heading across the deserts into Central Asia, as a means of providing rapid and effective military support for their garrisons and satellite states there. From this jumping-off point they were regularly sending military reconnaissance parties into Sinkiang, sometimes but not always disguised as scientific expeditions. They flaunted their presence in Kashgar with a consulate-general far outstripping the British one in size and visibility, not least by his large, permanent entourage of Cossack bodyguards. This was enhanced by the fact that the Chinese garrison of the province was – in Fleming's assessment – a Gilbert and Sullivan act, mostly fuelled by opium consumption. No one felt it would be long before the Russian economic domination was reinforced by outright annexation.

In fact, Fleming thought this would have happened earlier, had it not been for extraneous events such as the Russo-Japanese war of 1904, the outbreak of the First World War, the Russian Revolution, and the years of Allied intervention provoking civil war within Russia. Indeed, the annexation could have even have been expected to happen in Tsarist times, and Fleming found it ironic that the dreaded Tsarist troops, when they arrived in large numbers in Kashgar, came not as conquerors, but as refugees from communism. Now there were no further extraneous reasons to hold back the Russian incursions.

Things had taken a dramatic turn after an armed confrontation between the local militias in Urumqi, the northern capital of Sinkiang (which Fleming did not reach), and Russian intervention forces in 1934 (the year before Fleming's visit). But no word of this reached the outside world: Urumqi was remote and foreign visitors excluded. Where foreigners had managed to penetrate this isolation and witness the military events concerned – as was the case with some Germans and Swedish travellers – they had been arbitrarily arrested to ensure their silence. Avoiding the same fate, Fleming broke the news of these events to a wider world in his newspaper reports.

The position of the so-called White Russian contingents in Kashgar attracted Fleming's special attention. All their units had been systematically penetrated by communist agents, and the temporary government – who had the power to send them back to Russia at any time – was firmly controlled by the Bolshevik elements. So it had come about that while some of the Whites had fled from Sinkiang during the civil war fighting, those who remained were no longer White in any meaningful sense. Fleming concluded that the Soviet consulates and the Soviet advisers were in reality the only effective force in the province: Moscow was in control. The Bolsheviks were also establishing their long-term influence by infiltrating the schools, which had previously been firmly Islamic, with political instructors. Where this did not work, pupils were sent to Tashkent for more heavy-handed indoctrination, and while they were there fulfilled a dual role as hostages for the cooperative behaviour of those families who were left behind. Some of the richer and less amenable Turki families had already disappeared – probably arrested without trace. Fleming refers to a rabble of Soviet activists who were rustled up from neighbouring Kazakhstan if needed.

But what he noticed most was the absence of British, Indian and even Chinese goods from the bazaars. This was partly due to the Russians' exploitation of their nearby railheads, which allowed their goods to be imported without the hazards and delays of caravan crossings of the high passes. Fleming calculated that by the time he reached Kashgar, the volume of Indian merchandise on sale was about one twentieth of what it had been a few years before. The Russian goods replacing the Indian products were of noticeably inferior quality. Nor was the shift in provenance of the goods merely a natural consequence of rail and other links: there was a good deal of official interference to rig the market. Caravans from India were forced to pay several times more duty on their goods than imports from Russia. Delays were artificially engineered, meanwhile, to make the process even more costly and difficult. The British consulate-general, protest as it might, was unable to put an end to this unfair penalizing of British and Indian products.

Fleming concluded that some of these Soviet activities in Sinkiang were merely opportunistic efforts to gain power and profit by those on the ground. Some of the activities, however, appeared to be more sinisterly directed from Moscow. For instance, he found that "the only powers in the land are the Russian civil and military 'advisers'. Every department, every regiment, is in effect directed by a Soviet agent occupying a key position… the Province is run from Moscow". There was a persistent endeavour to squeeze out British interests. In fact, Fleming reported, many people thought that one day soon the province would apply to be an autonomous Soviet Socialist Republic – like its neighbours in Central Asia.

These thoughtful, political chapters about the state of affairs in Sinkiang in Fleming's book *News from Tartary*, and his series of *Times* articles on the same theme, were picked up for vicious attack by a journalist of the *Daily Worker*, the only official Communist newspaper in England at the time. The *Worker* claimed that *The Times* giving such unusual prominence to such articles showed how alarmed the

British establishment was at the "moral and commercial supremacy" established by the Soviet Union in that province. The *Worker* went on to argue that Fleming's articles were evidence of an aggressive British policy in Central Asia; a new 'Great Game', they implied, was about to commence. Fleming's articles and chapters on Sinkiang were certainly more political than the rest of his highly entertaining book, but they were hardly the "barrage of propaganda" the *Worker* claimed.

Later on, however, Fleming did pen a far more direct assault on Bolshevism; not in travel books or journalism, but in a spy thriller. In 1950 he began *The Sixth Column,* concerning a Soviet plot – "Plan D" – to undermine the British national character by subversion. A clandestine group of influential people, some British and some posing as Soviet defectors, were to encourage an atmosphere of bureaucracy, self-interest, dishonesty, small-mindedness and cowardice in the general public. This corrupting influence was to run in parallel with a propaganda campaign suggesting that Soviet communism was a harmless and benign system, and that all the ills and crimes attributed to it were no more than the aberrations of Stalin himself, who would not be around much longer anyway.

The immediate effect of such a brainwashing operation on the British would – so the fictional Soviets hoped – be their refusal to go on spending taxpayers' money on the defence budget.

It is not hard to discern the real concerns behind the plot. Fleming was disturbed by the extent to which the British fighting spirit, having survived the Blitz and won the Second World War, was now being eroded by the pervasive, claustrophobic atmosphere of Attlee's Labour government and its perceived advocacy of "a nanny state". The characters in *The Sixth Column* include, as the main villain, an English writer and broadcaster whose utterances carry enormous emotional weight with the British public. Although Fleming does not explicitly make the comparison (possibly because the popular Yorkshireman was still alive), J.B. Priestley – whose broadcasts were listened to by almost as large an audience as Churchill's – might have been the model for this powerfully influential character, though not of course for any of the treasonous traits of Fleming's villain. In the end, a group of characters, remarkably like Fleming's own circle of ex-military country gentlemen, succeeds in exploding Plan D.

In several respects *The Sixth Column*, while never a great success as a novel, was extraordinarily percipient. While Fleming was writing it, the British diplomats Burgess and Maclean were plotting their treasonous defection to Russia: plans as improbable and sinister as anything in Fleming's fiction. Also, when Stalin died a few years later there was a strong desire to read into the policies of his ultimate successor – Nikita Khrushchev – some of the more benign aspects of Soviet communism described in 'Plan D'. Most significantly, Peter dedicated the book and sent an advance copy to his younger brother Ian Fleming: within a year Ian was drafting the first of his James Bond novels – *Casino Royale*.

Peter Fleming was indisputably an adventurer. He also, indisputably, challenged the Bolshevik movement, by revealing the stifling economic effects of communism on Sinkiang, and by dramatizing its possible moral and psychological damage to British society in the 1950s. But he did not combine the two roles – adventurer and critic – in the same way that some others had done. It was his younger brother who would capture the worldwide readership, with his fantastical James Bond stories. But it was Peter Fleming who alerted the West to the true dangers of Communist plotting and intrigue.

Fitzroy Maclean

THE ROVING DIPLOMAT

Fitzroy Maclean

When the 25-year-old diplomat Fitzroy Maclean set out in 1937 – at his own request – from his first posting abroad in Paris to a second, less desirable role in Moscow, his friends thought he was making an unwise career move. While many intellectuals, notably – but not only – such dubious contemporaries as Guy Burgess, Donald Maclean (no relation) and Kim Philby, thought the Soviet Union was the new utopia, everyone agreed Maclean would find Moscow boring, constricting and unproductive. He would not, they said, be able to travel, and certainly not to the regions that most attracted him – Central Asia and the Caucasus.

Boring it was not to be. But Maclean soon realized it was no utopia, either. The Stalinist terror was already under way. Fear and mutual suspicion stalked the streets and haunted the homes of the Muscovites: children were denouncing their parents, and friends were betraying their friends to the secret police – the NKVD (the People's Commissariat for Internal Affairs), who were the successors to the Cheka of Bruce Lockhart's day. Even the most personal of conversations was unsafe, as everywhere – private houses as well as offices and embassies – was bugged by the NKVD. In the countryside, the kulak class of land-owning peasants were being rounded up or starved to death. In the cities, foreigners – especially Russian-speaking diplomats – were followed in the street, and even more closely if they ventured outside the centre of Moscow. And Maclean was already a Russian speaker. Having been determined to follow

Paris by a posting to Moscow, he had studied the language in the French capital[21], taking lessons from émigré Russians and reading the cornerstones of Russian literature that would remain his favourite reading for the rest of his life. When, many years later, he was invited on the BBC's *Desert Island Discs* radio programme to name the book he would take with him, he chose *War and Peace* in Russian.

The Russian Foreign Office, like the army, was one of the target areas for Stalin's purges. Maclean frequently found that the Soviet diplomatic contact with whom he had been speaking on the telephone one day would no longer be there the next. The man's Soviet colleagues would deny all knowledge of their former associate or his whereabouts; he would have disappeared, to Siberia or a firing squad, without trace. As he had been warned would be the case while still in Paris, Maclean found that social life was largely confined to the diplomatic corps: virtually no Russian would be rash enough to risk being seen speaking to, let alone accepting hospitality from, a western diplomat. Fortunately, Maclean found some kindred spirits in the newly established American embassy, which had a dacha outside Moscow where Maclean spent many weekends riding and walking through the forests. It was here that he was able to share his disillusionment with such young American diplomatic colleagues as George Kennan and Chip Bohlen, both of whom went on to influence American thinking about communism as Maclean did the British.

He would later note that "living in Moscow, even under the conditions to which we were condemned, one could in a few months find out more about the real character of the Soviet Union than one could hope to learn by reading all the books that were ever written on the subject". But the single event which did most to disillusion Maclean was the trial of the so-called dissident Nikolai Bukharin who, with a number of his fellow party members, had fallen out with Stalin.

---

21 When the author was learning Russian twenty years later, also prior to a posting to the Moscow embassy, Paris remained the best and safest place to learn the language: there was still a thriving Russian expatriate community there. The only problem was that one arrived in Moscow speaking with an outdated aristocratic accent and vocabulary.

The reason for the suspicion of Bukharin and his associates was obscure to Maclean at the time, and has remained obscure ever since; but it was partly that Stalin no longer believed in an early communist revolution throughout Europe, and was instead concentrating on the consolidation of communism within a single country – Russia. It was also partly down to Stalin's obsessive and paranoid fear of anyone rivalling his own dictatorial position. The "dictatorship of the proletariat" had become the dictatorship of one man.

Bukharin's trial took place in February 1938 in a courtroom which had previously been the ballroom of a clubhouse for Tsarist nobles. The trial was in progress for about nine hours a day for ten days, and Maclean, as the embassy's observer, sat in day after day at these protracted sessions. Bukharin – who had in his heyday been a close associate of Lenin's and one of the party's most serious philosophical thinkers – was charged with everything Stalin could throw at him: high treason, murder, spying and sabotage to name a few. With him in the dock were former heads of the Soviet government, of the NKVD and of the foreign ministry, as well as some lesser officials. Most of them – seeing how things were likely to go – promptly pleaded guilty. Others, after brief adjournments, when Maclean feared they might have been subjected to threats if not to actual torture, quickly changed their pleas to guilty, reeling off their confessions like well-learnt lessons.

Even the former head of the NKVD appeared as a broken man, declining to explain why he had changed his evidence, but leaving those who heard him in little doubt that he had been subjected to the same brutal methods which his organization had applied to so many others. Many of the prisoners seemed to be vying with each other to incriminate their fellow accused, and particularly to incriminate Bukharin. The picture that emerged from these bizarre proceedings was of some Trotskyist master-plot to conspire with foreigners in overthrowing the Stalinist regime, and of innumerable lesser plots to disrupt the country by means including the mass slaughtering of horses and the placing of powdered glass into consignments of butter destined for innocent Soviet workers.

The prosecutor was relentless in producing ever more unconvincing accusations. Predictably, the trial ended in death sentences for all the more important figures involved, including Bukharin. At one stage, Maclean was convinced he saw Stalin himself gazing down on the proceedings from a window high up in the courtroom.

The whole procedure had been a harrowing one for Maclean, as he had seen it unfold over the long days in court. Many years afterwards, he was to record that the nightmarish memory of the trial had haunted him for decades. His detailed, almost verbatim, account of some parts of the trial is a moving set-piece in his much later book *Eastern Approaches*, and there is no doubt that his immediate report of the proceedings to the Foreign Office was equally damning in its content and conclusions. But the most significant aspect of Maclean's reportage of the trial was his explanation of why the accused eventually acquiesced in the charges against them. The charges had been false, Maclean pointed out, but they knew they were going to die. If these people died protesting, they were weakening the Bolshevik revolution to which they had devoted so much of their lives. If they died acquiescing in those charges, though, then at least the Great Revolution continued on its way towards the glorious future in which they still believed, and their lives had been worthwhile. It was a conclusion that warned of the strength of revolutionary fervour in Russia. It was a wake-up call to dozy western opinion.

In his more normal relations with the Soviet foreign ministry, Maclean had further evidence of the hard-hearted and unscrupulous nature of the regime. There were a succession of "personal cases" affecting British and Russian subjects who – sometimes for romantic reasons – wished to enter or leave the Soviet Union. Despite his best efforts, Maclean could seldom get any but totally negative responses. Like his accounts of the Bukharin trial, all these events and activities were reported back to the Foreign Office in London. Two impressions were left on the senior diplomats in London: one was that the Soviet Union was indeed beyond redemption; the other was that Maclean himself was a more than usually percipient reporter.

But it is not for his reporting of the Bukharin trial, or for his handling of the "personal cases" and other routine problems of the embassy, that Maclean's time in Russia is remembered. It was his exploratory travels into Central Asia and the Caucasus (the first two of which preceded the Bukharin trial) that made his name. So difficult had it been for western diplomats to travel independently since Stalin's rise to power in the 1920s, that none tried to do so.

There was curiosity in London and Washington about the extent of control and the popularity – or otherwise – of the Bolshevik regime in these regions: Was there a degree of autonomy, or was everything controlled from Moscow? Were poverty and hunger resulting in seething discontent, or were the regions tranquil and subservient? Now Maclean opened a window – a difficult and heavy window – on a world both secret and fascinating. And few diplomats at any period and of any age would have had the determination and courage to do so. Nothing in his life, until his celebrated mission to Tito as Churchill's envoy in the Second World War, would resonate so clearly in the minds of his contemporaries and of his successors.

Turkestan and Central Asia were always Maclean's primary objectives, but since the Soviet authorities were never going to give permission to go there, he started exploring routes by which he might manage to reach them without having to produce any official passes.

Jumping on a train seemed the obvious way, but tickets and seats on trains to Central Asia required documentation not available to foreign diplomats. It was easier to get by train to Baku in the Caucasus, and from there Maclean reckoned he might be able to hitch a passage on a ship crossing the Caspian Sea and so arrive by a back route in Turkestan. All went well as far as Baku, but here he found it impossible to sail across the Caspian and so decided to press on to Lenkoran, a fishing village further south on the Caspian coast.

Here he was confronted with further evidence of the brutal nature of the Soviet regime.

Turko-Tartar peasants were being rounded up at bayonet point by the authorities and shipped compulsorily across the Caspian to Turkestan. The reason for this arbitrary action was at first obscure, but it was explained to him – by an unusually chatty and be-whiskered comrade – that it was part of a more general policy to uproot parts of the local populace and transplant them in other corners of the Soviet Union. The logic was that in this way, no single indigenous population would be sufficiently consolidated to cause trouble. Already Maclean was learning about practices of the Stalinist regime hitherto unrevealed.

Lenkoran proved no better a jumping-off point for Central Asia than Baku. All space on Trans-Caspian ships was taken up with the deportees. Deciding that he would at least try to see something of the hinterland, Maclean hired a horse from a local blacksmith and set off to ride into the hills in the direction of the Persian frontier. He had not gone far when an approaching Tartar cavalry patrol turned out to be intent on capturing him and he was arrested at gunpoint. Protestations that he was a diplomat and therefore immune to arrest fell on deaf ears: his captors had never heard of diplomats and said that if he went on protesting he would be shot on the spot. That action – Maclean declared – would have very unpleasant consequences for them. Not so unpleasant as it would for him, his captor responded with relish. Even when Maclean managed to unearth his Soviet diplomatic pass, it did not help – none of his captors could read a word of Russian. When they reached the nearest NKVD station, matters were not much better; the only paper in Maclean's possession possessing of any resonance for them was an official-looking document that was, in fact, a pass to the May Day parade in Red Square. The word "pass" was just decipherable by these illiterate Tartar militiamen, and Maclean offered to translate the rest to them. He did so "with such improvements as occurred to him", inventing as he went along solemn warnings about the impropriety of arresting diplomats, and ending by declaring the document to be signed by the People's Commissar for Foreign Affairs. A combination of bluff and steady nerves had once again carried the day.

Soon after this episode, a steamer arrived at Lenkoran which conveyed Maclean – sleeping on deck with "a Tartar horde" – back to Baku. From there he took a train inland to the capital of Georgia – Tbilisi. Maclean's arrival here was the start of his life-long affection for Georgia and the Georgians. The scenery was a romantic blend of mountains, ravines and fast-flowing rivers, and the inhabitants were among the best-looking people on earth – the men all dashing warriors and the women long-renowned as the jewels in the crown of most oriental harems.

Standing out looking ugly and ill at ease among the Georgians was a party official and former Soviet ambassador called Comrade Stark. When Maclean innocently mentioned to him the fall from grace of another party official, Stark visibly blanched as he envisaged his own fate being similarly in the balance. His fears soon proved to be all too well justified. The dread of purges stretched far beyond the confines of Moscow.

While in Tbilisi, Maclean was told of an Englishwoman who had been living there for more than twenty years. He sought her out, and found that she was the daughter of an Indian army colonel and had taken a job as a governess with a well-off Georgian family before the revolution; she had stayed with the family, teaching one generation of children after another, surviving the First World War, the upheavals of the Bolshevik coup, the Allied intervention and the reoccupation of Georgia by Stalin's forces. Her only sadness was that the family for whom she had been working for so long, and who used to own the large house where they still lived, were now reduced to living – with her and a sick child – in a single room. Maclean was to realize and record that even in Tbilisi the hardships, so well described later by Boris Pasternak in *Doctor Zhivago*, were proving as extreme as they were in Moscow and in other parts of the Soviet Union better known to the West.

Maclean's first foray into the unvisited parts of the Soviet Union resulted in a report which was widely circulated in London and which encouraged his masters, at the embassy and in London, to support him making further excursions into the unknown. The Caucasus had proved an ineffective springboard for Central Asia, so he started to think of alternative lines of approach. The Trans-Siberian railway seemed the most promising. He decided to take a ticket to the far end of the line, and then to jump train somewhere in Siberia and try to work his way south into Central Asia from there. Although he did not expect to be able to remain at large for long, it was worth a try. He broke his journey briefly at Sverdlovsk, a newly developed town on the far eastern side of the Ural Mountains previously known as Ekaterinburg and as the site of the 1918 murder of the last Tsar Nicholas II and his family. Although purporting to be a model of a new Soviet industrial city, in reality Maclean found that it was shoddily constructed and that the tarmacked roads soon petered out into the muddy tracks they had been before the revolution. Provincial industrialization was unimpressive.

Having managed to get a seat on a train going on to Novosibirsk, he found things little better there: the unsmiling "industrialized peasants" were poorly clothed, badly shod and living in dilapidated shacks. This was where he had decided to leave the Trans-Siberian line for good and head south towards Turkestan. After queuing for no less than ten hours, he managed to get the last ticket for Birsk – three hundred miles away, at the foot of the Altai Mountains and bordering Outer Mongolia. Not surprisingly, after so many hours hanging around the ticket office, he had identified the two NKVD officers who were following him. To his relief, they "escorted" him onwards, rather than intercepting him and putting him on a train back to Moscow.

He was always careful not to antagonize his minders unnecessarily; putting him on a train back to Moscow would have been a dire disappointment, but worse could have happened. In those days of ruthless purges of the tiresome elements in society, there was always the possibility of a shove through an open carriage door as the train went through a tunnel, and a subsequent story about a drunken diplomat having fallen onto a railway track in some remote area of Siberia or Central Asia. The masters to whom his minders were responsible were not a squeamish lot, and doubtless the minders themselves had participated in fairly unsavoury operations in their time. This was, after all, Stalin's Russia and not the Faubourg-St-Honoré, where Maclean had worked in Paris.

When he reached Birsk he found little to detain him there, and he was soon on his way further south. His companions on the train regaled him with horror stories about life further east in Siberia. They were not talking about the gulags, but about the collective farms where the machinery was broken and it was a struggle to support life at all; here, so far from Moscow, people spoke more freely about the realities of the Soviet system.

Even more disturbing was the fact that cattle trucks were attached to trains, which turned out to be full of Koreans being transplanted from the far eastern corner of Russia to Central Asia. The reason for this further enforced migration was that the Soviet authorities thought that Koreans might sympathize with the Japanese in the event of a further Russo-Japanese war. To secure a place on the next leg of the railway journey, Maclean managed – by a mixture of bravado and smooth-talking – to enlist the help of an NKVD officer who was anxious to avoid an embarrassing public showdown. By now the scenery was changing from the bleakness of the fringes of Siberia to the rolling steppes of Kazakhstan; the ugly concrete buildings and the ramshackle hovels being replaced by round felt tents – Kazakh yurts; in the distance the Tien Shan Mountains (known as the Mountains of Heaven) decorated the skyline. Maclean had achieved his objective: the long-sought heart of Central Asia.

Alma Ata, where Maclean disembarked from his train, was the first attractive place he had encountered on his travels: the apple orchards stretched to the mountain studded horizon; poplar trees lined the canals; melon plantations abounded; the whitewashed houses were well kept and, most unusual of all, the local population, both Russian and Kazakh, seemed reasonably contented with life. Even a Pole, with whom he spoke on the back of a truck going between the station and the town, and who had just emerged from an unexplained five-year spell in a labour camp, seemed optimistic about the future. But despite the more cheerful surroundings, the heavy hand of the Soviet regime extended here too. Finding accommodation in Alma Ata or even in the surrounding hills was entirely dependent on the help of his NKVD minders, who were as anxious as he was not to be reduced to sleeping on park benches or going all day without food.

In one friendly peasant house, Maclean was surprised and pleased to find that a child's story book contained proper fairy stories rather than Communist propaganda. Leaving the peasant house, he climbed further into the hills, and at 6,000 feet enjoyed enticing views over the distant steppes. This was certainly a more appealing side of Russian life than anything previously encountered. But he did not wish to linger: the whole objective was to reach Samarkand. The train was so crowded that the NKVD followers failed to get on board; this was just as well, since Samarkand was officially banned to foreigners in a way which Alma Ata had not been. The last stretch of the rail journey between – Tashkent and Samarkand – was spent crouched on this overcrowded train, "swaying dangerously on the little iron platform between two coaches".

Samarkand lived up to the high expectations which Maclean had for so long cherished. He described in detail in *Eastern Approaches* the Registan (the heart of the ancient city), the madrasas (Islamic schools), the mosques, the bazaars and the celebrated tomb of Tamerlane. He noted few Russians among the predominantly Uzbek population – the men in their robed national dress and the women heavily veiled. People seemed content to sit around gossiping and drinking tea. But even here, Maclean noticed that small children were being marched up and down while singing Soviet songs in adulation of Stalin. He thought it would not be long before the dead hand of communism had reached out even to this oasis of Islamic culture and tradition.

When he broke his homeward journey at Tashkent, Maclean found this city – many times the size of Samarkand – was an altogether more violent and dangerous place. He had been warned by an elderly female ticket collector on the train that he would find Tashkent full of hazards and temptations and when he tried to sleep on a park bench – for want of anywhere else – he was again warned about the risks of even dozing off in such a dangerous environment. As he made his way through the jostling crowds, avoiding camel caravans, people were continually offering to buy his overcoat or even his trousers. Had he been sleeping, doubtless he might have been stripped of these objects without the offer of payment. Bread shops were the scene of fights, and even getting onto a tramcar could not be achieved without a scuffle. It was little surprise to find that one of the most substantial buildings in the centre of the city was a prison, its crenellated parapets patrolled constantly by NKVD police. Tashkent was a reminder that the long arm of the Soviet Union stretched out to the major centres of population – if not to the smaller towns and fortresses – in as stark a form as in the Urals and Siberia.

This trip had taken longer than Maclean's permitted leave from the embassy, so he queued all night for a ticket for the train back to Moscow, wishing as he did so that he could have joined a caravan and pressed on to Bokhara or to Kashgar, over the Tien Shan mountains in China. This was an ambition for the future. For the present, as he trundled reluctantly across Russia, he observed that the train going the other way was made up of reinforced cattle trucks full of prisoners bound for Siberia.

In the event, after a long winter in Moscow (the time of the Bukharin trial), the Foreign Office in London, impressed with Maclean's report of his Turkestan foray, encouraged him to make another Central Asian expedition. And where they wanted him to go coincided with his own desires: Kashgar and Chinese Turkestan (the province known as Sinkiang) were causing anxiety both in the Foreign Office and in the India Office. The Russians had interfered in this region actively in Tsarist times, but following the revolution had withdrawn their Consul-General and his provocative Cossack escort, being too preoccupied with Allied intervention and other matters nearer home. Now however, in the 1930s, the Soviet government was reasserting its interest in this distant and remote region. Indian traders were being forced out by more aggressive Russian ones, and the British Consul was losing influence in contrast to his Soviet opposite number. The Great Game may have petered out with the advent of the First World War, but the India Office and the Viceroy in Delhi were still nervous about an increase of Russian military and commercial activity so close to the border of the British Raj. Both Percy Etherton, in the 1920s, and Peter Fleming, earlier in the 1930s, had reported their concerns. Someone with diplomatic standing and an interest in the region should be dispatched to make representations to the Chinese governor and restore British influence before it was too late. The obvious man for the job was that adventurous traveller and reporter Fitzroy Maclean.

Armed with a Chinese diplomatic visa, Maclean set out with many misgivings for Sinkiang. The Soviet authorities had, on this occasion, clearly been given instructions to allow him to pass without impediment to the Chinese frontier. But once across the Chinese frontier, things became more difficult. The roads were even rougher; no one seemed able to read his visa or understand his passport; the onward lorry to Urumqi (his immediate destination) had broken down; the local governor knew nothing of his visit and could not allow him to stay on Chinese soil; he had to retrace his steps, humiliated, angry and frustrated. Back in Alma Ata he visited the Chinese consulate and observed how the consul sought the permission of the Russian authorities even to refer the problem to his own superiors: Maclean could see for himself just how far Soviet influence dominated this frontier scene. The political purpose of his trip was more apparent than ever; the chances of achieving it less than ever. And indeed, when a message was eventually received from Urumqi, it was to the effect that Maclean was not welcome. The Soviet authorities simultaneously decided that he could not stay in Alma Ata (although in the previous year there had been no such ban); there was nothing to do but to comply with the orders to mount a train back to Moscow. Maclean resolved that on his next trip – whatever the Foreign Office might suggest – he would not give the Russian authorities prior notice of his intended route. Where there was not an officially declared presence there need not necessarily be an officially declared expulsion.

When he had managed to reach Samarkand the previous year, Maclean had determined to complete his Central Asian travels by next visiting Bokhara – the sacred city from which the light was reputed to shine not down from heaven but up towards heaven. He also aspired to cross the famous Oxus River – immortalized as the majestic wandering river in Matthew Arnold's poem 'Sorab and Rustum' – and enter Afghanistan. Strictly speaking, his official mandate to travel was probably limited to the confines of the Soviet Union, but to press on across the Oxus into Afghanistan could be justified as exploring an intriguing frontier and possibly opening up an alternative route back to Moscow. Most trips to Afghanistan and the Oxus by British diplomats or explorers started in India, but were unable to reach Bokhara because of difficulties in entering the Soviet Union. Maclean had the advantage of starting in Russia, and therefore only needed an exit visa (operative at any frontier point) and an entry visa to Afghanistan. Having obtained these, he started off, as before, by train through Orenburg, Tashkent and Samarkand, finally alighting at Kagan, from where he had hoped to take one of the occasional trains running along the former emir's state railway. Maclean was anxious to press on as fast as possible, before he attracted the notice of the local authorities, who were more likely to stop him than his assiduous NKVD minders – the latter being more intent on monitoring what he was up to than frustrating his travels. He was therefore disconcerted to find that he had missed the only train of the day and there was no bus service. Not daunted, he caught sight of a lorry loaded with bales of cotton and apparently moving off in the right direction. A short sprint enabled him to catch up with the lorry, and a flying jump landed him among the cotton bales. One of his NKVD followers managed to catch up and also leap on board. Unfortunately, the sight of two men jumping onto a moving truck encouraged other random pedestrians to do the same; soon the lorry driver realized he was giving a free lift to an intolerable number of hitch-hikers. He stopped and a police car with a uniformed officer caught up with them. Maclean – still accompanied by his NKVD fellow traveller – walked off into the trees beside the road; the police officer, preoccupied with the truck driver and disinclined to look for the mysterious foreign passenger, eventually drove off, leaving Maclean and his NKVD "escort" behind on the road.

Maclean decided that, after all these aborted efforts, there was only one sure way of reaching Bokhara, and that was to walk. He set off down the track through cotton fields punctuated with simple shacks, his reluctant escort following grumpily behind, reflecting that once away from the settlements life in the surroundings of Bokhara had probably changed little since Tamerlane's time in the fourteenth century. Occasionally, there were forks in the track and Maclean was worried that he might take the wrong one and spend the night wandering forlornly through the steppes. But usually, just in time, there would be a string of Bactrian camels whose drivers appeared more likely to be heading for Bokhara than for anywhere else, and so he followed in their path. As the light was fading and he was beginning to get seriously concerned, he noticed a slight brightness in the sky. It may not have been the celestial light shining up from Bokhara to heaven, but it was evidence of some settlement over the horizon. Topping a rise, he found laid out before him the walls, watchtowers, domes and minarets of this most sacred and elusive city.

What had made Bokhara so elusive in the Soviet era as well as in previous times was that it remained a stubbornly eastern enclave. Maclean wandered through the narrow alleys, explored the bazaars and stood awestruck at the foot of the Tower of Death from which prisoners had been thrown by the emirs. But he noted that here, unlike in Tashkent or even Samarkand, the Stalinist regime had made no attempt to modernize or Sovietize the place. The ugly offices, police stations and blocks of flats for party officials that dominated so much of Russia were absent from Bokhara. The policy had been that since the place was beyond conversion to the drab Stalinist model, it should be neglected and left to wither away in its own Islamic ruins. Unlike most of the provincial towns of the Soviet Union, Bokhara had not grown in size; on the contrary, it was half the size it had been before the revolution. Perhaps the saddest evidence of this was in the bazaars, where previously colourful crowds had jostled around the piles of oriental carpets, sipping Turkish coffee and exchanging gossip; now, Maclean noted, the only flash of colour was provided by the striped robes of the inhabitants, and even these were manufactured by "collectivized seamstresses working under the auspices of some State combine".

Maclean, who was already well versed in the history of European visitors to Bokhara, said he could have spent days or weeks happily exploring the corners of this faded city and retracing the links with his predecessors. But he was still intent on crossing the Oxus and penetrating into Afghanistan, and the longer he stayed in one place the greater the chances of the local authorities and putting him on the next train (or series of trains) back to Moscow. His two new, but restless NKVD minders, bored by the ancient city and exhausted by the rigours of nights spent in the open, were only too ready to aid his departure.

The most useful aid they could supply was finding places on the succession of trains from a nearby station to Termez, the point on the Oxus River at which Maclean planned to cross over into Afghanistan. Their efforts were redoubled when Maclean told them if places were not available on the train, he would simply walk back to Bokhara. One experience of trying to keep up with him, in their dark suits and their uncomfortable cheap yellow shoes, had been more than enough for these reluctant escorts. Places were found on the train, but only in the "hard" class. Stretched out on a wooden bench, Maclean found sleep almost impossible, not so much because of the hardness of the bench as because of the unstoppable flow of questions and conversation from his fellow travellers from Tajikistan. To make matters worse, they were all moved from their hard benches to wooden racks above to make room for a vodka seller, and soon his product had further enlivened the whole cabin. Sleep was not an option.

Once arrived at Termez, Maclean reversed his usual practice: instead of trying to avoid being identified by the local authorities, he went out of his way to introduce himself. He was confident they would want to move him on – out of the Soviet Union and into Afghanistan – just as quickly as they could arrange it. At first all seemed to go well. The officer commanding the local militia sent him speedily on his way by car to the frontier post. Here, apart from a few garrison buildings, the banks of the river were enveloped in a broad band of ten-foot-high reeds, said to harbour an alarming amount of predatory wildlife, including tigers. But, as so often, things were more complicated than anticipated. There were only three paddle boats in which the river – a mile wide at this point – could be crossed, and all of them were broken down. While he was waiting for a motor to be transferred to the least seriously broken of the craft, Maclean talked to the captain of the frontier guard about his gun dog and his enthusiasm for shooting. It transpired that the captain's favourite species of game were "Trotskyists and Diversionists", although he also took his gun out in search of pheasants, wild boar and tigers. But it was the Trotskyists – either trying to enter or leave his country illegally – who provided the most frequent reason for shooting trips. When finally the paddle steamer was ready to make the crossing, it took half an hour of dodging sandbanks to reach the far shore. While the Soviet shore had been punctuated by watchtowers, the Afghan shore appeared deeply forested and deserted – a forbidding landing place. But as they approached the shore, a few armed Afghans appeared from nowhere. The Soviet paddle steamer dumped Maclean unceremoniously in the mud and, having re-counted their crew to make sure there were no defectors, pushed off as if from an infected land.

His new hosts could make nothing of Maclean's passport or documentation and had no common language with him. But they were not unfriendly. After orientation towards Mecca and a break for prayers, he managed to make them understand that he wanted to move on to the town of Mazar-i-Sharif (the first staging point on the way to Kabul). After a night spent on the banks of the Oxus, two horses were found and he set off with an Afghan guide to ride first through the tiger-infested rushes and jungle, and then over a barren plain. Once they were briefly apprehended in a local fort which Maclean feared might be a brigand stronghold; it turned out not to be, and they were soon allowed to go on their way. This was bleak terrain, campaigned over by invaders from Philip of Macedon to Genghis Khan, and Maclean was relieved when after a sixty-mile ride, his lame but stout-hearted horse reached Mazar long after nightfall. At the only inn, no one spoke any of the multiple European languages with which he was familiar, but he managed to encounter a Russian couple who were, he fancied, much more forthcoming than they would have been when under the constraints of living in the Soviet Union. There was a lone motor truck in the town, but he was not surprised to hear it was broken. Worse was the news that there was currently a cholera outbreak in this part of Afghanistan and that he would be unlikely to be allowed to leave Mazar.

However, a friendly local doctor agreed with Maclean that he and his driver could be certified as already having had cholera (and therefore immune) and could leave in the hastily repaired truck. So hastily had the truck been repaired that no sooner were they well beyond the reach of mechanical help than a leak appeared in the petrol tank. This was repaired with the help of local villagers by stuffing the hole with a mixture of cotton rags and raisins ground up together into a rough paste. As soon as they were off again, further troubles developed with the steering gear. This time it was a collar stud that replaced the broken part. Thus, temporarily patched up, and with a good deal of the luck that seemed to attend Maclean on his adventures, he and his truck driver negotiated the precipitous hairpin bends of the foothills of the Hindu Kush and, at three in the morning, reached the village of Doaba, where he had arranged to meet the British minister from the legation at Kabul.

At an Afghan government rest house, Maclean managed to enjoy a good night's sleep and although the plumbing was not working, was able to rinse himself in buckets of water before the legation car arrived to take him to meet the minister. The discomforts and perils of the outward journey were over. The minister's wife turned out to be "a fellow clanswoman" whom he had known since childhood; they travelled on together to Kabul, where a series of excellent meals and a great deal of useful information were very welcome. But his plans to return via the same route were upended by the fact that the Soviet embassy declared entry across the Oxus now totally forbidden owing to the cholera outbreak. Maclean would have to return by a very roundabout route – via India, Iraq, Iran and the Caucasus. After many vicissitudes, Maclean arrived at the bridge at Djulfa over the Aras river between Iran and the Soviet Union. The Iranian frontier guards saw him onto the bridge and locked the gate at their end; but the Soviet guards at the far end had no intention of opening their gate and were unresponsive to his shouted appeals. Meanwhile, the Iranians said they could not allow him to return to Persia; he was suspended between countries over the rapidly flowing Aras. (The author was stuck on the same bridge twenty years later when trying to make the journey in the reverse direction: frontier bureaucracy changes little.) After an alarmingly long wait, a Soviet staff car arrived at the bridge and Maclean was allowed across. He was back in the USSR, but his troubles were not at an end yet. He managed to reach Yerevan, collecting on the way the habitual NKVD minders, and was impressed by the way that the Armenians[22], even under Soviet rule, had managed to preserve something of their traditional buildings and prosperity. From Yerevan he went on to Batumi on the Black Sea, where he found the population upset by the fact that their most celebrated product – mandarins – were nowhere for sale. The entire crop had been sent under order to Moscow and the inhabitants felt they were being penalized for last year's crop, which had, due to inclement weather failed to fulfil the quota expected in Moscow's master plan.

Tbilisi, the Georgian capital which he had enjoyed so much the previous year, was his next stop. He found the place more regimented than on his previous visit. When he accidentally stumbled into a prohibited zone, he was arrested at gunpoint and obliged to hold his hands up for a long period, until a senior officer who, unlike his subordinates, understood Maclean's papers and the concept of diplomatic immunity, allowed him to continue on his way. That way was in fact on the back of a truck, through snow and bitter cold, over the Georgian military highway (built by the Tsars) to the rail head where he could finally entrain for Moscow. As Maclean slipped back into the comfortable routine of diplomatic life in the capital, he realized

---

22 Armenians have a reputation for looking after themselves in all circumstances. When Khrushchev was asked by a cheeky western journalist at a press conference in Moscow in 1959 what he would do if Mikoyan (his deputy) defected while on a visit to America, he replied "I don't know what I'd do. But Mikoyan will be all right. He's an Armenian. He'll become President of the USA!"

he had observed a great deal about how Stalin's regime was working in the more remote corners of his vast empire. He was to tell his conclusions first to his ambassador and the Foreign Office in London and later – through his writings – to the world at large.

Many others before Fitzroy Maclean had exposed sinister aspects of the Soviet Union: the internationally predatory nature of the Bolsheviks, the imperial ambitions towards Sinkiang, the urge to stir up anarchy and confusion in western monarchies and republics, and the ruthlessness of the regime towards its opponents. What Maclean had uniquely achieved in his coverage of the Bukharin trial was to reveal Stalinism – the latest twist in the revolutionary saga that began with Lenin – as pernicious in other ways too. In the ruthless purging from the ranks of committed Bolsheviks any supporters who got even minutely out of line, or who had grown in strength to represent a threat to Stalin himself, the regime revealed its true colours. So, too, in the exploitation of those whose philosophical commitment to the regime inhibited them from rocking the boat even in their own defence, did Soviet justice demonstrate to Maclean a little of the new nation's blind zeal and fervour.

And Maclean told the world. It is easy in the post-Cold-War era to forget just how little knowledge of the Soviet Union, and how little criticism of it, was current among intellectual circles in Britain and the West in the 1930s. As Orlando Figes has pointed out in his memorable history of Russian culture – *Natasha's Dance* – such renowned and widely read authors as H.G. Wells, George Bernard Shaw, Thomas Mann and André Gide wrote about the new communist society with an enthusiasm almost entirely unclouded by reservations. Vladimir Nabokov, himself a refugee from Soviet Russia, found that at Trinity College, Cambridge, pipe-smoking, naive socialists viewed Russia's past history as uniformly reprehensible and her present Bolshevik regime as wholly commendable. This was the distorted moral climate into which Maclean's reporting was injected.

The diplomat's tenacious and adventurous efforts to penetrate Central Asia and the Caucasus, lands closed to all western observers since the revolution, revealed aspects of the regime which would colour western thinking about communism for many years to come. No one had previously known of the mass forced migrations of Turks and Tartars out of the Caucasus, and of sections of the far eastern population out of eastern Russia. No one had previously seen for himself the shoddy and temporary nature of much of the Soviet "development" of provincial Russia. No one had witnessed towns too Islamic to fit into the Soviet pattern being allowed to decay to the point of ruin and annihilation. No one had seen the effects of the dead hand of Soviet central planning on the collective farms and indigenous agricultural production of distant corners of the Soviet Union, until Maclean witnessed it himself or heard about it first-hand from encounters with travelling companions who would never have dared speak so frankly in the ultra-oppressive atmosphere of Moscow.

In 1958, I found myself, as the ambassador's private secretary, faced with the intriguing task of introducing Maclean to Khrushchev at an embassy reception. In the two decades since his travels, Maclean had become an MP and an acclaimed war hero on account of his mission to Tito's guerillas in German-occupied Yugoslavia. In the USSR, meanwhile, it was a moot point as to how people viewed him. In some circles, he was the writer who had described the country in a distinctive, but unflattering way. In others, he had been a fearless ally against Germany in World War Two, one of the few foreigners to have been awarded the prestigious military Order of Kutuzov.

I was equally unsure about Khrushchev's possible reactions to Maclean. The Soviet leader, had, of course, been highly critical of Stalin himself, so perhaps he might view Maclean as an ally. Then again, perhaps the diminutive Ukrainian peasant might feel belittled by the towering, imposing Scot, and become more aggressive than usual.

As the two men shook hands, Maclean told Krushchev that he had been writing about 19th-century travellers in Central Asia (a reference to his newly published book *A Person from England*); Khrushchev looked at him quizzically: "So you're an historian now!" he murmured and moved on. Maclean had certainly been many things, but being an interpreter – a whistle-blower – on the Soviet Union to the rest of the world in the 1930s had surely been one of his most significant contributions. As the *Spectator* said of him when reviewing *Eastern Approaches*, "seldom has such talent been brought to the service of adventure".

A PERSONAL EPILOGUE

Fitzroy Maclean was serving at the British embassy in Moscow and gathering material for his *Eastern Approaches* just twenty years after the Russian Revolution. When I was the junior diplomat in the political section (the chancery) of the embassy, it was forty years. The event was celebrated with much marching and trumpeting in Red Square, and I watched in awe as the Presidium of the Soviet Union stood in a carefully selected line above the embalmed bodies of Lenin and Stalin. Even then I felt strong links to some of the adventurers and writers who had confronted the early Bolshevik regime, and, as time went by, was to find links to more and more of the protagonists in this book.

Stephen Graham had been an author much cherished by the publishers for whom I worked when I first left school and before going to university. I was flattered at being made the editorial contact with him, and used to visit him in his book-lined and dishevelled house in Soho. When our editorial conversations were over, he would reminisce about the Russia which he knew so well and which I had never yet visited, and, to speed our conversations on their way, he would reach for a volume of Dostoevsky from the shelves above him and reveal behind it a bottle of slivovitz, the deadly Serbian plum brandy. He was, like Peter Fleming and for that matter, like myself, in love with Russia as well as a totally committed antagonist of the Soviet Union.

When, after Cambridge, my first appointment in the diplomatic service was to Moscow, the Air Attaché at the embassy was a certain Air Commodore Donald MacDonell, DFC. He was a former Battle of Britain fighter pilot and the hereditary chief of the Clan

Glengarry. Rather more surprisingly, it transpired that he been born at Baku on the Caspian coast of the Soviet Union, where his father, Ranald MacDonell, had been running a network of British agents and attempting to prevent the Bolshevik takeover of the Caucasus. I remember hearing tales of his father's exploits, and wish in retrospect that I had paid more attention, because his father was to become a major player in the events which many years later would attract my researches.

I had read *Eastern Approaches* before I even arrived in Moscow and was fascinated to meet its author when he returned to the city for the first time in twenty years – in 1958. We found that, quite apart from the job that I was then doing and he had done before, Sir Fitzroy Maclean and I had much common background: we both came from the western Highlands of Scotland, and had both seen active service with Scottish regiments in conditions of guerilla warfare (in his case in the Second World War in Yugoslavia; in mine on national service in Malaya). We both spoke Russian and were mildly obsessed with Russian literature and with the stories of the Great Game. It was not altogether surprising that we travelled together in parts of Central Asia and that I learnt much from the experience. He was to remain a good friend until the end of his life, inviting me regularly to Strachur in Argyllshire, and accepting invitations from me to embassies abroad.

Robert Bruce Lockhart I knew at one remove. His nephew, Jock Bruce Lockhart, was playing a deeply significant and sometimes controversial role at the embassy in Tehran during the latter years of the last Shah, and at that stage I was the desk officer for Iran (or Persia, as we still called it) in the Foreign Office. Jock would treat my desk and my room as his anchorage in London, and spent many hours sitting on my desk telling me stories not only of Persia but of Russia in his uncle's day. He had inherited his uncle's flair for sailing close to the winds of danger, and for winning the confidence of those who ruled the country where he worked. It all seemed one intriguing story of the struggle for power and influence.

I met Peter Fleming more than once, but he was someone I did not really know. I was better acquainted with his younger brother Ian

– the creator of James Bond – whose step-daughter married one of my colleagues in the Moscow embassy shortly after the time I was there in the late 1950s. I ushered at the wedding, at St Margaret's Westminster, and afterwards met Ian Fleming on a number of occasions, sometimes at his house in Victoria Square. He was forever asking questions about life at the embassy in Moscow. Did bachelors – as I then was – manage to have any Russian girlfriends? Were Russian girls always trying to trap or embarrass us? Did the KGB try to entice NATO diplomats into black-market deals with a view to blackmailing them? Were they especially suspicious of those who spoke Russian? Did they use hidden microphones in our houses and flats to learn about our individual vulnerabilities? How did we throw off KGB minders if we needed to? The questions were unending, and the answers – however discreet – often seemed to be reflected in some aspect of the next Bond novel. It made one feel that the line between reality and fiction was not always clear.

When it came to the English or Scottish governesses who had lived and worked with Russian aristocratic families before, during and after the revolution, they had of course long departed the scene – some for that great nursery in the sky – long before I arrived in Moscow. St Petersburg, or Chekhovian country houses, would in any case have been their more natural habitat than busy, grubby, commercial Moscow. But there were survivors, some of whom still occasionally visited Russia and others who remained in contact with the Russian communities in Paris or London, communities often centred round the Orthodox churches in the Rue Daru or in Kensington. From these survivors one heard stories – both elaborations of old ones (as so engagingly recounted in Harvey Pitcher's *When Miss Emmie Was in Russia* or in Eugenie Fraser's *The House by the Dvina*) and sometimes exciting ones completely new to me. Their experiences not only reinforced one's admiration for these women, but also confirmed one's impression that they had played a not-insignificant part in exposing the iniquities of Bolshevism.

But the book that did most to form my vision of Russia during the revolutionary years – more even than Bruce Lockhart's memoirs or

Fitzroy Maclean's *Eastern Approaches* – was Boris Pasternak's *Doctor Zhivago*. I read the book in 1958, when it first came out in English translation and before any Russian edition was available. This was while I was serving at the British embassy in Moscow and I managed to meet Pasternak on several occasions, always being careful to do so unobserved by the authorities.

Having read the book – it was long before the film came out – I could not understand why Khrushchev and the Soviet leadership were to take so strongly against it, to expel Pasternak from the Soviet union of writers and deny him his Nobel prize. Zhivago himself is depicted as not initially being against the revolution: he describes its outbreak as "like a breath that has been held too long… everyone was revived, reborn, changed, transformed… socialism is the sea, and all these separate streams, these private individual revolutions are flowing into it – the sea of life".

When the revolution moves into its more Bolshevik and restless stages, Zhivago does admittedly become more critical towards some aspects of the scene. He says "those who inspired the revolution aren't at home in anything except change and turmoil". As the civil war against the White forces gets underway, he becomes even more critical: he feels that "people imagined it was out of date to follow their own moral sense, that they must all sing the same tune in chorus". But in describing the disillusionment in the years immediately following the Leninist coup, Pasternak was not describing Khrushchev's Russia of the 1950s; Khrushchev had himself already denounced the worst excesses of Stalinism, and no longer was the country in the turmoil and terror of the Zhivago years.

What Pasternak did supremely well was to portray sympathetically the confusion and the deprivations endured by ordinary professional Russians, by people like Zhivago – himself a medical doctor – who welcomed long-overdue social changes to an autocratic, corrupt and outdated system of government, but who found the ensuing upheaval difficult to survive.

By the 1950s Russia had come through these dark times; starvation and terror were things of the past, the railways were running without strikes, the Soviet 'Sputnik' was in space (before any American spacecraft) and Russia was again a superpower. Pasternak's book widened and deepened the understanding of an outsider like me, as well as the understanding of a younger generation of Russians (when the book became available to them) who had not lived through these events, of the phenomenal endurance and resilience of the ordinary Russian man in the street. It increased one's respect for Russia and Russians. In my case, it also increased my respect for the British adventurers who had confronted and exposed this confused and bewildering scene. They had suffered what Zhivago suffered: the empty shops, the failed communications, the permanent doubts about who could and who could not be trusted. They had not only survived, but also opened a window on Russia to the outside world, as surely as Peter the Great opened a window on the outside world to Russia when founding St Petersburg.

Even before reaching Russia, I had become familiar with some aspects of the pre-revolutionary scene there, and intrigued by the background against which the characters in this book had been operating. To learn the language, I had been sent by the Foreign Office to live with a White Russian émigré family in Paris for several months; the logic being that living with a family in the Soviet Union would have rendered me vulnerable to compromise. The family chosen for me were Georgian aristocrats: the father – Prince Amilakvari – had escaped from his estates in the Caucasus in 1918 and had come with his family to Paris. Having been unable to take any money or valuables out with him, he was reduced to becoming first a taxi driver, and then a private soldier in the Foreign Legion. Being the natural leader that he was, however, Amilakvari had risen to the rank of brigadier and by the time of the Second World War was commanding the Legion at the battle of El Alamein.

He was killed while heroically leading his troops into battle, and became a legend in the Legion. His family lived in a small flat behind Les Invalides and it consisted of a beautiful young princess, who was his daughter, and her aunt – also a princess – who chaperoned her all too assiduously. Life was entirely lived among the émigré community;

elderly Orthodox priests dropped in for tea at all hours of day and night and gathered round the samovar; not only their extended family but also all their friends appeared to be Russian. I had formal lessons in the mornings, but in the afternoons either repaired to the Bois de Boulogne to read *Anna Karenina* on my own, or visited an ancient great aunt – one Princess Gorchekova – who lived in one room above the projection room of a cinema, and read aloud to her (very loudly to combat both the noise of the film's soundtrack and the great aunt's deafness). The plan was that she should correct my pronunciation, but in fact she interrupted only to comment on the families and places mentioned in Tolstoy's story: "Never go there," she would say, "the food's always cold and the daughters are very plain." Predictably, I ended my stay in Paris feeling familiar with the practices and manners of pre-revolutionary landowners, and having the accent – and indeed the vocabulary – of an upper-class Georgian. I might have been living out a small part in a Chekhov play. I was captivated by the *fin de siècle* environment, and enchanted by what I had learnt of the Russian way of life. But when I reached the Soviet Union after my stay in Paris, it was hardly surprising that the Comrades smiled – or scoffed, depending on their temperament – at the way I spoke to them.

One of the factors which provided a link between me and some of the people depicted in this book was that, although both I and most of them were very junior while in Russia, we had intermittent encounters with a Russian leadership which was remarkably accessible. Bruce Lockhart and others met Lenin and Trotsky frequently for substantive conversations in 1917. In 1957 Khrushchev, who as First Secretary of the Communist Party was in the process of establishing himself as the sole and dominant leader of Russia, would summon my ambassador frequently – often in the middle of the night – and harangue him in the Kremlin about the provocative nature of the British presence in West Berlin. On these occasions, the ambassador would take me with him, as I was his diplomatic private secretary and would be expected to take a record of the meetings. So Khrushchev knew who I was and would often include me in his parties at the Kremlin and – if he could not find my ambassador – would sometimes say substantive things to me, as Trotsky did to Lockhart. On one occasion, for instance, he told me that our NATO proposals for verifying disarmament agreements by some overflying of each other's countries was equivalent to "not being content to go into my sitting room and my dining room, but pushing into my bedroom. I don't know you well enough, so keep out… b***** off!" In other words, he was expressing a fairly clear rejection of our proposals. He would usually couch his remarks in deliberately offensive language – the equivalent of hammering with his shoe on the table (as he famously did at one UN summit in 1960). He was always more polite to my dog – a large wolfhound who, like me, lived in the embassy – than he was to me or even to my ambassador. He wanted to shock, and I suppose knew that he could not shock a wolfhound. But one got to know the man, and just as Lloyd George had pressed Lockhart for his opinion of Lenin, so Harold Macmillan pressed us to tell him whether Khrushchev was another Stalin or someone with whom he could do business.

I had a stronger link with Anastas Mikoyan who, as Chairman of the Presidium of the Supreme Soviet, was effectively Khrushchev's deputy. Mikoyan had been the only one of the Soviet commissars in Baku in 1918 who, unlike the other twenty-six, had not been shot, allegedly on the orders of Teague-Jones. How he survived had always been a mystery; but Mikoyan was a natural survivor who also lasted through Stalin's purges in the 1930s. The tough Armenian was known to Ranald MacDonell and Teague-Jones in Baku in 1918, and to me in Moscow in 1958; they had found him elusive; I found him unexpectedly communicative. On one occasion, when I was making a reconnaissance for Prime Minister Macmillan's visit to Russia in 1959, Mikoyan took me on a personally conducted tour of the Winter Palace in Leningrad. He led me into a little unfurnished room and told me, "This, my boy, is where the Russian Revolution happened". It was the room in which, after storming the palace, the Bolsheviks had arrested Kerensky's ministers, and the young Mikoyan had himself been present.

On another occasion he invited me to lunch at his dacha outside

Moscow, where the vodka flowed as freely as in Stalin's days, and where Khrushchev teased Mikoyan for being "a typical Armenian, who always knows how to look after himself". The cast of characters who ruled Russia had changed in forty years, but Mikoyan uniquely had not.

Another aspect of the Russian experience which I shared with many of the protagonists in this book was a penchant for travelling around the vast country by train. Trains are somehow at the heart of Russia; they play an important role in much of Russian literature, from *Anna Karenina* to *Doctor Zhivago*. They are the best way of seeing the country; I travelled from Moscow to Samarkand by rail across the steppes; on other journeys I spent days on end looking out of the train windows at pine forests, and became more aware of the scale of the country than I would have done by any amount of flying. And trains are sociable in Russia. Every coach has its samovar; when not drinking tea or looking at the unchanging scenery, one plays chess with strangers. Everyone wears pyjamas – by day as well as by night – on the transcontinental routes, which gives one a sense of being in the uniform of a long-distance traveller, especially at the brief station halts. Normally taciturn Russians become conversational in carriages, restaurant cars and corridors. Many of the protagonists in this book spent much time on overcrowded trains, if only travelling between St Petersburg and Moscow in their different disguises and with their different passports. I was never in disguise, but I nonetheless managed to get to know strangers better on long-distance trains than in any other way.

Yet another link with the British heroes of the revolutionary years was my familiarity with the mansion overlooking the Kremlin (from directly across the Moskva River) which is now the British embassy. It was visited and described by Lockhart and others as a house where they dined and where memorable events took place. Once – all too memorably – a Russian dinner guest took a telephone call and, learning that his girlfriend had rejected him, spun his revolver and shot himself dead: a classic case of Russian roulette. No such tragedies took place in my day, but my wolfhound once held back organized demonstrators trying to climb over the embassy gates and was pelted with bottles for his pains. We well knew that Khrushchev wanted us out of the house, which was both the chancery and the ambassador's residence, and where I as private secretary lived in the mews, since he was irritated by seeing the Union Jack flying opposite the Kremlin every time he looked out of his office window.

Game hunting – elk, bears, wolves – was also an ongoing activity. Frederick Bailey was not the only British adventurer who enjoyed hunting and shooting when his other duties allowed him to do so. Such pre-revolutionary sports were still practised in my time in Russia, and the gamekeepers and ghillies who accompanied us on our shooting trips from the diplomatic dacha on the Volga (some hundred miles north of Moscow) had often escorted sportsmen and aristocrats bent on the same activities before the Bolsheviks came to power. When I was there, anyone over the age of fifty could well remember those pre-revolutionary days. Elk and bears were still to be found in the forests, and our ghillies would tell us how as impoverished young men they longed to acquire a valuable bear skin. Their descriptions of how they did this were along the same lines as those (recounted in earlier chapters) told to English-speaking governesses. They could not afford rifles, so they would set off into the forests in winter armed only with a spear or lance, looking look for traces of dripping water under fallen trees, which were evidence of a hibernating bear. They would then prod beneath the tree with their spear and, if they had poked a sleeping bear, it would emerge, furious and half-blind with gummed-up eyes. It would rear up and attempt to claw off the head of whoever had disturbed it, and this was the one and only chance the ghillie had to kill the beast with his lance. If he missed or faltered, he would lose his head. The risks, our companions told us, were well worth taking for the sake of a bear skin that could be sold to a landowner as a rug for his sledge on winter expeditions. The Scottish governess – Heather – had been shocked by these tales, and so was I. But my shock and my credulity were enhanced, on one occasion, when my ghillie removed his fur hat (not a luxury, but a winter necessity) and showed me a deep scar across the top of his head. "A narrow escape," as he put it.

Wolf-hunting was an even more frequent pastime. In this case again little had changed in forty years: the hunter, assuming he could afford a rifle, would go in a troika (a sledge drawn by three horses) round the edge of a forest dragging behind the sledge an unfortunate piglet in a sack, which would squeal as it bumped over the snow. The squeals would arouse the curiosity of the wolves, who sensed an animal in distress as likely prey. As soon as the wolves had emerged sufficiently far from the cover of the woods to be silhouetted against the snow, the hunter would shoot at them from his moving sledge. This was no easy feat, of course: failure to shoot the wolf or wolves could result in them attacking the occupants of the sledge as well as the piglet. The only time I was taken on such a troika trip, I was deeply upset by the outcome. All went well to start with, except that, from the beginning my concern for the piglet was ignored. The wolves duly emerged from the forest along the Volga bank; my host missed his shot at the leading wolf, which continued bounding over the snow towards our troika. Just when the wolf was near enough to constitute a real danger to all of us on board the sledge, my host leant over the back of the sledge and cut the rope joining it to the piglet's bag. The wolf stopped its pursuit and tore open the bag, devouring the squealing piglet. As we sped away, I saw that the snow was stained with blood over a large area, and I never accepted an invitation to go on such a trip again. (In one of the Flashman novels, a similar incident occurs, except that it is not a piglet but a woman passenger on the sledge who is sacrificed to placate the pursuing wolves.)

Life had not changed much in rural Russia between the 1920s and the 1950s. The sporting activities that had diverted the young adventurers who found themselves in Russia at the time of the revolution still diverted busy Cold War diplomats forty years later. And when more exciting pursuits did not beckon, we still wandered in the forests in search of mushrooms as Russians have always done, like characters out of a Turgenev novel.

But the experiences which above all helped me to understand and sympathize with my predecessors were our endeavours to throw off the stifling attentions of our KGB minders. Most NATO diplomats were closely followed by the KGB during the height of the Cold War. Russian speakers were particularly closely shadowed, which suggested the Soviet security services were more interested in whom one talked to than in what one saw; they did not so much fear that we might photograph a bridge or a military vehicle as that we might hear outpourings of disaffection from disgruntled Chechens or Georgians, Ukrainians or Latvians. As innocent diplomats, we were, for our part, not up to anything nearly as provocative or dubious as some of the secret agents whose activities have been recounted in previous chapters. But there were nonetheless moments when one did not want to arrive at one's destination with an unwelcome tail of KGB snoopers. I remember for instance calling on Boris Pasternak at his home in the country to discuss (together with a Swedish colleague) how he would react to the award of a Nobel Prize for Literature (*Doctor Zhivago* had been published in English only the previous year). The last thing we wanted was to embarrass or endanger him by exposing him to accusations of improper contact with western embassies.

On occasions such as that, it seemed both legitimate and sensible to shake off our minders. There were various recognized ways of doing this. One was to get on a train on the Moscow metro and then, just as the doors were closing, to step off, leaving one's followers to move away on the train. A more controversial way of shaking off a following KGB car was to set out with four people in a diplomatic car and drive out of town. Soon the KGB following car (always comprising three officers and a radio aerial) would be identified; the diplomatic car would stop and all four passengers would walk off in separate directions, leaving the ignition key in the car. One of the four would soon find that he was not followed, and he would then return to his car and drive it to a pre-arranged rendezvous where the four diplomats would now meet up with their car. The three KGB officers, however, would now be without theirs, and the diplomats would then drive off unobserved to their destination. Similarly, diplomats would sometimes leave an unwanted suitcase on a train, while ostensibly stepping onto a station platform only to stretch their legs, allowing themselves to be left behind while their followers travelled on with the suitcase; the town could then be explored unhampered. (The author did this in Yerevan, being possibly the first westerner into the Armenian capital since the Second World War.) Such clearly devised plans were not unnaturally viewed with suspicion by the Soviet authorities and resulted in closer and more intrusive surveillance; they were not to be recommended except *in extremis*. But the mere fact that certain diplomatic colleagues – usually from other embassies – were employing such methods made me feel some understanding for Bailey when I learned that he'd shaken off his Cheka followers by slipping into a house by one door and emerging from another in a different set of clothing.

Moura Budberg (Lockhart's sometime mistress) told me towards the end of her life that she had on occasion thrown off Cheka minders by a method still practised by at least one young and attractive female NATO diplomat forty years later. She would stop on her walks through Moscow and look in shop windows until she had identified her follower. She would then approach a uniformed policeman and, fluttering her eyelids flirtatiously, say in her best Russian, "Please, Mr Policeman, I'm frightened because there's a nasty man stalking me." As the policeman stopped and questioned the Cheka agent, and the latter, with much whispering and furtive showing of cards, sought to establish his identity and mission, the lady in question would quietly slip away into the crowd – no longer followed.

For all these reasons – my familiarity with the places, the people, the way of life in Russia, the hazards and embarrassments of being under surveillance – I hope to have interpreted the exploits of a previous generation of British adventurers with some measure of understanding.

SELECT BIBLIOGRAPHY

BAILEY, Lt. Col. F.M. *Mission to Tashkent* (London: Oxford University Press, 1946)

BAILEY, Geoffrey. *The Conspirators* (London: 1961)

BARING, Maurice. *The Puppet Show of Memory* (London: W. Heinemann, 1922)

What I Saw in Russia (London: W. Heinemann, 1927)

BERBEROVA, Nina. *Moura: The Dangerous Life of the Baroness Budberg* (New York: NYRB Classics, 2005)

BROWN, Archie. *The Rise and Fall of Communism* (London: Harper Collins, 2009)

BUCHAN, John. *Mr Standfast* (London: Hodder & Stoughton, 1919)

Huntingtower (London: Hodder & Stoughton, 1922)

Memory Hold-the-Door (London: Hodder & Stoughton, 1940)

CHAMBERS, Roland. *The Last Englishman: The Double Life of Arthur Ransome* (London: Faber & Faber, 2009)

CALDER, Robert. *Willie: The Life of W. Somerset Maugham* (London: Heinemann, 1989)

W. Somerset Maugham and the Quest for Freedom (London: Heinemann, 1972)

CRANKSHAW, Edward. *The Shadow of the Winter Palace: Russia's Drift to Revolution* (New York: Viking, 1976)

DAWE, Rosamund. *A Memoir of an English Governess in Russia, 1914–1917* (Chichester: Bishop Otter College, 1973)

DUKES, P. *Red Dusk and the Morrow: Adventures and Investigations in Red Russia* (New York: Doubleday, Page & Co., 1922)

EAGER, M. *Six Years at the Russian Court* (London: Hurst and Blackett, 1906)

ETHERTON, Lt. Col. P.T. *In the Heart of Asia* (London: Constable & Co., 1925)

FIGES, Orlando. *A People's Tragedy: Russian Revolution, 1891–1924* (London: Jonathan Cape, 1996)

Natasha's Dance: A Cultural History of Russia (London: Allen Lane, 2002)

Revolutionary Russia 1891–1991 (London: Pelican, 2014)

FLEMING, Peter. *News from Tartary* (London: Jonathan Cape, 1936)

FRASER, Eugenie. *The House by the Dvina: A Russian Childhood* (Edinburgh: Mainstream Publishing Co., 1984)

GATHORNE-HARDY, Jonathan. *The Rise and Fall of the British Nanny* (London: Hodder & Stoughton, 1972)

GRAHAM, Stephen. *Changing Russia* (London: John Lane, 1913)

Russia in Division (London: Macmillan, 1925)

Part of the Wonderful Game (London: Collins, 1964)

GREENE, Graham and Hugh. *The Spy's Bedside Book* (London: Rupert Hart-Davis, 1957)

HART-DAVIS, Duff. *Peter Fleming: A Biography* (London: Jonathan Cape, 1974)

HASTINGS, Selina. *The Secret Lives of Somerset Maugham* (London: John Murray, 2009)

HILL, George. *Go Spy the Land* (London: Cassell, 1932)

The Dreaded Hour (London: Cassell, 1936)

HOPKIRK, Peter. *Setting the East Ablaze: On Secret Service in Bolshevik Asia* (London: Oxford University Press, 1984)

On Secret Service East of Constantinople: The Plot to Bring Down the British Empire (London: John Murray, 1994)

HOWE, Bea. *A Galaxy of Governesses* (London: Verschoyle, 1954)

JONES, Stinton. *Russia in Revolution: Being the Experiences of an Englishman in Petrograd During the Upheaval* (London: Herbert Jenkins, 1917)

KETTLE, Michael. *Sidney Reilly: The True Story of the World's Greatest Spy* (London: Corgi, 1983)

KINVIG, Clifford. *Churchill's Crusade: The British Invasion of Russia 1918–1920* (London: Hambledon Continuum, 2006)

LOCKHART, Robert Bruce. *Memoirs of a British Agent* (London: Putnam, 1932)

My Scottish Youth (London: Putnam, 1937)

LOCKHART, Robin Bruce. *Reilly: Ace of Spies* (London: Penguin, 1967)

MacDONELL, Donald. *From Dogfight to Diplomacy: A Spitfire Pilot's Log 1932–1958* (Barnsley: Pen & Sword Books Ltd, 2005)

MacDONELL, Ranald. *And Nothing Long* (London: Heinemann, 1938)

MACLEAN, Fitzroy. *Eastern Approaches* (London: Jonathan Cape, 1949)

Back to Bokhara (London: Jonathan Cape, 1959)

McLYNN, Frank. *Fitzroy Maclean* (London: John Murray, 1992)

MASSIE, Robert K. *Nicholas and Alexandra* (London: Victor Gollancz, 1968)

MAUGHAM, W. Somerset. *Ashenden, or the British Agent* (London: Heinemann, 1928)

A Writer's Notebook (London: W. Heinemann & the Book Soc., 1949)

NOEL, Edward. 'A Prisoner among the Jungali Bolsheviks' from *On the Run: Escaping Tales* (London: Rich & Cowan, 1934)

Oxford Dictionary of National Biography (Oxford: Oxford University Press)

PASTERNAK, Boris, *Doctor Zhivago* (London: Collins and Harvill, 1958)

PITCHER, Harvey. *When Miss Emmie was in Russia: English Governesses Before, During and After the October Revolution* (London: John Murray, 1977)

REILLY, Sidney. *The Adventures of Sidney Reilly, Britain's Master Spy* (London: E. Mathews & Marrot, 1931)

SERVICE, Robert. *Spies and Commissars: Bolshevik Russia and the West* (London: Macmillan, 2011)

TEAGUE-JONES, Reginald. *The Spy Who Disappeared: Diary of a Secret Mission to Russian Central Asia in 1918* (London: Gollancz, 1990)

WALPOLE, Hugh. *The Dark Forest* (London: M. Secker, 1916)

The Secret City: A Novel in Three Parts (London: Macmillan, 1919)

The Crystal Box (London: 1924)

WELLS, H.G. *Russia in the Shadows* (London: Hodder & Stoughton, 1920)

YOUSSOUPOFF, Prince Felix. *Lost Splendour: The Amazing Memoirs of the Man Who Killed Rasputin* (London: Jonathan Cape, 1953)

ACKNOWLEDGEMENTS

The people to whom I owe most for giving me the idea of writing this book, and indeed for making it possible for me to do so, are those characters in the book whom I knew at later stages in their lives – Stephen Graham, Fitzroy Maclean, Peter and Ian Fleming, the Bruce Lockhart family and others, as described in the Personal Epilogue which constitutes my final chapter.

But there are many others who helped me along way, and I would like to record my indebtedness to them. The Rt. Revd and Rt. Hon. Lord Williams of Oystermouth (best known as Dr Rowan Williams, former Archbishop of Canterbury and present master of Magdalene College, Cambridge) generously shared his wisdom and knowledge of the Russian Orthodox Church and Russian literature with me. Giles Udy and Canon Michael Bourdeaux also were very helpful regarding relations between the Church and state in Russia and elsewhere. A number of my former diplomatic colleagues who served with me or at different times at the British Embassy in Moscow shared their recollections of times past; these included Sir Roderic Braithwaite, Sir Kenneth Scott and Selby Martin. Tania Illingworth (née Tolstoy) directed me towards some useful background reading about the period before and during the revolution. Anyone writing about this period in Russia, and the legacy of Russian culture, owes much to Orlando Figes for his authoritative works on the subject.

Gosia Lawik and her colleagues at the London Library have as always been consistently helpful in assisting me in the tracing of source material.

The Select Bibliography at the end of the book lists those sources on which most of my facts are based. I have not included Giles Milton's fascinating book *Russian Roulette* (2013) because – although it includes some of the same characters as my book – I had drafted all the chapters about them before the publication of his. Not surprisingly, I found we had fastened on some of the same exciting incidents from the same sources, but our approach to them is from a different angle: he concentrates on the spies and spying and the role of MI6, while I concentrate on the steps which my protagonists took to expose the machinations and iniquities of Bolshevism to a more public world of western governments and opinion. Indeed, my cast includes many characters who were innocent of any intelligence role at all. As the centenary of the Russian Revolution approaches, there will doubtless be many more books appearing about the personalities and events concerned – as there have been about the centenary of the outbreak of the first world war. Those were stirring times.

I also want to record my appreciation of Toby Ward for his percipient drawings of so many of the characters in the book; his interpretation of them will help the reader to recognize their often eccentric personalities.

ARCTIC

NORWAY
SWEDEN
FINLAND
Murmansk
ESTONIA
LATVIA
LITHUANIA
Riga
Archangel
Leningrad
(St Petersburg, Petrograd)
OLAND
MOSCOW
Kiev
URAL Mts
U
S
River Ob
Odessa
Sverdlovsk
(Ekaterinburg)
River Volga
Stalingrad
(Volgograd)
Novosibirsk
Omsk
Black Sea
Tbilisi
TURKEY
Yerevan
Baku
Caspian Sea
YRIA
IRAQ
Alma Ata
Tashkent
Ashkabad
SINKIANG
Tehran
Mashad
PERSIA
AFGHANISTAN